THE BEST O|

EDITED BY **MICHAEL SMITH**

A Dutton Paperback

E. P. DUTTON & CO., INC. NEW YORK 1969

CONTENTS

ILLUSTRATIONS

ILLUSTRATIONS

INTRODUCTION

1.

The hard part of being a critic is seeing what's happening on the stage. You have to see for yourself. In the present there are no stable, reliable, generally accepted, true standards of judgment or vision. Objective criticism is lies.

It's not only a matter of political content or social values. The nature of our experience is radically changing, and art doesn't reach us in the old ways. The electric crescendo of sensory input can no longer be switched off. Neither can we ignore the global context of our everyday lives. The theatre obviously needs some kind of technical regeneration in order to hold its own with the newer media; otherwise it will lose what little remains of its audience. Already theatres feel like museums. What we lack is a vision of the form a rejuvenated theatre might take. Most training is still geared to psychological realism. The theories of Brecht and the exhortations of Artaud have influenced practice far less than the expert articles would suggest, and the brilliant radicalisms of Beckett, Ionesco, and Genet turn out to be personal styles. Naturalism is dead; long live what?

In America the vacuum is occupied by something called "Broadway standards," against which all theatrical proficiency is measured. But Broadway standards—of writing, direction, acting, design—are with some exceptions barely adequate to Broadway artistic ambitions, which are hopelessly confused with desires for profit and personal advancement. We compete not toward excellence but for attention.

The theatre is in decline. We are not likely in our life-times to see anything good. The audience is deserting it—less than two percent of the population of the United States ever goes to theatre—and they can't be blamed. Most theatre

9

is dull or inept or both. Caring about it is asking for frustration.

Still the theatre is alive. I am one of many people who give it much or most of their time, energy, and concern—whose lives, not only livelihoods (often not *even* livelihoods), are structured around and conducted in terms of theatre. I make a living from the theatre, but my involvement goes deeper than that fact can explain: it is the central, almost obsessive metaphor of my daily life.

For all the changes around it, though, the established theatre—that which most people would identify as "the theatre" entire—goes on much the same. It is sustained stunned by those who will not change and wish the world wouldn't, who manage to think it settled down when they did, who because they are many and rich can seem to succeed in wishing the present out of being, who are generously grateful for the theatre's reassuring stability, however empty it has necessarily become. Its condition and theirs is beyond calm therapy. If it is to survive, the theatre, like the society of which it is part, requires change as extreme and unpredictable as revolution.

2.

Criticism of nonart is nonsense. Happily, the commercial theatre—Broadway and Off-Broadway—isn't the whole story, even in New York. There has to be a place to begin, to experiment, to grow, to prepare the revolution, and that place is Off Off-Broadway, brought into being during this decade for and partly by new playwrights, who have in turn proliferated beyond all expectation. More new plays are being written and performed now than at any other time in American theatre history. How good they are remains to be seen—but it is a quantitative renaissance at least.

By the early 1960s Off-Broadway was getting established and starting to be reviewed in the daily papers. This enlarged the audience and was considered a good thing, but before long it meant Off-Broadway was subject to the same hit-or-flop rules as Broadway. Whatever sense these rules may make for a commodity theatre, they are death to experiment; however competent the "major" critics may be as entertainment guides, they are the wrong men to seek out and nurture the seeds of a possible new theatre. The Living Theatre, for example, which for several years was the headquarters of experimental theatre in New York, alienated the uptown critics by its handcrafted, personalist production methods and its desperate political commitments and never got the audience it deserved and needed; the closing of the Living Theatre in October, 1963, was a near-fatal blow to Off-Broadway.

The critic is victim as well as villain, as the situation forces him to take positions for or against plays; what he says in support of these positions—the meat of criticism—is relatively unregarded. Yet the bare yea or nay is least important to him. Very few plays are triumphs, more are outright fiascoes, but most fall somewhere within a wide range of mediocrity. One is properly concerned less with a play's relative and immediate merit than with what it reveals of the theatrical experience and of the nature of human experience now and forever. A work of art is an expressive object, not a commodity.

But publicity is necessary to the theatre. Playwrights, actors, directors, designers can do only part of their work in private: they need the danger and occasion of coming together and working in public, before an audience. In isolation their work is incomplete and unreal and they won't continue to do it.

Productions of new plays began turning up five or six years ago in the most unlikely places, and they turned out to be more than local news, because nothing comparable was happening anywhere else. Off Off-Broadway was being born, in Greenwich Village and on the Lower East Side, and by circumstance I was its prime publicist. Here there were no press agents, and there was almost no money, and for two or three years no publication but *The Village Voice* paid any attention. Then the daily newspapers began sending reviewers down occasionally, which led to mentions in the large-circulation magazines, which attracted the notice of foundations, publishers, and even a few commercial producers. Soon the new playwright, far from being neglected, was getting all the attention he could reasonably want, and sometimes more than he could take. We had created a climate of anticipation, and it was paying off.

It was a fact that much of the new work was tentative, lacking in craft, technically crude. But critical standards aren't simply a matter of good versus bad; the issue is change. The changes in the theatre's structure are already fact. What remains to be seen is the possibility of change in its nature.

3.

Almost all the theatre I see is imitation theatre. The theatre I care about is mostly imaginary, but I've seen it made real.

Imagination gets its nourishment from reality. The reality of the established theatre in America is all habit—habitual goals, habitual procedures, habitual satisfactions. Its advocates might speak of traditions, but it has no advocates. The theatre has consumed its traditions, and its habits are their ash.

"The theatre"—do the words mean anything at all? One thinks of an intricate hierarchy. For Americans Broadway is at the top (though constantly threatened by the West End). The ladder descends from this heaven through regional repertory, Off-Broadway, university theatre, summer stock, Off Off-Broadway, novice, amateur, and student theatre—to the child who recognizes the images on the television screen as actors acting, people like himself playing games of imagination, and warily eyes the first rung. But the ladder leads nowhere. It's no longer worth the climb. The crisis, or the joke, is that everyone now agrees that Broadway is nowhere— it's not even controversial any more. Still we are sucked in. The conspiracy continues by default, by inertia, by seduction, by desperation. Broadway standards. Broadway aspirations.

I have nothing much against Broadway as an entertainment industry or a social institution. But I'm trying to talk about theatre, and if theatre is an art, then Broadway is rarely theatre. Its practitioners are nourished by ego thrills; its devotees eagerly succumb to nostalgia; its aspirants dream of glory and wake to predictable disillusionment. Decadence is glorious, of course, and so it shines over the bishops, the priests, the vestry, the humble altar boys, down finally to the congregation, which knows divinity isn't just a candy and stays away. Well, no, not entirely, not quite yet. Go to Broadway for a report from London, for a fairly glamorous night out, for comfortable "culture," for diversion (if you're easily diverted), for familiar jokes and shallow, reassuring insights, for know-how, for the hits. Not for theatre.

Still we are all part of it. We snuggle into the structure for all the world as if we trusted its comfort. The siren voice I hear, though I should be deafened with my own opinions, is Broadway's.

Almost all the theatre I see is imitation theatre. But I have seen the real thing. Not often but again and again it is suddenly there before me, sometimes utterly unexpected. Imaginary theatre is real theatre; what exists is the phantom. It has other disciples besides me, visionaries, mavericks, lunatics, revolutionists. Some see through present habits to the truth they bury alive; others see beyond them to possibilities of theatre experience that have never happened before, because nothing has ever happened before. They are doing something else, and they are the ones who keep me interested. The vision eludes them too, and they all falter sometimes, cop out (even to worry about copping out is a cop-out), mistake themselves for players in the game. But their concern is theatre, and they are doing theatre, really doing it, and they are its hope.

The theatre has split into two parts. This is possibly the only hopeful reality about the American theatre today. A few more promising playwrights aren't going to mean much if they have to work within the structure that already exists. But a few things have been happening which suggest that the present structure of the theatre can safely collapse now, that it is no longer the all and essence, that theatre can and does exist without that structure and is, on the whole, better off for it. Anarchy is a real possibility.

Still the fission exists mainly as a state of mind. The theater is still a legitimate career, more legitimate now than usual, in fact. People still want to be professionals. That means they want to be successful, which involves them in competition: many must fail for a few to succeed—we are thinking in free-enterprise terms. You aren't a professional in the theatre unless you make a living from it and that isn't easy; it's one of the toughest livings there is.

The other reality of theatre is the experience of making and performing and witnessing it. It is a shared act of imagination, an imaginative experience in which the audience participates with the artists. The key word is experience. It is this which holds the meaning.

There are still people who manage to remember why they got into it in the first place. Theatre isn't a holy vocation, like the priesthood, or something you can take up with a martyred sense of mission, like nursing, or a quick way to high living, like hustling (supposedly), or a solid buck, like stenography. It's something you love. Liking it may be enough in high school, when you get your first taste, but it has to turn into love before you stake your life on it. There's simply no other justification for doing it. Once you're into it you can make up the fancy reasons and work out ways to make it sound serious, because you're a grown-up now. But if you lose or forget that original liking and love, you're not going to do what you set out to do, what you want to do (nobody *has* to), and what you're in is imitation theatre— to you and probably to the audience too.

The issue is personal commitment. Liking and wanting are the signs of involvement and concern. They are the essence of seriousness.

The question is whether you like the idea of it or like actually doing it. Do you love it as an experience, or do you covet it as an ego dream? Do you want the thing itself or the things that can come with or from it? This is the point at which the theatre divides in two. And it is encouraging to see this division becoming a matter of public action, not just of private points of view. The fact remains that most people in the theatre devote most of their time, effort, and ingenuity to placing themselves in the structure, and relatively little to developing, refining, elaborating the experience they came for—with the result that when they do finally get in, the main thing they're concerned with is fitting, filling, and keeping that hard-won place, as if it were the point. But it's hard to forget the authentic experience once you've had it.

The experience transcends the footlights. Some people locate it specifically in the connection between actors and audience, but for me the theatrical experience centers in the collaborative act of imagination. The feeling is thrilling and immediately recognizable. I can get it whether I'm in the audience, or directing, acting, lighting, or working over a script. It's the creative ecstasy. It is the act of, by mutual consent and participation, turning something imaginary into something real. I can't get that feeling by myself: it's like love.

It *is* love, in fact. Here the two halves of a true life, love and art, are actually united.

Only after this personal seriousness is realized, I think, is it possible to move on to the serious *uses* of the theatre. I am antipathetic to the whole idea of purposiveness and always more concerned with what and how than with what for. The theatre, like other art forms, is not just an experience and an artifact but also a medium of expression and communication. It not only *is* something, it *says* something, whether or not that's its intention. It is a statement and an act as well as an event, and it can aim at having an effect beyond the time-space boundaries of the experience. It can be used for any number of legitimate and serious purposes—political, social, ethical, moral, etc. It is extraordinarily broad and powerful in its potential: it can be as specific as literature, as abstract and emotionally direct as music, as thrilling as sport, as mysterious and awesome as religious ritual, as irresistibly involving as a mass rally, all at the same time. This power is both frightening and inspiring to contemplate—but don't worry, don't get too excited, not yet. The power stays obstinately potential. For some reason, nobody can manage to get it all going. I don't know if anybody ever has. Still, the possibility is clearly there, and the aim of much serious theatre is to tap these power reserves and affect audiences and society. In *Mysteries and Smaller Pieces* the Living Theatre chants, "Change the world!" Brecht tried too.

4.

In Off Off-Broadway there isn't, or wasn't until recently, much fame or fortune or status around to compete for. Satisfaction in the doing was the only satisfaction to be had. Lack of money, on the surface a limitation and a hang-up, seemed also to have advantages. With neither money nor careers at stake, caution is unnecessary, you can do anything.

In contrast to other amateur theatre, Off Off-Broadway happens in New York. I know it's reverse parochialism, but I am not sanguine about the decentralization of the American theatre, at least not yet. Audiences outside New York don't have the opportunity to be *au courant*. Apart from rare spirits who flourish in isolation, and especially for those just starting out in theatre, it's almost essential to serve time in New York. Otherwise you'll never know where you are. You have to see what's been done and what's being done; the audiences that see your work will be aware of its context; and you can find people to work with whose ideas are entirely different from your own.

The term Off Off-Broadway designates, rather misleadingly and arbitrarily, an assortment of people, places, and programs that have started functioning in New York since about 1960, mostly devoted to the production of new plays by otherwise unproduced playwrights. Off Off-Broadway productions occur in coffee houses, churches, lofts, and any other available spaces, only rarely in theatres recognizable as such: these are theatres not in architecture but by virtue of what happens.

Out of this inconspicuous milieu has come a solid and amazingly extensive record of achievement: for several years Off Off-Broadway has given production to more than a hundred new plays per season. Most of the work is on a small scale, most of the plays one act long, most of the excellence on the level of promise rather than fulfillment. But Off Off-Broadway has provided the desperately needed opportunity for a large number of people to get a quantity of real experience, working before public audiences, that they could have found nowhere else.

Still, theatre has a larger place to occupy in society than can be satisfied by Off Off-Broadway. It sounds simple-minded, but it's a question of size. Theatre is a public art, and everyone who has worked Off Off-Broadway must know the comfortable but slightly unreal feeling of playing for a private audience. It's not how many that matters so much as who. Off Off-Broadway audiences often seem too unde-manding: maybe they pay too little. They agree too easily. They're too cool. They take the most outrageous point of view in stride because in context it's no longer outrageous but just what they'd expect. Broadway is corrupted by its part in the world of business, but at least it faces the de-mands of nonpartisan customers and is taken for an aspect of "real life"—the profit motive is the touchstone of Ameri-can reality. Off Off-Broadway has no such authentication, and in a very real sense it is not taken seriously. It tends to be its own reality. It tends to become a world closed unto itself; it's a tiny world, and those who live and work inside that world for too long are threatened with preciosity. Eccen-tricity becomes the norm. The danger, specifically, is that inventive tricks of style—"avant-garde" mannerisms—may be valued more than substance; experimentalism becomes a value in itself. The end of this road is a theatre which speaks only about theatre and only to theatre people.

Everybody has to find his own romanticism, or allow him-self to be found by it. It takes time, and it's not easy to stay loose on such a trip, without beginning or end. You guess where you're going by looking out the window as the stations flash by. Where did you get on? You look at your ticket and it explodes.

The experience of Off Off-Broadway has demonstrated clearly if redundantly that the accepted methods and aims of theatrical procedure are no longer adequate but have become irrelevant to the concerns and appetites of the present, of the generation that has grown up since, say, the Korean War, after the breakthroughs of Beckett, Ionesco, Genet. The frontiers of the theatre, like so many other frontiers, have been pushed so far back that they've virtually disappeared, but the established theatre has shown little interest or competence in moving into the new territory. Maybe it shouldn't be expected to. But neither can the theatre artists now coming of age be expected to limit their ambitions to the accomplishments of the past.

A crisis is essential, but it calls for a difficult decision by the artists involved. They must abandon the desire for conventional success, especially when it comes within reach. It calls for sacrifice without the ego comforts of martyrdom, because the decision must be made for self-serving reasons. It is an incredibly hazardous moment: they must first create a new aesthetic and then a new institution to express it. Broadway won't die; it has to be assassinated.

Whether they know it or not, those who have been working in Off Off-Broadway have made the first step, and they are in the best position to continue the adventure. But Off Off-Broadway is in constant danger of turning back into the showcase gambit it began as. Undeniably it's a place to get experience and exposure and to begin the climb up the fabled ladder to what once may have been paradise but is no longer. So they must choose. They must pull down the ladder and burn it, in effigy or for warmth. They can't climb, they have to learn to fly: this is the twentieth century. The immediate obstacle is ambivalence. It's understandable; I share it. We all want the best of contradictory worlds, and we've found out often that we can get it. We can have a good time protesting the war in Vietnam, for instance. But the good times get thin and finally distasteful, and the protest begins to make us feel pitiful. Are we moralists of hedonism, or merely comforting ourselves with righteous gestures? We have to like living with ourselves, especially if we want anyone else to like living with us. Are we being courageous or imaginatively cowardly? Are we artists or opportunists?

Then there is a higher opportunism, a higher hedonism, in which we seek to fulfill and please ourselves in truth. And ambivalence is a part of truth: ambiguity, in fact, sometimes seems the only possible truth. I am ambivalent even about ambivalence. It is also a cop-out.

About all the critic can do is pay attention and try to see what's happening. But his very presence is dangerous: he is the carrier of an insidious disease. The going thing swallows even its critics: it seduces those who would destroy it—now Judith falls for Holofernes. One proceeds with trepidation, wondering if it's possible not to become an agent of the enemy, wondering if virtue has to be its own only reward, wondering if it's possible to keep the faith without keeping it a secret.

MICHAEL SMITH

Sundance
August 5, 1968

FORENSIC AND THE NAVIGATORS

(BY SAM SHEPARD

Forensic and the Navigators was done in the smallish
upstairs room at St. Mark's Church in-the-Bouwerie,
where Sam Shepard had his first plays staged five years
before, also under Ralph Cook's direction and with
Lee Kissman in a leading role. He's been writing a
couple of plays a year since then, brilliant and original
and clear to the point of perfect mystery. *Forensic
and the Navigators* is characteristic in its detailed but
ambiguous exposition, its fugitive lucidity, its soluble
realism. It's like real life: you can't tell what's
going on. The whole thing may be a smoke dream, but
the smoke that fills the theatre at the end is real.
So are the people, for all their elusiveness as dramatic
characters, and so is the paranoia of our times, which
Shepard expresses better than anyone else now writing.

M. S.

Forensic and the Navigators was first produced by Theatre Genesis at St. Mark's Church in-the-Bouwerie, Tenth Street and Second Avenue, New York, on December 29, 1967. It was directed by Ralph Cook with the following cast:

FORENSIC: Robert Schlee
EMMET: Lee Kissman
OOLAN: O'Lan Johnson
1ST EXTERMINATOR: Walter Hadler
2ND EXTERMINATOR: Beeson Carroll

Lighting: Johnny Dodd
Stage Manager: Ann Held
Electrician: Soren Agenoux

The play was followed without interval by a concert of songs by the Moray Eels (Peter Stampfel, Antonia Duren, Richard Tyler, Sam Shepard).

OPPOSITE: Robert Schlee (Forensic) and Lee Kissman (Emmet) in *Forensic and the Navigators*

Black space. A small table center stage with a long white linen tablecloth that goes almost to the floor. An old-fashioned oil lamp in the center of the table. An office-type swivel chair at opposite ends of the table facing each other. Forensic sits in the stage right chair with a note pad and pen in front of him. He has long blond hair, a brown cowboy hat, a long red scarf, a black leather vest, jeans, and moccasins. Emmet sits at the other end of the table with a small portable typewriter in front of him with paper in it. He has long black hair, a green Cherokee headband, beads around his neck and a serape, jeans, and cowboy boots. An elaborate Indian peace pipe sits in the center of the table in a large glass ashtray. The stage is black. Sound of Emmet's typewriter clacking. Silence. Emmet and Forensic sing in the dark.

EMMET AND FORENSIC: We gonna be born again. Oh Lord.
We gonna be born again. Good Lord.
We gonna be born again.
Lord have mercy now.

We gonna be saved tonight. Oh Lord.
We gonna get saved tonight. Good Lord.
We gonna be saved tonight.
Lord have mercy now.

They sing both verses three times through then stop short. Silence. Sound of Emmet's typewriter. The oil lamp slowly glows and becomes brighter. The light comes up full. As the characters become visible they both relax from their writing and lean back in the chairs like executives. They stare at each other.

FORENSIC: Where's that woman Emmet. Ya' can't count on her to get ya' a hot meal on the table 'afore six A.M. then could ya' tell me what kinda good is she. Tell me that one Emmet.

Emmet just stares at Forensic then begins to type.

FORENSIC: So as far as you're concerned we're really cutting out of here. I take it that that's the story so far. Do I take it right Emmet. Right or wrong. Do I take it right or wrong.

He stands and slams his fist on the table, Emmet stops typing and looks at Forensic.

FORENSIC: Boy I'll cut you down! Answer me right or wrong!
EMMET: If you have to be stubborn do it outside Forensic. I'm writing a letter.
FORENSIC: Who to then. Tell me that much. Jesus, I feel so far left out of what's going on since you and everyone else decides we ain't goin' through with a whole plan that's been goin' on since we was ten years old.
EMMET: Sit.

Forensic sits.

EMMET: Now, I'm writing to my mother and for me to do that I have to have my wits. Would you like a smoke.
FORENSIC: Your mother. Jesus. All right. I'll light it.

Forensic picks up the peace pipe and lights it.

EMMET: It's no good being disappointed Forensic. We've been through that. We have to just lay low for a while. We need you a lot so don't go feeling left out of things. Right now we have to take care of certain business. We have to transfer the guns and the equipment. We have to individually escape. We have to be quiet. We have to do these things before we make any moves. If we make any other moves we're screwed and that's the end of that. We have to switch our sensibilities so that we're not even pretending. So that we are transformed for a time and see no difference in the way we are from the way we were. We have to believe ourselves.
FORENSIC: Here. (*He hands the pipe to Emmet, who smokes it.*)
FORENSIC: It's just chicken Emmet and you know it. It's downright yellow and cowardly. We could blow that whole place up in less time than it would take to go through a sensibility switch. Besides there's people in there now who are really trapped for real. What about them. We're out here switching disguises while they only think of ways to escape. We could blow that whole mother fucker sky high and you know it.
EMMET: Here. (*He hands the pipe to Forensic, who smokes.*)
EMMET: Don't talk like a dumb kid Forensic. You got any

idea whatsoever what this project looks like from the outside, objectively without emotion. Why it looks overwhelming Forensic. It's a fucking desert fortress is what it amounts to. They've rebuilt it since the time of the Japanese you know. It's not the same camp at all. New plumbing, double inlaid wire fencing that fronts a steel wall thirty feet high without doors.

FORENSIC: How do they get in then and what difference does the plumbing make.

EMMET: By helicopter and the plumbing difference is that since its reconstruction we have no idea what the design is underground which makes internal explosions almost out of the question.

FORENSIC: Then bomb the mother fucker.

EMMET: And kill all the inmates. RIGHT! BOMB THE MOTHER FUCKER AND KILL ALL THE IN-MATES! THAT'S WHAT YOU'RE SAYING! THAT'S WHAT YOU'RE SAYING FORENSIC! OUT OF MY SIGHT! GET OUT OF MY SIGHT! I DON'T WANT TO SEE YOU EVER AGAIN.

He stands and lunges toward Forensic as Oolan enters wearing a white hospital gown like they have for the insane and sandals on her feet; she holds a frying pan with a single pancake in it, she circles the table flipping the pancake and catching it in the pan.

OOLAN: You boys should have told me what hour it was getting to be. Why my goodness sakes I look at the clock and the time is getting to be way past the time for you boys breakfast. And you both know how up tight the two of you get when breakfast isn't just exactly when you get the most hungry. So here it is. Hot and ready.

She flips the pancake onto the table; Forensic and Emmet stare at the pancake as Oolan smiles; Emmet sits back in his chair; Oolan picks up the pipe and smokes it.

EMMET: How many times I gotta tell you I don't eat that buckwheat Aunt Jemima middle-class bullshit. I want Rice Krispies and nothing else. Is that clear.

FORENSIC: Get that pancake off the conference table you stupid girl.

OOLAN: Here. (*She hands the pipe to Forensic then picks up the pancake and eats it slowly as she watches them.*)

FORENSIC: Emmet, you're as soft and flabby as you say your enemies are.

EMMET: You're pretty much of a shit yourself. Shit face.

A loud knock that sounds like somebody banging on a steel door with a sledge hammer; Emmet and Forensic stand suddenly and pull out small ray guns that they have concealed in their crotches; Emmet motions to Oolan to answer.

OOLAN: I can't, my mouth is full.

Another loud knock; Emmet motions again, more angry this time; Oolan forces the pancake down and fixes her hair; she faces upstage and answers.

OOLAN: Who is it. Just one moment please.

Another loud knock; Emmet motions again, really mad; Oolan crosses upstage.

OOLAN: Yes. Hello. Who is it please.

LOUD VOICE (*over microphone*): IT'S THE EXTERMINATOR, LADY!

She looks at Emmet, who waves his ray gun and shakes his head.

OOLAN: Um— We don't want any. Thank you anyway.

LOUD VOICE: DON'T WANT ANY WHAT. IT'S THE EXTERMINATOR. OPEN UP!

OOLAN: O.K. Wait just a second.

She turns to Emmet and shrugs her shoulders; Emmet and Forensic duck under the tablecloth and disappear; another loud knock.

OOLAN: Coming! Just hold tight.

Two huge Negroes appear in the light, they are dressed like California Highway Patrolmen with gold helmets, gas masks, khaki pants and shirts, badges, boots, gloves, pistols, and both are carrying large tanks on their backs, with a hose and nozzle attachment which they hold in their hands; they just stand there and look around the room.

OOLAN: Um— We haven't had any rats here since last February, March, around in there.

1ST EXTERM: Well they told us to cover the place from top to bottom.

2ND EXTERM: You'll have to leave mam.

OOLAN: Fuck you. This is my home.

Emmet's voice is heard from under table.

EMMET: Cool it Oolan.

The Exterminators wander around casing the joint.

OOLAN: Um— Don't you think you hadn't better check it out with your home office and see if you got the right place. I mean it would be awful if you got the wrong place. Don't you think. What do you think fellas.

1ST EXTERM: This is exactly the place little girl.

2ND EXTERM: The table gives it away. Without the table or with the table in another place maybe it would be cause to call the home office. But with the table in the place it is and looking the way it does there is absolutely no doubt we have the right place.

They both turn upstage and adjust the nozzles and synchronize watches; as they do this Forensic and Emmet lift the table from underneath and move it upstage right so the table looks like it moves by itself.

1ST EXTERM: Now we have to synchronize our watches and adjust our nozzles and get ourselves ready.

2ND EXTERM: You'd better get out of here lady. Without a gas mask you're as good as dead.

FORENSIC'S VOICE (*from under the table*): Sing something Oolan.

OOLAN: What.

EMMET: Anything.

Oolan starts singing "Ahab the Arab" and looking at the audience; the Exterminators turn and cross to Oolan; she keeps singing and smiles at them; they see the table and cross up right and stare at it; they cross back to

Oolan and stare at her then back to the table; this happens several times as Oolan sings.

1ST EXTERM: ALL RIGHT STOP THAT SINGING!

Oolan stops and giggles.

1ST EXTERM: Now what happened to that table lady.

Oolan turns around and looks at the table.

OOLAN: Oh my god! (*She faints in the arms of 2nd Exterm, who catches her.*)

2ND EXTERM: Great.

1ST EXTERM: Well put her down you dope.

He lets Oolan fall to the floor.

2ND EXTERM: We gotta think fast Forensic or we're screwed.

1ST EXTERM: What did you call me. Forensic? Is that what you called me. What kind of a name is that.

2ND EXTERM: I don't know. I don't know what came over me.

1ST EXTERM: Now look. Didn't you and I both see that table over here when we first came in here.

2ND EXTERM: Gee I don't know.

1ST EXTERM: What do you mean. Wasn't it you that said we could tell we were at the right place on account of the table being where it was, which was right here, not over there. Wasn't it you who said that to her. Answer me mushmouth. Was it me or you!

2ND EXTERM: It was me but it still seems like the right place even with the table over there.

1ST EXTERM: But we can't be sure now. Before we could be absolutely sure but now there's some doubt. Am I right. Am I right or wrong!

1ST EXTERM: I guess.

1ST EXTERM: So that means we'll have to call the home office before we can make another move. Am I right. Where's your phone lady.

2ND EXTERM: She's fainted or something.

EMMET'S VOICE (*from under the table*): There's a pay phone down the road.

1ST EXTERM: There's probably a pay phone just down the road so why don't you go down there and call while I stay here.

2ND EXTERM: Down the road?

1ST EXTERM: Yeah. Now hurry up! I'm going to be right
here waiting. Just ask them if it makes any difference
where the table is.

2ND EXTERM: O.K. You're going to wait here?

1ST EXTERM: Yeah. Now move!

*2nd Exterm. exits. 1st Exterm. looks around then moves
over to Oolan, who is still on the floor; he stares at her,
then takes off his helmet and gas mask; he takes off the
tank and then kneels down beside Oolan with his back
to the table; he stares at Oolan's face for a while, then
touches her shoulder; the table suddenly moves downstage right behind 1st Exterm.; he kisses Oolan on the
forehead, then takes off his gun belt and holster; he lies
down beside Oolan and stares at her, then puts his arm
around her; Forensic and Emmet come out from under
the table very quietly and slowly; 1st Exterm. kisses
Oolan on the lips; Forensic picks up the tank and gas
mask; Emmet picks up the gun and holster; 1st Exterm.
pulls Oolan close to him and hugs her; Emmet puts on
the gun while Forensic puts on the tank and gas mask;
this all happens while 1st Exterm. squeezes Oolan and
kisses her and strokes her hair.*

1ST EXTERM: Oh my darling. You mustn't worry now. We'll
get you out. I'll get you far away to a safe place where
we can be quiet and you won't even know. Just relax.
All you'll see is smoke filling up the valley. We'll be
very high up. Don't you worry about that. It was a tree
house but now it's a fort. It's very strong and beautiful.
You can trust it to keep you safe and sound. It's colored
just like the trees. Orange and yellow and green and
blue. And it makes sounds like birds and dogs and wild
boar. Really. If anyone comes you can see them from
two miles off. You can signal to me if I'm not around.
But I always will be. I'll never leave for a second. You
can count on me. If you could only see me now I know
you'd believe me. If you could wake up in my arms and
act like I was supposed to be here. Like I always was
here and always will be. If you could wake up like that
then we could go away from here now. Right this very
minute. We could leave and live in the trees.

Emmet has the gun on 1st Exterm; Forensic points the nozzle at him.

EMMET: All right Big Bopper, on your feet.

1st Exterm. jumps to his feet and raises his hands; Oolan gets up.

OOLAN: What a nasty rotten trick.

FORENSIC: Shut up! (*He crosses to 1st Exterm. holding the nozzle on him.*) So you a lover in disguise. Is that it Big Bopper. You really full of pizzaz but you just got led astray. Is that the story.

1ST EXTERM: Don't press that nozzle!

EMMET: Just keep your hands raised up there.

OOLAN: Don't press that nozzle! We'll all go up in flame!

FORENSIC: It's not a torch. It's gas. Toxic gas. Highly poison toxic gas that when you breathe it you're dead right away.

1ST EXTERM: Don't be ridiculous.

FORENSIC: WHAT! WHAT DID YOU SAY SMART ALECK! DON'T GET SMART MISTER OR I'LL GAS YOUR ASS!

EMMET: Take it easy Forensic.

FORENSIC: Well he's a wise guy.

1ST EXTERM: That gas is for roaches, rats, and varmints. Not people. It just gets you sick and makes your eyes water.

FORENSIC: What.

EMMET: Wait a minute. Now just take it easy.

FORENSIC: He's trying to come off like a killer of pests and bugs.

EMMET: Just don't get excited. We might find out something. Are you hungry mister.

1ST EXTERM: No.

EMMET: Well I am. Would you mind if the two of us sat down at the table and I ate some Rice Krispies while I ask you some questions.

1ST EXTERM: All right.

FORENSIC: What is this.

EMMET: Go fetch the Rice Krispies Oolan.

OOLAN: You know he has a friend somewhere out there in a phone booth who's going to come back here.

EMMET: Just get the Krispies woman!

OOLAN: Jesus. (*She exits.*)

EMMET: Now set yourself down here mister. Come on. Just fold your hands on top of your head.

1st Exterm. clasps his hands on top of his head and sits in the stage left chair; Emmet keeps the gun on him and sits in the stage right chair.

FORENSIC: Now what am I supposed to do Goddammit.

EMMET (*decides to involve himself again; becomes just like Forensic*): Now then mister I take it you've come a long way. Not just from down the block or down the road.

1ST EXTERM: Well yes. I mean that depends.

EMMET: I take it you have certain tools at your disposal which provide photographs and details of our layout here. Like table positions, etc.

1ST EXTERM: That goes without saying. What's the name of that girl.

EMMET: I'll give you a hint. It sounds like it might have something to do with tea but it doesn't.

FORENSIC: What the fuck am I supposed to do.

1ST EXTERM: Darjeeling?

EMMET: Now your home office must be getting pretty edgy to send a couple toughs like you, all equipped and everything. Hot and ready. They must suspect a move on our part, but the amazement is that we had no idea they had any interest in our project whatsoever. I mean you just show up out of the clear blue sky. We don't even have any dogs.

1ST EXTERM: Dogs?

EMMET: Doberman pinschers, German shepherds, wire-haired pointing griffins, circling the place, sniffing for trouble, ready to tear out a throat of those that smell of a different turf. Do you understand. No young blond dopey muscle boys practicing jujitsu on the front lawn. We're vulnerable as all get out. We've left ourselves with our drawers down. That gives you all the room to plunge in and you have. Which means for us that we temporarily have to abandon the idea of temporarily abandoning the project and throw ourselves once again into the meat of the game. You've forced our hand as it were.

1st Exterm. takes his hands down; Forensic starts circling the stage restlessly with the gas mask and tank still on.

EMMET: Keep up those hands.

FORENSIC: We don't need this. I'm telling you. We're not going to find out anything more or better by interrogation than we are by going out there and seeing for ourselves what the place looks like. What its potentials are for collapsing. We can't sit around all abstracted out of shape while they lie stacked up on top of each other behind steel doors. It just isn't fair.

1ST EXTERM: What's her approximate age.

EMMET: Thirty-two, twenty-one, thirty.

1ST EXTERM: Does she see many boys. Young ones. Do they come to her door. Do they sit outside in the driveway honking in their Cobras with their right arms coaxing and kneading and fondling the tuck and roll and their left hand pumping, squeezing on the wheel.

EMMET: Do you have a master's degree mister.

1ST EXTERM: Not at all.

EMMET: What qualifies you then for a job in the line of gassing.

1ST EXTERM: I'm past my prime.

FORENSIC: So he goes for the skirt does he. Perhaps we could make a deal.

EMMET: Forget it Forensic. We got her out of there once or don't you remember. Now you want to start the whole thing over. Put her in a position for being taken back. You don't think clearly. BOMB THE MOTHER FUCKERS! We got her out and she stays out and she ain't going back for no kind of deal. Not even for the most precise, delicate ground plan of the new plumbing system that they just recently put in. Not even for that.

1ST EXTERM: You mean to say that you'd consider some sort of trade. Some information for her inspiration. I'll do it by jove. I'll do it just as sure as you're standing there.

EMMET: Keep those hands up.

Forensic tears off the gas mask and the tank and lays them on the floor; he goes to the table.

FORENSIC: Now you're talking.

Emmet hands the gun to Forensic, who holds it on 1st Exterm. Emmet stands and paces around; Forensic takes his place in the chair facing 1st Exterm, who takes his hands down and slowly begins to stroke himself and grope his own crotch.

EMMET: Out of the question. Absolutely out of the question. We can't jeopardize her position. It's ridiculous. She'd be right back in solitary or something worse. She'd be stacked up right along with the rest of them.

FORENSIC: Big Bopper you are on the brink of having for your very own the hottest little discotheque mama ever to come on the set.

Oolan enters with a bowl, milk, and a box of Rice Krispies; she crosses to the table.

EMMET: Oh good. It's about time. Bring it down here.

He crosses down right and sits cross-legged on the floor; Oolan goes and stands beside him.

1ST EXTERM: Oh that's fantastic. I'll tell you anything.
FORENSIC: O.K. First off, do you have a map of the plant.
1ST EXTERM: Map? Map. Yes I do. Of course I do. But I don't think the plumbing is included in the detail. I mean—

He pulls out a map and hands it across the table to Forensic, then goes on groping himself as he watches Oolan.

FORENSIC: Let me see it. Come on, come on.

Forensic opens the map and spreads it on the table in front of him.

OOLAN: Emmet you'll never in a million years guess what I just a little while ago figured out in the kitchen.
EMMET: Come on, come on. Krispies woman. Gimme Krispies.
OOLAN: I know but it's about that. It's about Krispies and the complaint you've had against them all these years. The complaint being that you always lose a few of them because as soon as you add milk to a full bowl they rise up and overflow the bowl and fall on the floor. So what you've had to do all this time is fill the bowl half full, add the milk, mush the half filled bowl down into the milk so they get soggy and don't rise, then add more

fresh Krispies on top of those and then a little more milk
and then mush the fresh ones down so that the whole
bowl is soggy and then finally add the sugar and then
finally you get to taste the very first spoonful after having
gone through that long painful process.

EMMET: Yes, I know, I know. That why I always have
good woman fix Krispies so that man not have to go
through so much pain.

OOLAN: I know but what I'm saying is that I've solved that
whole problem.

EMMET: Good, good.

OOLAN: I'll show you how to do it.

EMMET: Good.

OOLAN: O.K. Now first I pour the Krispies in. All the way full.
(*She fills the bowl with Rice Krispies.*) Now I put both
my hands gently but firmly on top of the Krispies like
this. (*She puts her hands on the Krispies and looks at
Emmet.*)

EMMET: Yeah?

OOLAN: Now you pour the milk.

EMMET: Over your hands?

OOLAN: Yes. Go ahead. Don't be afraid.

EMMET: I don't want somebody's grimy hands in my cereal.

OOLAN: Just pour the milk.

*Emmet picks up the milk and pours it over Oolan's
hands; she smiles at him; he sets down the milk and
looks at her; she takes her hands off the cereal.*

OOLAN: See?

*Emmet picks up a spoon and starts eating ravenously as
Forensic speaks.*

FORENSIC: Listen here, this is no use to us. It's all in some
sort of code or something. Everything's mixed up according to this. Hey what are you doing. Hey! Hands above
the table mister. HANDS ABOVE THE TABLE!

*1st Exterm. quickly puts his hands on the table and
faces Forensic.*

FORENSIC: Look, you're going to have to earn this woman
mister. This map doesn't show anything whatsoever

where the central stockade is, where the ammunition's kept, where the officers stay, where the guard towers are, where the electric source is, not to mention food and what means of transportation they have in case of a pursuit. None of that's down here. How do you account for that. What's this map for.

1ST EXTERM: I don't know. They hand it to us. The first day we get uniforms, helmets, guns, tanks, gas, and they hand us that map. One apiece. We each get one to study when we go home. We each are told to memorize the details of this map and to make sure we have them by the next morning because we are going to be thoroughly tested and retested on these details. But we never are. Each morning we're never tested and each evening we're threatened that we will be tested the next morning. But we never are. (*He puts his hands down and starts groping again.*)

FORENSIC: Ah ha! I get the picture.

He picks up the map and stands; he walks around the table to 1st Exterm. and begins interrogating him; Oolan just watches Emmet as he devours the Rice Krispies; each time he finishes a bowlful she fills the bowl again and he goes on eating.

FORENSIC: Let's just see what kind of homework you claim you've been doing then. You wouldn't mind that I'm sure. After all you've studied so hard night after night and each morning you've been disappointed. So it's about time you had a chance to show your stuff. Don't you think?

1ST EXTERM: Does she care about things like popularity and lettermen's jackets?

FORENSIC: Now pay attention swabbie!

1st Exterm. snaps to attention in his seat, he salutes and puts his hands on the table; Forensic circles him with the map in his hands.

EMMET: Good. Krispies. Good.

FORENSIC: What's the capital of the state of Arizona!

1ST EXTERM: Phoenix.

FORENSIC: How much barbed wire does it take to encircle four hundred acres!

1ST EXTERM: Nine thousand two hundred and seventy square yards.

FORENSIC: How many guns on the east wall facing the western barricade.

1ST EXTERM: Forty-five.

FORENSIC: On which side are the women kept!

1ST EXTERM: Southwest corner and northeast.

FORENSIC: Two parts? The women are split in two parts?

1ST EXTERM: Yes sir.

FORENSIC: Which two again. Again! Which two!

1ST EXTERM: Northeast and southwest.

FORENSIC: And the men!

1ST EXTERM: Northwest and southeast.

FORENSIC: And the dogs!

1ST EXTERM: Right in the middle and all around the edges.

FORENSIC: Which edges! Make yourself clear Forensic. Which edges!

1ST EXTERM: Every edge. All the way around.

FORENSIC: On the sides then. All around the sides. Wouldn't that be a better way to put it.

1ST EXTERM: Yes.

FORENSIC: And are they chained, tied, on leashes attached to men, running wild, vicious, kind. What kind of dogs.

1ST EXTERM: Dobermans, shepherds, griffins.

FORENSIC: Where's the light source now. Where does it come from. How much wattage. What kind of lamps.

1ST EXTERM: Three million kilowatts, underground, double spots, ninety-inch strobes—

FORENSIC: Wait a minute. Underground? Underground! What's underground.

1ST EXTERM: Light source sir.

FORENSIC: Underground light source. How. What kind. How is that possible!

1ST EXTERM: Underground streams sir.

FORENSIC: Water?

1ST EXTERM: Yes sir. That's right sir. Water.

FORENSIC: I'll be damned. How deep.

1ST EXTERM: What.

FORENSIC: How deep down! The water! How many feet.

1ST EXTERM: Oh. I can't reveal that kind of information sir. That's not part of the test.

FORENSIC: Ah ha! (*He grabs the pen off the table and marks a big check on the map, then sets down the pen.*) Not part of the test indeed! You were doing so well for so long.

1ST EXTERM: What do you mean. That's not part of the test. How deep.

FORENSIC: All right, all right. We'll go on. Now then, how many guards are standing on the right wall facing the embankment overlooking the pond.

1ST EXTERM: Wait a minute. I know how deep it is but I'm not supposed to tell.

FORENSIC: Never mind. How many guards.

1ST EXTERM: Don't you want to know how deep.

FORENSIC: How many guards!

Emmet gorges himself faster and faster as the interrogation gets more intense; Oolan keeps filling the bowl; Forensic paces around the table.

1ST EXTERM: Sixty feet deep!

FORENSIC: AH HA! What kind of pumps! Hydraulic, electric, gas. What kind of pumps!

1ST EXTERM: Vacuum sir.

FORENSIC: They run on air then. DO THEY RUN ON AIR!

1ST EXTERM: Yes sir.

FORENSIC: AND IF THE AIR WERE TO BE CUT OFF WHERE WOULD IT BE CUT OFF AT!

1ST EXTERM: At the throttle sir.

FORENSIC: AT THE THROTTLE! WHAT DOES THAT MEAN, AT THE THROTTLE. DON'T YOU MEAN AT THE THROAT. CUT IT OFF AT THE THROAT! DON'T YOU MEAN THAT. ANSWER YES OR NO!

1ST EXTERM: Yes.

FORENSIC: THEN HOW DO WE GET TO THE THROAT FORENSIC!

1ST EXTERM: Through the back sir.

Loud banging again as before; Emmet jumps to his feet with the package of Rice Krispies clutched to his chest;

1st Exterm. jumps up and grabs Oolan holding her tightly as though a bomb is about to drop; Emmet and Forensic rush around the stage not knowing what to do.

EMMET: Hide the Krispies! Hide the Krispies! What'll we do.

FORENSIC: Under the table Emmet!

EMMET: Oolan!

1ST EXTERM: Leave her alone!

FORENSIC: Under the table Oolan!

EMMET: Take the Krispies! Take the Krispies!

Oolan grabs the Krispies from Emmet and hides under the table; 1st Exterm. follows her; another loud knock.

FORENSIC: Not him! Just her! Just Oolan!

1ST EXTERM: Leave her alone!

EMMET: Yes! Who is it please!

2ND EXTERM. (*voice over microphone*): IT'S THE EX-TERMINATOR, LADY!

EMMET: I'm no lady mister! I'm a man!

FORENSIC: Don't talk like a dumb kid Forensic. Open the door.

EMMET: Fuck you. This is my home. Give me that gun.

FORENSIC: Stand back Emmet or I'll blow you wide open.

Emmet lunges at Forensic and grabs the gun; they struggle with the gun; another loud knock, 2nd Exterm's voice.

2ND EXTERM: OPEN THIS DOOR OR I'LL BREAK IT DOWN!

Emmet and Forensic struggle all over the stage with the gun; long loud ripping sound of door being crashed in; at the end of the sound 2nd Exterm. falls onto the stage; he is still dressed in the uniform but without gas mask and tank; a pause as Emmet and Forensic look at 2nd Exterm; they both have hold of the gun and neither of them lets go until the end of the play; 2nd Exterm. gets up slowly and brushes himself off; he looks around the stage.

2ND EXTERM: Boy is it ever weird out there. Have you guys ever been out there.

FORENSIC: Out where.

2ND EXTERM: Out there. You haven't got much time though. I should tell you that right away. Fair warning and all that sort of stuff. Now what's happened to Forensic.

He starts looking around as Emmet and Forensic tug at the gun.

EMMET: What's weird out there mister. I've been out there before and there hasn't been anything weird. What's so weird.

2ND EXTERM: The whole thing. The road and everything. The phone booth. The road. Do you suppose he left or something. I suppose so. It's better I guess.

FORENSIC: What's better. What's weird about the road. Make yourself clear!

2ND EXTERM: Especially the road. Just walking along in a gas mask and looking the way I look and everything. I mean there's not many people but if you run across anybody while you're out there it's really weird. But you'd better get out before it's too late. They'll be here before you can say Jack Robinson.

EMMET: Who?

2ND EXTERM: I suppose what he did was he just decided to quit the whole business. I suppose that's it. He just got tired of waiting around. Left his gear and everything. In fact we must have decided the very same thing at the very same time but we just happened to be in different places is all. That's it I'll bet. I'll bet that's what happened. Just as I put down the receiver and folded the glass door open and stepped outside and looked down at the tank and the mask leaning up against the tree trunk and a semi roaring by, just as he, standing around this table hears the same semi roaring by and takes off the mask and sets down the tank, just as I leave the tank and the mask leaning up against the tree trunk and start following the semi down the road, just as he leaves the room with the tank and the mask sitting here on the floor and starts walking toward— We must have passed each other somewhere. That's it. I'll bet that's what happened. He starts walking toward the phone

booth and I start back toward the house and we missed
each other on the road. I'll bet you that's the way it
happened. But you guys had better get out. They're
going to gas this place once and for all.

*Very slowly blue smoke starts drifting onto the stage;
it keeps up until the stage is completely covered and all
you can hear is voices of the actors; it gradually pours
over into the audience and fills up the entire theatre by
the end of the play; it could change colors in the course
of filling the place up, from blue to pink to yellow to
green.*

FORENSIC: Who is! You're out of your mind! Gimme the gun
Emmet.

EMMET: He's lying Forensic! Can't you see that. He's not in
any hurry to get out so why should we be.

2ND EXTERM: I suppose if I just wait around he's bound to
turn up. Fat chance of finding him this time of night,
walking along in the dark. Barely see your own nose in
front of your own face. Nice place you boys have.

*He sits in the stage left chair, puts his feet on the table
and leans back with his hands folded behind his head;
Emmet and Forensic tug at the gun.*

FORENSIC: He's not either lying. He's called the home office
and found out where the table's supposed to be and
they're sending men out to help him. He's waiting
around for his men. Now gimme the gun Emmet.

EMMET: He just told you that he left all his gear back at
the phone booth and he came back to meet his buddy.
They're deserters Forensic!

2ND EXTERM: Yep. A place like this could get a man dreaming about settling down. Finding some roots. A kind
of headquarters. A place to come back to.

FORENSIC: This is our home!

2ND EXTERM: Where's that woman Emmet!

EMMET: What?

2ND EXTERM: That woman you had here before.

Oolan giggles under the table; nobody hears.

EMMET: Oh she—

FORENSIC: Don't tell! Don't you tell him anything!

2ND EXTERM: The trouble is, what if he's arrived at the phone booth, found my tank and mask leaning up against the tree trunk and thought the same thing as me at the very same time but in two different places. What if he's set himself down inside the phone booth or up against the tree and he's waiting for me thinking the same thing as me; that it's too damn dark to go walking back on that road at this time of night. What if that's the way it is.

EMMET: Then you'd better walk back and get him.

2ND EXTERM: No, no. You don't understand. If either one of us makes another move like the moves we've already made then the whole thing could go on forever. Now is a very crucial time. We have to each think individually what the other one is going to do or we'll just miss each other again and again and we'll finally give up and go our separate ways. Do you get what I mean.

FORENSIC: Maybe he doesn't even want to meet you though. Did you ever think of that.

EMMET: Shut up!

2ND EXTERM: Maybe you're right Forensic. Maybe you're absolutely right. Maybe he doesn't. That means he could be somewhere altogether different from the phone booth. That means he could be anywhere.

FORENSIC: That means he could be right under the table even.

EMMET: Will you shut up!

2ND EXTERM: He most certainly could be Forensic. He most certainly could. Right under my very nose. Right under the table. But that means I'm right then. That both of us are thinking the very same thing at the very same time. But if he's under the table then we're also in the very same place. I hardly think that could be true Forensic because if it were then it could mean only one thing. That he not only doesn't want to meet *me* but he also doesn't want *me* to meet *him*.

1st Exterm.'s voice is heard from under table; Oolan giggles; Emmet and Forensic tug at the gun.

1ST EXTERM: Now you got the picture.

2nd Exterm. stands and paces around the table; he addresses the table.

2ND EXTERM: Then I take it the whole thing's off. Do I take it right! Do I take it right or wrong!

1ST EXTERM: Right! You take it absolutely right.

2ND EXTERM: Then we just split up and go our different ways.

1ST EXTERM: That's up to you. I'm staying here.

EMMET: Will you give me the gun!

2ND EXTERM: I called the home office you know.

1ST EXTERM: I know, I know.

2ND EXTERM: Then I take it you know what's going to happen.

1ST EXTERM: You take it right.

FORENSIC: What's going to happen!

2ND EXTERM: And even so you're willing to stay. Even knowing what's going to happen. You're going to stay here.

1ST EXTERM: Yes I am. I've fallen in love.

EMMET: What's going to happen!

2ND EXTERM: You don't care if we win or lose then. You don't care if I stay or go. You just don't care. YOU JUST DON'T CARE FORENSIC!

FORENSIC: Yes I do! What's going to happen.

1ST EXTERM: Why don't you leave. You don't have to stay.

2ND EXTERM: Me? Alone? You want me to go running out there alone and go skipping up to them in my fancy new uniform and wave and throw kisses maybe and say hey fellas you've got the wrong house, you've got the wrong farm, you've got the wrong lawn. There's nothing here to exterminate. It's just us. It's just us and a few of our gang. Really. Try the next ranch. Try next door or down the road a piece. Down where they've got all the dogs. Down where you hear all the screaming 'til late in the night. We don't even play the phonograph after eleven o'clock. You can ask them if you like. Just down the road there. They'll tell you. Not a complaint in over thirty-five years. You can come in and look but it's just like I say. It's just a bunch of friends not knowing what else to do. Having breakfast now and then. It's pretty dirty but come right on in. Sure, search wherever you like. You won't find a thing. What do you think we are. Patsys or something. What do you think. Sure, tear up the bed, tear off the sheets, rip out the drawers, tear off our clothes. You won't find a thing. Guns? Guns? You think we have guns? Not on your life. Where would we hide guns. Under the floor. Under the floor! You hit the nail right on the old head. Guns under the floor. Under the table. Guns all over the place. See for yourselves. Every turn you make there's another gun. Automatics, elephant guns, Marlin four hundreds. Knock yourselves out. Well I'm not going to do that Forensic. I'm not going out there ever again. I'm staying right here!

Loud banging is heard as before; the smoke by this time has filled up the stage and poured over into the audience; the banging keeps up in short intervals and develops a kind of mounting rhythm; this lasts for quite a while as the smoke gradually begins to thin out; finally as the smoke disappears the actors are all gone plus the table and chairs so that the audience is looking at empty space at the end.

MOON

a play in one act

《BY ROBERT HEIDE

"Each day is dark and dreary,
  But the night is bright and cheery."
——from *When the Moon Comes over the Mountain*
    sung by Kate Smith

Moon is meticulously written in a style that might as
well be called superrealism. Robert Heide is
preoccupied with the experiences of alienation and
pointlessness and transmits them with exquisite intensity.
His characters make contact only when they panic.
Under his own direction, *Moon* was a plastic, hysterical
largo, played at a pace measured to the rhythm of
metapsychological despair—boredom forced to be
expressive. Only with the arrival of Christopher, the
Parsifal figure, does the space-age moon regain its
reflective power to light the heart.

M. S.

Moon was first presented at the Caffe Cino, 31 Cornelia Street, New York, on St. Valentine's Day, February 14, 1967. It was directed by the author with the following cast:

SALLY: Jane Buchanan
SAM: Victor LiPari
INGRID: Jacque Lynn Colton
HAROLD: Jim Jennings
CHRISTOPHER: John Gilman

Lighting design: Donald Brooks

A return engagement opened on January 30, 1968, with the following cast:

SALLY: Linda Eskenas
SAM: Robert Frink
INGRID: Lucy Silvay
HAROLD: Jim Jennings
CHRISTOPHER: John Gilman

Lighting design: John P. Dodd
Film sequence: Bill Stern

Lucy Silvay (Ingrid), James Jennings (Harold), and Victor LiPari (Sam) in *Moon*

Environment

The set should be a maximum of simplicity and symmetry meant only to "represent" symbolically an apartment in the Village.

The room and the objects in it are of a dark bilious color.

In contrast, blazing white light like the high-power-intensity lighting that might be used inside of a microscope.

On the wall: a square of multicolored plastic with two transistor knobs which represent dials used in the play to turn sound "on" and "off."

The usual areas and objects: windows (fourth wall), shelves, tables, seating arrangements, kitchen facilities—a range, coffee pot, cups, etc., the outer hallway and door into the apartment.

Characters

SALLY, A young woman in a loose-fitted black sweater and skirt, an unmade-up appearance, ballet slippers.

SAM, a young man in a turtleneck sweater, baggy pants, sandals or slippers; he does not bother combing his hair.

INGRID, a girl dressed in the latest and most exaggerated of the newest fashion, with emphasis on breasts, legs, and shoulders; flat shoes. She enters and leaves wearing a black fur coat. Her dress is silver. She carries a large handbag filled with pillboxes, makeup, poppers, anything imaginable.

HAROLD, a tall young man in dungarees, a leather jacket, heavy workman's shoes that are coated with mud.

CHRISTOPHER, the young man upstairs; white pants, white shirt, a clean scrubbed appearance, a look of innocence.

The characters, with the exception of Christopher and Ingrid, wear black.

Sam is reclining on the daybed, back to audience.

Sally sits closely on a low stool.

Sally breathes heavily, twitching and playing restlessly with her hands.

She stares full force at Sam as if she expected some movement on his part. She makes a quiet, gurgling sound in an attempt to attract attention.

Sam remains tight-faced, his head buried deeply into an open book. It is not discernible whether or not he is actually reading. He seems tense, withdrawn.

Abruptly, Sally jumps up as though she were about to let out a scream.

She paces wildly like a confined beast.

Her body seems to heave as if she even felt "trapped" in it.

Quickly, she switches on the phonograph.

Over the speaker system we hear "2,000 LIGHT YEARS," The Rolling Stones.

Sally dances wildly attempting to distract Sam. She soon becomes caught in a free-form dance. Perhaps she is rehearsing for a dance class.

The record begins to repeat itself.

About one quarter of the way through the second playing, Sam rushes up and shuts off the machine with forceful intent and anger as if he might begin to let loose a rage at any given moment.

SAM (*loud, nervous*): There are times I'd like some . . . silence . . . around here . . . peace of mind . . . quiet!

Pause.

SALLY (*pacing back and forth*): I . . . ha . . . ha . . . feel nervous . . . fidgety myself. There's somehow a tenseness . . . a heaviness in the air. I don't know. I mean . . . (*slight pause.*) I'm not sure what . . . Oh nothing . . . I guess I'm just a little on edge . . .

51

She sits down. Pause.

SAM (*sitting*): What happened last night . . . to us? I don't
    seem . . . I'm not able to remember . . . anything.

SALLY (*getting up. Confronting him*): You became violent
    . . . you had consumed a great deal of liquor . . . it was
    strange . . . I mean—I had never known you to become
    so violent before. You came at me and . . .

SAM: Let's not talk about it. Let's go into something else . . .
    some other subject . . . something less . . . strenuous.

SALLY (*moving further into him*): Maybe you're feeling
    guilty . . .

SAM: I don't want to talk about it . . . whatever it is . . .
    you want to go into it . . . I don't! That's final . . .
    whatever it is—I say!

SALLY: Whatever what is? (*Pause.*) Look! Will you just talk
    to me? Talk! (*Pause.*) Well, I can't take it!

SAM: Take what?

SALLY: Your silence. Your withdrawals. Your . . . noncom-
    munication. I'm fed up.

Pause.

SAM: I'm sick . . . I feel sick. I have a hangover. My head is
    bad. All day I . . . oh, what's the . . .

SALLY: Does that mean we can't talk . . . say anything?
    (*Pause.*) Maybe you'd rather be alone. Have your with-
    drawal . . . alone. It feels stuffy in here. Hot. Close. I
    can't breathe. (*Beginning to go out. Moves frenetically*)

SAM (*gets up. Pulls her down. Slaps her*): Sit down! Relax
    your complicated little anxieties. Have some coffee. Later
    we will discuss whatever it is that needs discussing be-
    tween . . . ourselves . . . between us. For now, let us
    discuss only everyday things. My mind . . . (*Slight
    pause.*) Later I will be . . . prepared to face . . . to look
    at the ugliness . . . the abstractions . . . the truth of
    things. Here, smoke a cigarette.

SALLY (*putting cigarette to her mouth and lighting it ner-
    vously. Quickly, she extinguishes it. Gets up moving
    downstage*): Today is not such a good day for me. I feel
    . . . nervous . . . ha . . . ha. Sometimes I don't know
    what is happening to me either . . . what is the matter
    with me. Something stirs up inside of me . . . like some

blind instinct I can't control . . . inside of me. I feel I could burst open . . . explode. I get to feeling desperate. I want to run somewhere . . . away . . . I just don't know . . . where . . . out to the store . . . to a movie.

SAM (*behind her*): Just try to remain calm . . . try . . .

Slight pause.

SALLY (*more composed*): Let's begin again . . . a new conversation . . . not relating to yesterday at all . . . uh . . . tell me . . . I mean . . . let us forget those few moments of anxiety we just had . . . begin again. Calmly. Can we? Can we begin again calmly? Yes. (*Pause. Sally puts her head into Sam's lap as she sits on the floor.*) What kind of day . . . tell . . . what it was like . . . earlier . . . what you did . . . what went on?

SAM (*reserved*): Just a day. The usual happenings. Statistical reports. Office rituals. Making additions and additions and pushing buttons . . . then . . .

Pause.

SALLY: What?

SAM (*half to himself*): Oh, nothing . . . I was thinking about things not really adding up . . . anywhere . . . in my head . . . I mean . . . my life.

SALLY (*jumping up*): Is that some personal inference to me? Are you meaning to infer . . .?

SAM (*in a rage. Grabbing her*): Look, will you shut up before I break your arm? Shut up, I said!

A pause. A transition.

SALLY: Did you see today's paper? Did you see the paper . . . read the news today?

SAM: I didn't feel like looking at it . . . my head and all. I had two Bromo Seltzers. What an idiotic party! Stupid people! "Hello, and what do you do with your life, young man? How are you justifying your existence?" Blah! Social events! (*A slight pause. Sam moves onto the floor.*) Anything in it?

SALLY: What?

SAM: In the paper . . . anything in it . . . today's paper . . . of interest . . . that I should know . . . be informed about?

SALLY (*circling around him*): Only the usual everyday chaos
. . . problems. Someone shot five people . . . in Texas
. . . I think it was. A young man. Eighteen. In a beauty
parlor it was. Five women. He said he did it for the
publicity, to get his name in the paper. He wanted to
be a celebrity . . . become recognized . . . I guess. Something about high food prices having something to do
with the high cost of war or . . . something. Some
paintings . . . old masterpieces . . . were stolen. (*Slight
pause. She gets onto the floor with Sam. The lights go
down.*) The moon. There was a feature article on the
moon. (*Laughing to herself.*) It's strange . . . funny
. . . I mean.

SAM: What's funny?

SALLY (*playful*): I mean . . . I was just thinking . . . you
can't really talk about the moon the same old way anymore like people used to in Shakespeare's plays and all.
You can't say . . . with poetic emphasis . . . "O Moon!"
like in *Romeo and Juliet* or (*Singing now, somewhat
flatly.*) "It's only a paper moon . . . hanging over a card-
board sea" or (*More throaty. Matronly like Kate Smith.*)
"When the moon comes over the mountain" . . . I'm
really crazy about Kate Smith aren't you? (*Low.*) Moo
. . . Moooooooooon. (*Dramatically—staring forward.*)
"The cow jumped over the moon . . . hey diddle . . .
diddle . . . the cat and his fiddle . . ." or something.
The whole idea struck me as just "funny" . . . somehow
. . . I guess . . . ridiculous. Moon. Blah! I mean there it
is . . . really just there . . . if yah wanna look at it.
No longer just some romantic 1920's singsong abstraction
. . . something to aspire to . . . to look at from a great
distance through a telescope. Wait. Here's a picture.
I'll show you. (*Goes to handbag and brings out a news-
paper—sits back down.*) Here. (*Pointing.*) I mean
doesn't it look odd and bumpy and all? See . . . here!
Right here is this diagram . . . the first moon city. Moon
city. They plan to build it . . . to live there . . a whole
lot of people . . . on the moon—eventually . . . soon
. . . in the not-too-distant future. And later, Mars . . .
Venus. Whole communities under a huge air-condi-
tioned–oxygenized plastic bubble! It's kinduv fantastic
. . . I think . . . I mean living up there in space and all

. . . I mean not that we're not in space too . . . right here . . . already, now . . . I mean . . . well . . . people . . . the idea of it . . . real people . . . you and I maybe . . . and everybody . . . living on the moon. It would be like being a real pioneer . . . up there. The first experimental community . . . mmmm.

SAM (*bursting her dream bubble, he gets up. Brighter light*): So when do we make reservations?

SALLY: Huh?

SAM (*going back to his novel*): Reservations . . . numbskull. Plans? Don't we have to make plane or rocket reservations . . . or something?

SALLY (*deflated. Sad. Bewildered by her own enthusiasms*): Yeah . . . yes . . . I guess so. (*Pause. Angrily.*) Probably it won't happen for some time though . . . even . . . in our own lifetime, I mean. A moon community. Maybe it will.

SAM (*taking over the room like an actor*): Probably it will turn out to be just another Levittown, U.S.A. . . . if "we" get there first before the Reds . . . if that matters anymore . . . the U.S.L.B.J.H.H.H.R.M.N.F.Q.U.—P.? . . . with shopping centers, five and ten cent stores, Grand Unions, bowling alleys . . . superhighways, movie houses. . . . (*Slightly deflated.*) . . . beauty parlors. (*Pause. There is a prolonged silence in which the two characters do not utter a sound. Finally Sam brings things back to some notion of reality.*) My book . . . the book I was reading . . . did you see it?

SALLY (*looking*): What? Oh. Book. Uh . . . no . . . let me see . . .

SAM (*looking around the room*): I don't know where it is. (*Finding it.*) Ah, here it is!

(*He sits down. Begins to read. Pause.*)

SALLY: Can we hear the radio?

SAM: No! I'd rather it remain off if you don't mind. I'd rather listen to just . . . silence.

SALLY: Okay. Okay. Don't yell! (*Slight pause. Nervous.*) Would you like some coffee?

SAM: If you're gonna make some . . . if you're having some . . .

SALLY (*in kitchen area*): Is the book good?

SAM: What?

SALLY (*looking for a confrontation*): Damn you. Will you
    listen! I said—is the book you are reading any good?

SAM: It's okay.

SALLY (*angry*): Well, why are you reading it if it's just okay?
    Haven't you any better way to live out your existence?

SAM: How?

SALLY: Mmmm. I don't know. You said once you wanted to
    paint a picture or something.

SAM (*ignoring her last statement*): No. I mean it's good . . .
    I guess. (*Slight pause.*) Anyhow, I know how it ends.

SALLY (*curious*): How?

SAM (*perturbed*): How?

SALLY (*demanding*): How?

SAM (*scratching his head*): Mmmmm. Well . . . you really
    wanna hear? Well . . . this couple have been making it,
    see. I mean both of them are married . . . I mean each
    one to someone else like; but they are having this affair
    see . . . with one another, that is. Get it?

SALLY: Yeah. Dope!

SAM: So they are driving back from this weekend on the
    French Riviera, St. Tropez, I think. It's French . . . the
    book . . . I mean it takes place, see, in France. Well,
    the whole book is about how they can't . . . either one
    of them . . . have an affair . . . even . . anymore.

SALLY: What?

SAM: Anyhow, they are suffering from a kind of modern
    metaphysical boredom . . . and all . . . living in an in-
    creasingly mechanized and alienated world. They feel
    alienated from one another . . . alienated even to them-
    selves . . . see . . . each individual self. They can't get
    together . . . yet they can't really be apart either. He . . .
    the man, is married to this famous chanteuse named
    Cleo who is never at home cause she has this . . . her
    career . . . and so he feels, existentially speaking, that
    he is in her eyes—like an object, like an old table or
    chair—very Sartrean—I mean, they talk a lot about life
    being one big nothing and all . . . in the book . . .
    (*Slight pause.*) or was it Heidegger.

SALLY (*under her breath*): —Heidegger.

SAM: See, he, the main character, is a philosophy student.
    So, anyhow, he doesn't feel related to this wife who is

so obsessed . . . up tight . . . having this "overneed" for her career. She sings these very sorrowful songs; (*Sally jumps up making a screeching sound. Looks stage front. Looks into fourth wall mirror.*) and, when she's not doing that, she is looking in the mirror—checking out her image and all. Well, she doesn't like sex either . . .

SALLY (*loudly*): Who? Who!?

SAM: Cleo . . . even though she's supposed to be some sex image to her fans. They write her dirty suggestive letters which she, in turn, answers. (*Sally mimics letter writing.*) See. It makes Henri . . . that's our hero's name . . . feel disgusted . . . even though he never brings the subject forth . . . out into the open. So Henri takes up with Françoise . . . see. She's married . . . kinduv . . . to this uncle of hers who's this novelist . . . older. Anyhow, he knows about the affair. In fact, he encourages it. See, he's bored too . . . with everything.

SALLY (*worried*): Then what happens?

SAM (*running amok*): Well, it gets complicated cause everywhere they go . . . well . . . it gets more and more frenetic . . . the tension . . . the plot . . . hysterical . . . and Françoise thinks she is pregnant by some oriental houseboy too. (*He grabs Sally. They play out the "game" of the novel fully. They mimic driving a car together.*) Well . . . being bored and all she drives off on this highway into this Mack Truck . . . (*Sally screams.*) in a red Porsche—sort of like James Dean. It ends with a double funeral where Cleo sings Chanson de Mort . . . The Song of Death . . . (*Lights down. At this point we hear the voice of Cleo singing in French over the loudspeaker with full orchestra. This goes on for one full minute. Lights up.*) but everyone is bored even there too. I mean, what does death mean if you're really hip and all. Anyhow, to make a long story short . . . Cleo meets the uncle . . . at the funeral, which the uncle paid for . . . heh . . . heh . . . and they grab hands . . . (*Sally and Sam grab hands. Hollywood music ensues loudly. They "act out" a "Hollywood ending."*) touch one another. They feel . . . well . . . through the death of Françoise and Henri they have a reawakening . . . a kinduv catharsis into . . . being able to "really" feel and all. You know, like maybe things are not so

bad after all? So anyway, they go off and make it or
something. I mean it ends on a kinduv positive note . . .
y'know . . . (*Music off.*) but not too positive . . . he
he . . . he. Hey, are you listening?

SALLY: I thought you said you just read the end?

SAM (*in a fury*): Yeh, I did . . . but I read this review of it
in *The Village Voice*. I mean, they gave the whole story
and all. That's what made me wanna read it. They said
it was . . . well . . . subtle in its exploration of character
relationship . . . that's what made me wanna read it.
I mean . . . (*Intense. Angry.*) people feel alienated. They
don't know how to get together. Oh, Christ . . . I don't
know! Don't ask me questions about what I'm reading.
I lost my goddamn place!

SALLY (*dreamy*): Maybe they'll make a movie out of it.

SAM: Yeah . . . they are already with Jean Seberg and Mar-
cello . . . no . . . it's not him . . . somebody like him
. . . Belmondo . . . no. It's . . . what the hell is his
name? Trig . . . Trig . . . Trigonet . . . Jean Louis
Trintignant. . . . I wish I had a name like that. Yeah.
(*Movie soundtrack music pours forth. The lighting goes
kaleidescopic.*) Brigitte Bardot will be Cleo and maybe
Charles Boyer for the uncle. Ha ha. A super-technicolor
panavisti . . . spectacle . . . in pornovision!

On the word pornovision *Sam and Sally roll around on
the floor together in "mock" copulation. They breathe
heavily, remaining on the floor. They make sounds, then
separate, exhauted still on the floor.*

SALLY (*entering movieland*): Jean Louis Trintignant. Wasn't
he in *The Sleeping Car Murder?* Didn't we see that at
the Eighth Street . . . or was it the Garrick?

SAM: Did we see that? Did we see that one?

SALLY: Yeah . . . I remember . . . you fell asleep in it.

SAM: Oh, was it good?

SALLY: Okay . . . I guess . . . It's not my type of thing.

SAM: Who got murdered?

SALLY: Murdered?

SAM: Yeah. *Sleeping Car Murder.* Murder mystery. Who got
murdered?

SALLY (*getting up*): Six people . . . I think . . . two homosexual lovers plot the whole thing to get this lottery

check from this actress . . . Simone Signoret. She is in
love with one of them . . . not knowing he's gay . . .
or knowing . . . and thinking she can change his direction . . . I don't remember which. Ha.

SAM (*moving restlessly*): Oh, yeah . . . and one of them
works for the cops or something . . . as a detective . . .
and he's working to try to solve the case!

SALLY: Then . . . you weren't sleeping?

SAM: Well, partly.

SALLY (*running after him, tickling him*): How does it end?
I'll *murder* you, you ass! How does it end? Tell me.

SAM (*rolling on to the floor*): Stop it! Cut it out! Stop!

SALLY (*straddling him*): They don't make it. They're gonna
live happily ever after on some South Sea Island in a
rose-covered cottage on Simone Signoret's money . . .
but they don't make it . . . they get caught and they
don't make it. Ha! Ha!

SAM (*half sarcasm, half humor. Getting up*): Tough! Nobody makes it, bitch.

SALLY (*serious now. Angry*): They don't? Why not?

SAM (*flying into fantasy*): Cause I say so and I'm the President and I have the power and I'm gonna blow up the
whole world anyway. Blow it up. (*Throwing imaginary
hand grenades.*) Boom. BOOM! Booom.

SALLY (*confronting*): You're a paranoid-schizophrenic living
in Greenwich Village with delusions of grandeur and
an inclination toward anticipating disaster out of every
situation. Ha. How's that for a penny analysis?

SAM (*furious*): I could be Jesus Christ and you wouldn't
know the difference.

SALLY (*in a full-fledged argument*): He was another paranoid
too.

SAM: Says who?

SALLY (*moving in circles around Sam*): Albert Schweitzer,
baby . . . in this book I read—A *Psychiatric Study of
Jesus*. He said there is a lot of evidence to support that
old J.C. may have been another psychotic with another
Christ complex out to save the whole world just like
you . . . or maybe destroy it.

SAM (*throwing his arms around her as if they were about to
ascend into space*): Boom. Boom. Boom. Then we could
go live . . . pioneer on the old green cheese moon.

SALLY (*breaking off. Sitting*): Ah, who cares. I'm sick of the whole world anyhow. Why pretend anything else.

Pause.

SAM: You sure you read that book correctly?

SALLY: Whadahyamean?

SAM: I mean you're always reading things into things. Your imagination. Your fantasy projection transferences. (*No reply. Pause.*) How about lighting a joint? (*Goes to kitchen where he gets joint.*)

SALLY (*after him in the kitchen*): Go ahead! You light it! Transcend existence. Catatonize yourself. What do I care!

SAM (*grabbing her. Pulls her down*): What!?

SALLY: Go ahead! Break my arm too.

SAM: Nobody's breaking your arm. (*Slight pause. Sally waves her arm at Sam in jest and anger.*) Let's sit down and keep quiet . . . shut up . . . for a while.

SALLY (*a last stand*): You'd like to avoid all communications with me . . . just blow pot all day long . . . reach Nirvana or something . . . who knows what or where you want to get to. The moon. Dreams. Movies. I'm sick of it all. It's all just *"lies"* anyway. (*Hysterical.*) Lies! (*Screaming.*) Lies!

SAM: . . . Now, calm down. You're having one of your free-floating anxiety attacks again. Just calm down sweets . . . love . . . valentine.

SALLY (*biting*): At least it's not free-floating paranoia or simple-schizophrenia or some swimming-in-a-sea-of-ambiguity . . . like you.

SAM: Your terminology is really flying. You sound like some coffee klatch in the dorm after Psych I . . . at NYU. The girl who's always waving her hand in the last row who knows all the answers but none of the . . . Now, just calm yourself. Here. (*Hands her a joint.*) Light it. (*She does. He sits.*) My nerves. My body is still depressed from all that rotten alcohol we drank last night. Put on some music . . . on the machine. Indian. (*Gets onto the floor in yoga position.*) I want to meditate . . . concentrate . . . groove . . . with something . . . spiritual.

SALLY (*standing over him*): Do I have to meditate? (*She puts on Indian raga music. They sit, eyes closed, at-*

tempting meditation. After a moment.) I can't concentrate on anything today. Somehow . . . I . . .

SAM: Shut up! Meditate . . . or just keep your trap shut! I can't talk anymore!

They remain silent, listening to the music, passing a joint back and forth to one another. After a long moment, Ingrid and Harold are heard by the audience— as it were, moving down the corridor outside the apartment. They are pushing and shoving one another, physically close to violence.

INGRID (*berating. Loudly, trumpeting*): What kind of people don't put their names on the bell . . . I ask you?! (*She passes back and forth looking at various doorways.*) I think what they told us was four-R . . . that means rear! These stairs are killing me. Maybe we should go back down . . . go have a drink somewhere by ourselves. Oh, wait. Here. (*Looking.*) There's nothing more embarrassing than knocking on the wrong door. (*She pulls out a nose popper and begins sniffing, trying to get higher.*) That man was naked and I think he was having sex in there . . . with a boy too. Sex has a very decisive, odoriferous smell I tell you. Don't you have anything to say? (*Moving close.*) I suppose you would like to have joined in or something, into the sexual act, but yet you can't raise it up when it comes to me. (*At this point Ingrid reaches into her handbag. She pulls out a pillbox and begins gulping pills. She offers one to Harold. He refuses.*) Now try to compose yourself. (*Slight pause.*) Act natural. Try not to indicate . . . to show . . . that we are having marital difficulties. It's not in good taste to wear your problems out in the open for public consumption as it were . . . this being a social situation. Now try to remember these simple rules . . . Oh . . . ha . . . ha . . . Here we are. Hello. Hello. (*Loud. Demanding*) Anybody home? Hello. Shhh. Shh.

SALLY (*disrupted*): Who's that?

SAM (*trancelike*): What? . . . Shhhh . . . Quiet! I'm thinking . . .

Sally, realizing a presence, gets up and turns off the music. Puts on ballet slippers.

INGRID (*a false cheerfulness*): Uh . . . Hi—You . . . uh . . .
    left your door open. Can we come in? (*Examining the
    place suspiciously.*) You shouldn't leave your door open
    . . . you know, with all the murders, rapes and robberies
    going on . . . in the city . . . uh . . . heh . . . mmmm.

*An awkward, silent heavy tension takes over the room.
The two couples stalk one another.*

SALLY (*polite, pulling herself together. Breaking the freeze*):
    Oh . . . well . . . come in . . . sit down . . . wherever you
    can . . . there's not much room. Let me have your coat.
INGRID: Yes. (*Removes her coat and scarf. Sally disposes of
    it quickly. Goes to Harold.*) Harold, your jacket!
HAROLD (*staring downward. A tight lip*): I prefer to keep it
    on . . . thank you.
INGRID (*moving toward couch*): A cold. Harold is afraid of
    catching a cold, aren't you Harold? (*No answer. A false
    merriment.*) I said to Harold . . . I bet you people
    forgot about having us over . . . er . . . the party . . .
    last night? Remember? Ha . . . ha . . . Well, we almost
    didn't come. (*An awkward pause.*) We had your ad-
    dress . . . your phone number. We were gonna call . . .
    first. We tried. Didn't we honey? Didn't we try?
HAROLD (*dull, not listening*): Yeah.
INGRID (*anxious. somewhat terrified*): You've had your phone
    disconnected. I said to Harold . . . "I bet you forgot."
    It was just a casual, meaningless suggestion on your part.
    Just drop by. And here we are . . . Heh . . . mmm.
    (*Slight pause. To Sam.*) Harold would rather have his
    face in the TV or be screwing nuts and bolts into his
    machines. It was my decision to venture out. (*Cornering
    Sally.*) You can still renege . . . shoo us off . . . if you
    want to be alone. Tee . . . hee.
SALLY (*trying to place her guests in her mind*): Oh . . . uh
    . . . no . . . uh . . . we don't mind. We were just
    . . . sitting . . . listening to some music . . . weren't we?
    Why . . . uh . . . don't you sit . . .?
INGRID: I'll just sit down . . . (*Accidentally falling.*)
    OOoooooooooooo!
HAROLD (*half to himself*): The clumsy never succeed.
INGRID (*getting up. Menacing*): What did you say?

HAROLD: I said . . . "The clumsy never succeed" . . . just an old saying from my mother.

INGRID (*Angry, staring long and hard*): Your mother! She certainly didn't teach *you* anything . . . about success . . . in the *real* world. (*Harold moves toward her with violent intent. Abruptly, she switches her attitude to the coquette, realizing she is with "others."*) What an interesting and cute apartment you have. Ha. Ha. Very bizarre. Very interesting. I'm sure our turning up is a complete surprise . . . I said to Harold . . . it was a casual suggestion . . . on your part. (*Desperate.*) Lots of people write their names and addresses on little pieces of paper and hand them to people they meet . . . at parties . . . never really expecting . . . acknowledgment . . . or a visitation.

SALLY: It doesn't matter. We were very drunk. Part of the evening is a complete blur . . . in both of our minds. Yes? (*Harold walks blindly into Sally. She stares full force at him, then breaks it off.*) Something happened which we don't remem . . . ber.

This last statement is followed by a long dead silence in which the four characters stare blankly, bewilderedly at one another. An uncomfortable tension takes over the room.

INGRID (*gazing at Harold and Sally*): Er . . . ah.

SALLY (*snapping her fingers nervously*): We . . . uh . . . were having some coffee. (*Pause.*) Would anybody like some coffee . . . or something?

HAROLD (*following her*): Yeah.

INGRID (*Nervous, trying to make conversation*): Harold doesn't say much . . . really . . . in company. (*Cornering, advancing toward Sally in kitchen.*) We were just married . . . a year it is. We're just beginning to get used to one another . . . understand our position in relationship to one another as to who has the upper hand and all that stuff. He's a little shy . . . awkward . . . ha . . . ha . . . in a social situation. (*Slight pause. Leaves kitchen. Sits next to Sam on sofa.*) What time did you people leave last night's festivities?

SALLY (*moving away from Harold's steady advances*): Time? What . . . time? I'm not sure . . .

INGRID (*angry. Sarcastic*): We left early. Harold got sick . . . mixing the drinks. Didn't you Harold? Didn't you get sick last night?

HAROLD (*with controlled violence, a smirk across his face*): Yeah.

INGRID: That's why we left early. I mean as opposed to staying on and on. Harold feels . . . that it's better to leave before things . . . people . . . become decadent as they very often do at parties He wouldn't like it . . . (*She moves closer to Sam putting her arm around his neck seductively.*) I mean . . . if somebody tried to screw . . . I mean . . . rape me . . . made advances or anything. (*More excited.*) Harold is capable . . . I mean Harold might . . . it is within his capacity to murder someone. Didn't you say you might murder someone Harold . . . if someone . . . I mean . . . made advances on me . . . on my person . . . at a party . . . or someplace?

HAROLD: Yeah.

INGRID (*going into her purse*): I carry this tear-gas gun. My Aunt Emma gave it to me . . . She sent it through the mail all the way from Kansas . . . that's where I'm from . . . mmm. You never know about men . . . she says . . . in New York City (*She gets up and pulls out gun, pointing it bluntly at Sam*) Yah wanna see it?

HAROLD (*grabbing her. They wrestle for the gun*): Gimme! . . . that!

INGRID: Harold! You're hurting me. It might go off. Harold!

HAROLD (*twisting her arm. Throwing her down*): Sit down!

INGRID: My arm!

SALLY (*ignoring the situation. Trying to remain cool*): I think coffee is ready.

SAM (*quietly*): You people like music?

INGRID (*going up to Harold*): We should apologize.

HAROLD (*breaking from her*): I'll do my own apologizing if there's any to be done. (*To the rest of the room.*) What my wife, Ingrid, is trying to communicate to you all is that I have . . . a kind of . . . violent personality . . . an uncontrollable temper. When I get worked up . . . (*Pause. He sits down. Lights go dim.*) You see, I was a Marine . . . in the Marines. (*Slight pause.*) Of course

... even as a kid ... well ... I'm not sure what it is. (*Slight pause.*) Back in Texas where I come from ... a man was murdered ... I mean to say that I don't conceal any longer this nightmare truth. I loved him ... I guess. He was my buddy ... in the Marines and after. We went everywhere ... together. Well, one night ... we shared a double bed ... (*Slight pause*) He was asleep. I was fooling ... kidding around. I put a pillow over his face. He had asthma or something ... respiration trouble. Anyway, in the fooling around ... he stopped breathing. I took the pillow off his face. His eyes were open ... staring ... at me. Later, there was an inquisition you see. I was set free. It was decided that what he had had was a heart attack. Somehow, in me ... I knew that ...

INGRID (*jumping up abruptly*): Oh ... Stop it! Stop telling everyone you meet that morbid and ludicrous story. You don't know ... you can't be absolutely certain that it wasn't an accident. You said that he had a heart condition ... or something. Why continue to implicate yourself any further. This wallowing in guilt.

HAROLD (*still "in" the story. Moves up*): There is ... there was ... an intention ... somewhere ... in me. There must have been. I don't understand.

INGRID (*quickly. Going at him like an attorney that is onto a victim*): We understand! It is obvious ... psychologically obvious ... a clear deduction that you were in love with this man ... that because of convention ... this love ... you could not consummate it. It turned then into hatred. You hated yourself and him for remaining unfulfilled ... repressed.

HAROLD (*loud*): Shut up!

INGRID (*moving in tightly*): Why lie! You can't express ... the truth. So you choose me with all my convenient sexual fears to share your guilt ... to continue to support your image of manhood ... punishing me for what was done to you by your family. I'm tired of playing the role of mother-substitute. I'm ...

HAROLD: Shut up I say ... you bitch!

He grabs her throat, pulls her to her knees and begins to strangle her with intent to kill. We hear Ingrid make a gurgling sound. Sam and Sally watch frozen in terror.

SAM (*finally*): This will have to stop! (*Sam pulls Harold off of Ingrid bodily, forcing him to yield his grip. They are on the verge of a fist fight.*) You will both have to leave . . . just *leave!*

INGRID (*still on the floor*): I'm sorry. Please. Let us stay. Just for a moment. Till we pull ourselves together. (*An awkward silence follows. Ingrid stays on the floor for a long while. Finally she gets up. Goes to kitchen. Gets a drink. Sits back on sofa.*) Harold has vivid fantasies. He goes to an analyst three times a week. These stories . . . he . . . prefabricates them to bring attention to himself. There is no basis in truth to what has been said.

Sam moves to the phonograph.

SAM (*nervous*): Do . . . uh . . . you like music? I'll put on a record.

SALLY: Not now.

INGRID (*sitting nervously, humiliated*): Yes . . . play it . . . anything.

They listen through a three-minute record. Very loud. Dave Clark 5, "Do You Love Me." During the record the lights go up. Ingrid swallows about seven different pills. Harold and Sally stare at one another. Harold is attracted. Sally is strangely drawn to his look. Sam begins to do a shaking rock and roll dance. Each character is caught in his own private world, lost, lonely, bewildered. At the end of the record, Sally puts on her coat and hat.

SALLY (*quickly*): Er . . . ah . . . ha . . . ha. Would . . . uh . . . you all excuse me for a moment? I think there is something I forgot to get at the store. (*She leaves.*)

INGRID (*desperate*): Where is she going?

SAM (*half dazed*): She said to the store. She sometimes leaves abruptly.

INGRID: Her leaving seemed peculiar just then. (*Ingrid looks at Harold. He is onto the sofa lying down, legs outstretched, reading Sam's book. Ingrid gets onto the floor herself. She heaves convulsively, making sounds. She has taken too many drugs. The room spins in her head. She gets half up after a long moment.*) I don't know. I'm not sure why . . . we came here. Harold . . . we must go . . .

home . . . now. (*Getting her things.*) I feel a sudden
panic seizing hold of me here. (*Going up to Sam.*) I
am sorry. Perhaps we will see you again . . . sometime.
Harold. Leave one of our cards. (*They put on their
things and proceed to leave.*) You invited us from the
party. (*She menaces Sam a final time.*) I said to Harold
earlier that you had probably forgotten. Goodbye. Come
along, Harold.

*Sam waves halfheartedly with his hand, his back turned
to the audience. There is a long moment in which he
walks about the room examining its various sections. He
goes to the phonograph: but does not play it. He walks
to window area [fourth wall], staring straight out. We
hear traffic sounds. Finally, he lies down, exhausted.*

*Enter slowly Christopher in white pants and white
sweater. He carries a loaf of bread in a pan.*

CHRISTOPHER: Er . . . ah . . . hello. (*No reply. Sam is asleep.
Finally, startled by a strange presence, Sam jolts up,
confronting Christopher.*) We . . . my friend and I . . .
we made some bread . . . upstairs. We just moved in.
We had nothing to do today . . . so we made . . . we
made some bread. (*Slight pause.*) There is a funny
smell in here. Well, I'll just leave it then. (*Begins to
leave.*)

SAM (*puzzled*): No. Wait.

CHRISTOPHER: Yes?

SAM (*goes to him*): Did you want something?

CHRISTOPHER: (*quietly*): No.

SAM: You moved in . . . upstairs . . . in the vacant rooms?

CHRISTOPHER: Yes.

SAM: What is your name?

CHRISTOPHER: Christopher. My friend is Joe. He's asleep.

SAM: Oh. (*Pause.*) Would you like some wine . . . or coffee?

CHRISTOPHER (*hesitant*): No. I must get back. I'm a painter
. . . see. I want to sort of get to bed early so I can get
up . . . in the morning . . . to get the light. The sky-
light . . . the light here . . . upstairs . . . is the reason
we took the space . . . it being on the top floor. I need
it for my painting. The daylight. Well, as I said . . . I
wanted to bring you down one of the loaves . . . we

made two . . . see who was living underneath . . . introduce myself . . . So . . .

SAM: What do you paint?

CHRISTOPHER (*moving about the room. Intense*): Circles
mostly. Just circles. You'll come up and see them sometime. I'm kinduv *obsessed* with circles, see. They are
meant . . . I guess . . . to represent . . . ha . . . ha . . .
the earth, sun, moon and all the other planets in the
heavens, the solar system. I use many brilliant colors,
electric colors, red, green . . . yellow . . . they hurt your
eyes if you look at them too long. (*Pause.*) Well . . . we
heard the music. We thought you might like some. We'll
see you again . . . come back down . . . maybe . . . tomorrow you'll meet my friend.

*Exit Christopher. There is a moment in which Sam
stares at the bread. He picks it up and puts it in the
breadbox. Enter Sally.*

SAM (*after a moment. Softly*): Where did you go?

SALLY: I don't know . . . I just had to leave . . . get out . . .
get some air. I brought back some milk. (*Puts paper
bag she is carrying down.*)

SAM: They've gone.

SALLY: Yes, I see.

SAM: I don't remember ever having met them. Do you? . . .
at that party?

SALLY: No . . . I . . . . (*Pause.*) I don't want to talk about
them . . . now.

SAM: What is it you want to do?

SALLY: I don't know.

SAM: What were you thinking about . . . what were you
doing . . . what happened to you while you were out?
Tell me. Talk to me. Philosophize . . . anything. I
feel . . .

SALLY (*entering the game*): Oh . . . not much happened . . .
really. I walked around the same block two . . . three
. . . times. I thought . . . if only there were someplace
to go . . . to . . . to run away to. I thought . . . I would
like to leave this city . . . go back to St. Louis—all the
time knowing . . . inside . . . I could never go back there
anymore. Backwards. I said to myself . . . "there is nowhere to go . . . nowhere left for you to run to." I

passed by the newsstand . . . on the square. The headline
on the evening paper glared up at me saying . . . "A
Man Walks On The Moon." (*She laughs.*) It struck me
as being funny somehow. Then, I ran back here . . .
right then. Right away. That's all.

SAM (*lightly in a matter-of-fact-manner*): One day . . . I
suppose . . . as you said earlier tonight . . . there will be
this community . . . a community of men who will be
living on the moon in a plastic bubble . . . but it will
not seem either strange or funny at all . . . to anyone
who will just . . . be . . . there—in that situation. And
things will not be that much different from what they
are . . . right here . . . right now. The truth is none of
us will really ever know anything about the deeper,
darker mysteries of existence. We will never know . . .
never . . . never really be certain about what it is we
really are searching for in this life anyway . . . in this
world. The endless questions . . . thoughts . . . that well
up deep down inside of us. As of now . . . at this point
in time and space we remain uncertain . . . except for
having reached the moon—maybe. Hallelujah!

SALLY (*holding him, a determined, firm attitude*): But if we
could be certain . . . maybe . . . someday . . . of something more . . . than just the beating of our hearts.
Listen! (*She puts his hand to her breast.*) Boom. Boom.
Boom. One day they will just stop pounding . . . but
for now . . . they just go on . . . and on. Boom. Boom.
Boom.

TOGETHER

SAM:	SALLY:
Boom	Boom
Boom	Boom
Boom	Boom
Boom	Boom

BLACKOUT

DR. KHEAL

BY MARÍA IRENE FORNÉS

Dr. Kheal appears before us. He knows everything and
we are his ignorant, stupid students. He is a foolish
figure but he has all the answers. Truth, beauty, love,
cooking—no subject is too abstruse. What he tells us is
astonishing in its banality and irrefutably noncommittal.
Whatever our own opinions, they are contemptible.
Still, something links us. What is this we recognize
as the arrogant professor loses his way and starts
raving, speaking eerie gibberish? Ah, it is our very
humanity, the very uselessness of wisdom, the sweet
triviality of what we can be sure of. Dr. Kheal is as
demented as we are.

M. S.

Dr. Kheal was first performed on April 15, 1968, by Philip Bruns at the Writers' Stage Theatre, 82 East 4th Street, New York, as part of a benefit for the New Dramatists Committee. Later the same evening it was performed by David Tice at the Village Gate, Bleecker and Thompson Streets, New York, as part of a benefit for the Caffe Cino. Both actors were directed by Remy Charlip, and the Tice version was subsequently presented by the Judson Poets' Theatre.

David Tice
in *Dr. Kheal*

There are a reading stand, a small table with a jug of water and two glasses, a blackboard, and a stand with various charts. Professor Kheal enters. He is small, or else the furniture is large.

The titles or subject matter should be shown by slide projections. Or perhaps they should be written on the blackboard by Dr. Kheal.

1. THE OUTLINE

DR. KHEAL: The professor picks up the chalk . . .

Dr. Kheal picks up the chalk.

. . . and writes

Dr. Kheal writes "The Outline" on the blackboard. He looks at what he wrote and decides to draw a line alongside the edges of the blackboard.

He looks at the class with an air of superiority and counts to three, demanding their attention. One, two and three. He asks his first question.

He mouths a question and then puts his hand to his ear as if listening to the answer.

Wrong.

Pointing in different directions..

Wrong. Wrong. Wrong. Wrong. Then, suddenly, someone shouts his answer from the back. Others join him. They all shout at once. It becomes a loud and fast thing. The teacher speaks rapidly trying to reply to each; Wrong, wrong, wrong, wrong, wrong, wrong, wrong. Damn it! You're wrong.

Suggesting a voice from the distance.

"Dear professor, perhaps you have the wrong answer."

He looks at the audience fiercely.

My answer wrong? It couldn't be that my answer is wrong.
   I am the master. Let us proceed.

He looks among his papers. Then talks to himself.

How could my answer be wrong? . . . Hmmm . . . Did I
   have an answer?

He thinks.

Nonsense, I don't need an answer. I am the master . . . Let
   me see . . . Let me see . . . I'll find an answer. Hmmm
   . . . Hmmm. How is that possible? I don't even remember the question. Was there a question?

To the audience.

Was there?

To himself.

Hmm. Of course there was. There's always a question, but
   the question is always what the answer is.

To the audience.

Raise your hand if you know the answer . . . Ha ha. There
   you are! There are many of you, but the multitude is
   often wrong.

He starts to erase the blackboard.

Is it not?

*He looks to see if someone replies. He then erases the
blackboard.*

2. ON POETRY

Now, poetry is for the most part a waste of time, and so is
   politics, and history, and philosophy . . . nothing concrete, nothing like a well-made box . . . which is concrete and beautiful and you can put things in it. But
   what can you do with poems . . . tell me . . . and with
   politics . . . and with history, and with philosophy . . .

You can wrap them up, shove them up your ass, and what do you have?

He moves his hands as if he were doing a magic trick which ends with the middle finger up.

. . . Nothing . . . Ha ha ha ha ha ha.

Invaded by an immense poetic feeling.

But if you can make a box, think, have you not made a lyrical thing?

He thinks he hears someone speak. He squints, and looks over his glasses, then, ignores the possible speaker.

Poetry, on the other hand, is just a few words put together. Just a few. Just words. There, is poetry . . . And then they say there are poets . . . poets of this sort, poets of that sort, and poets of the other sort . . . But who, tell me, understands the poetry of space in a box. I do . . . Abysmal and concrete at the same time. Four walls, a top, and a bottom . . . and yet a void . . . And then, there is the smell of wood, that sober smell. Who understands that? I, Professor Kheal, I understand it clearly and expound it well.

He takes a deep breath.

3. ON BALANCE

He goes to the blackboard and draws a figure as follows:

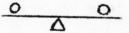

He moves away, looks at the blackboard, looks for his glasses in his pocket, puts them on, and points to the blackboard.

Balance can save your life. Imbalance can destroy it.

Lost in his thoughts

. . . What is balance . . . Balance is a state of equilibrium between opposing forces. The harmonious proportions of elements in design. Balance is keeping my pants up. My groin in place. Any more questions?

4. ON AMBITION

Then, of course there is the question of will. Oh, will, will, will, will. Always will. Tell me, does anyone here know the answer? . . . Does the thing happen, or does one do it? Of course sometimes it happens and other times one does it. I dont mean . . . just anything . . . ordinarily . . . I mean how . . . what . . . which . . . Is *it* made . . . Can it be made . . . what . . . Life, of course . . . Life. No, I don't mean birth. I mean life. Can I make my own life? Of course not, you fool. A well planned life is pitiful. Doesn't it seem richer if the firmament puts its silvery hands in it? In your life.

He puts his hand to his ear.

What?

He listens.

Not modern? Mo . . . dern? . . . You scum, you turd, you stale refuse. Worse than that, plastic face.

He blows air through his mouth.

That is what I think of you . . . I'll take your will and chew on it, like a little oyster, or a clam. Chew, chew, chew, chew, chew your little will, yum yum . . . Can you make a clam? I'll chew your little entrails.

He darts his tongue like a satyr. He puts his hands over his groin with a scared look.

Can you make a clam? I don't mean stuffed clam. I-mean-make-a-clam. What would you like? A show of hands? All right. Let's have a show of hands. Those in favor of the firmament leading you by the hand raise your hand.

He counts.

All I can do is peepee before you.

He raises his leg like a dog and then shakes it.

And the rest. What do you think? Is there another alternative? Either you do it, or else it does itself, life that is. What other way is there? None.

He looks with suspicion into a few faces.

None. There is no other way. All right.

5. ON ENERGY

Here is the next question.

He unrolls a chart that reads: "How does one do a million little things?"

How does one do a million little things? . . . What is the answer? How does one do a million little things? . . .

He waits a moment for the answer.

One at a time.

He is pleased with the incisiveness of his answer.

Now.

He unrolls the next chart. It reads: "How does one do a million big things?"

How does one do a million big things? . . . Hmmmm . . . Does anyone know the answer?

He waits a moment.

One at a time. Ha ha ha ha ha . . . What a surprise . . . Surprised, everyone? Now, the last of the three.

He unrolls the next chart. It reads: "How does one do one big thing?"

How does one do one big thing? . . . Ha ha ha ha ha ha ha,
    Extraordinary question, isn't it? I'll answer it.

He goes to the blackboard and makes this drawing:

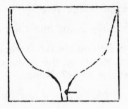

Pointing to where the arrow indicates.

Start here.

He fills in the space indicated as follows.

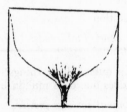

He darts his tongue like a satyr.

Would you have guessed? Never.

6. ON TRUTH

Now . . . words change the nature of things. A thing not
    named and the same thing named are two different
    things. Ha ha ha ha . The ways of the Devil . . . that
    son of a gun . . . Someone once said "In the beginning
    was the word." Guess who? The Devil . . . clever
    bastard . . . he'd say anything. In our time he is still
    renaming things . . . Freedom . . . ahhhhh . . . you
    see. I'm right . . . Happiness . . . Today who dares to
    say the word without some kind of

Mocking their manner.

"Intellectual Hesitation."

Still in mockery.

"Happiness . . . happiness . . . what is happiness?"

Back to himself.

And I show them my teeth.

He opens his mouth wide, then puts his fingers in his mouth.

And I say to them. There, is happiness. My teeth are good.

Forcing his hand in the mouth of an imaginary person.

And I put my whole hand in their mouths and I call them every name in the book. Violent. I am. I get angry. But it doesn't matter. I am always right. You see, most people believe that truth is the order in which they live. Others, the bright ones, believe that there is no truth at all but only an arrangement. Both are mistaken. Ha ha ha ha ha ha.

Now, truth is not at all the way we understand something to be . . . Why? The moment you name it it is gone. A chair. You name it; "Chair" and there it is, still a chair. A dog. You name it; "Dog" and it comes. But truth . . . you name it and it vanishes. What is truth then? Anyone knows?

He stands like a bullfighter and makes three rapid passes.

There is truth. Three quick passes. Name it here, here, and here. Surround it, and you'll have it. Never touch it. It will vanish.

7. ANECDOTE

On my way here this evening someone said to me . . . "Dr. Kheal, is being poor a sign of stinginess?"

He opens his mouth as if to laugh, but makes no sound.

I said, "No, it isn't."

Pause.

But of course it is.

Pause.

Ha ha ha ha.

8. ON BEAUTY AND LOVE

The morning was fine. I cleaned the bathroom, then the kitchen. What else is there but cleanliness.

He looks over his glasses, expecting objections.

And then, I lay down to rest with my head on a high pillow. "Gee, look at my belly going up and down. I must be alive." Well . . . in that case . . . I go to my dresser, I look in the mirror. "Gee, look how pleasant my face is in the mirror, I must be beautiful." Ha ha ha. Well, we each have our way. I know that we can only do what is possible. I know that. We can only do what is possible for us to do. But still it is good to know what the impossible is.

There is a pause. He is looking at the impossible.

Beauty is . . . beauty . . . beauty . . . beauty . . . what are thou that drives me out of my mind. Beauty? . . . Shall I tell you?

He sees Crissanda in front of him.

She speaks in riddles, like the gods. *ksjdnhyidfgesls.* She says: "I am the supreme lover. Ahhhh. I bring you bliss . . . You are trying too hard . . . Listen to me . . . Listen . . . Listen . . . I know . . . Ohhhhhh . . ." The fool, she knows nothing. It's the way she talks, in riddles, like the gods. *ksjdudyehrnchs.* And then, she says: "Don't move your hands when you talk, it tickles me . . . from across the room the movements of your hands tickle me." And I laughed. Ha ha ha. And she looked at me surprised, and her little eye wandered and was lost. "Where are you?" I said, "My little one . . . Crissanda . . .

Crissanda . . . where are you? I didn't mean to laugh."
And she said: "Crazy people are fools."

*He is startled. His eyes open very wide. They are filled
with tears.*

And she left. "Crissanda, Crissanda," I called after her. No.
She was gone. What happened? What happened? I
know what happened and yet I cannot say. I do not
know the words to speak of beauty and of love. I, who
know everything . . . Some things are impossible.

He goes to the blackboard.

Love, as we know it, increases daily. Let us say the average
level of love is 100 degrees. We add a daily increase of
10. We subtract 7 for daily wear and tear and we have
a daily increase of 3 which is cumulative. In 10 days we
have an increase of 30 which has raised the level to
130. We have a big fight which reduces the level by
50, leaving love at a low level of 80. However, the daily
increase of 10 minus daily wear and tear of 7 continues
. . . producing a true increase of 3 which is cumulative.
After 7 days we have an increase of 3 times seven which
is 21. Added to the low level of 80 we have 101. Back
to normal.

He has written the following:

$$
\begin{array}{ccc}
\begin{array}{r} 100 \\ +10 \\ \hline 110 \\ -7 \\ \hline 103 \\ - \end{array}
&
\begin{array}{r} 10 \\ \times 3 \\ \hline 30 \\ +100 \\ \hline 130 \\ -50 \\ \hline 80 \end{array}
&
\begin{array}{r} 7 \\ \times 3 \\ \hline 21 \\ +80 \\ \hline 101 \end{array}
\end{array}
$$

Here is the arithmetic of love. Ha! You think that is contradictory? Love and mathematics. Don't you know that
you can take a yes and a no and push them together,
squeeze them together, compress them so they are one?
That in fact that is what reality is? Opposites, con-
tradictions compressed so that you don't know where
one stops and the other begins? . . . Let us proceed.

9. ON HOPE

And here, is a picture of hope.

He unrolls a chart with this figure:

Man stands in his life, "Grotto." Always, with a sense of
being enclosed. He thinks of freedom, open space, air,
sun. The only way out is always narrow, always arduous
and frightening to cross. He dares. He fills his lungs
with air. He swims. He is courageous. He reaches the
point where, if he goes any further, he won't be able
to return. "Point of no return." If he continues he might
find the exit, if there is an exit . . . if the exit is within
reach of his endurance. That is the point. Does he continue? Does he return? There, is the picture of hope.

10. ON COOKING

Have you ever cooked brussels sprouts? The miniature cab-
bage? Toy vegetable. Have you ever seen how beautiful
they are?

11. SUMMING UP

And now, to conclude, I'll sing you a song.

    The other day
    Looking at a weird looking spider,
    With legs ten times longer than its body,
    Who moved in the most senseless and
    Insane manner,
    I said, "Spider, you are spastic and I am
    A superior beast."
    There! That is what it is all about.
    Man is the rational animal.

THE NEXT THING

[BY MICHAEL SMITH

The Next Thing was inspired by the Ljuba Welitsch
recording of the last scene of Strauss's *Salome*. It was
originally written in three long scenes, to be played
out of chronological order. The present form of the
play—in eleven discontinuous sections—was devised by
Jacques Levy, who directed the original production.
Levy also invented, with my connivance, a final dumb
show in which the murder, originally not shown,
was enacted several times in slow motion over the
recorded dialogue of the last scene. The intentions
of the play were ritualistic and obsessive from the
start, and I loved the production. I hope, incidentally,
that this is my last study in family hang-ups.

M. S.

The Next Thing was presented by the Open Theatre at La Mama Experimental Theatre Club, 122 Second Avenue, New York, on March 23, 1966. It was directed by Jacques Levy with the following cast:

SUE: Kay Carney
ARTHUR: Ed Setrakian
MOTHER: Barbara Vann
HAROLD: John McCurry

Music: Robert Cosmos Savage
Set: Gwen Fabricant

OPPOSITE: Barbara Vann (Mother) and Ed Setrakian (Arthur) in *The Next Thing.* Photo: Ted Wiechers

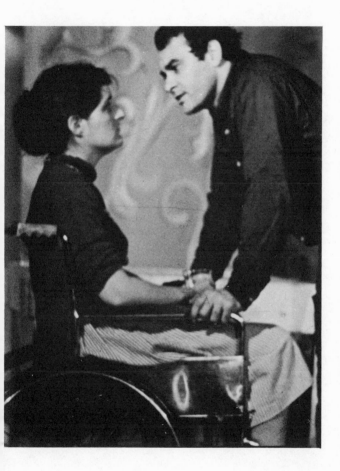

The living–dining room of a large, comfortable apartment. At dinner. Arthur and Sue are at the ends of the table, in profile to the audience. Mother is in the middle, facing front. An awkward pause.

SUE: You can't possibly be serious.

ARTHUR: Well, perhaps not. Perhaps not.

SUE: Eat them?

ARTHUR: Think about it. It bears thinking about.

MOTHER: Eat what?

SUE: Isn't there a legend about this? Didn't some king feed somebody his children?

ARTHUR: Ahh—belch, belch—that was delicious. Succulent, I'd call it, passably succulent. Give my compliments to the chef, will you, king? By the way, what was it?

SUE: Braised boy.

ARTHUR: Your majesty? I beg your pardon? Beef, you say?

SUE: Boy.

ARTHUR: Ah yes. Well, ahem, I thought that's what you said. Yes. Well. Arabian, I suppose. One of the dominion peoples, no doubt. Damn savages. I mean to say, they eat us, why shouldn't we . . . uh . . . *The ghastly truth begins to dawn on him, the sins of his fathers begin to be betrayed in the pallor of his cheek, the palsy of his hand. Whose boy? he asks. Whose boy did you say? His host smiles humorlessly.*

SUE (*smiles humorlessly*): I'm afraid so.

ARTHUR: AIIEEEE!!, he cries. He leaps up from his seat at the banquet table, seizes the poignard from its leathern sheath, and with a terrible scream plunges it to the hilt into his own entrails and gargling hideously falls to the inlaid marble floor dead. AARRRRGH!

He crashes to the floor and plays dead.

MOTHER: All right, get up.

ARTHUR: I'm dead. By my own hand. Dead and damned.

MOTHER: No, you're not. Neither one. Get up.

ARTHUR (*plays tantrum*): I wanna be dead! Come on,

Mommy, you said I could be dead if I drank my milk.
I wanna be dead! (*Plays dead.*)

SUE (*whispers to Mother*): Is this . . . typical? I mean, at
dinner?

ARTHUR (*gets up*): You don't have to whisper. It's extremely
rude, and frankly, Sue, I'm surprised at you. If you and
Mother wish to talk privately, just say so and I will
excuse myself from the table. While I am here, however,
dead or alive, simple decency dictates that you should
include me in the conversation. Is that clear? Is that
absolutely clear!!? All right! Good!

An awkward pause.

SUE: As you were saying.

ARTHUR: Thank you. As I was saying, there's no excuse for
killing people unless you want to eat them.

MOTHER: Except in war.

ARTHUR: I *mean* in war. Why do people start a war? Because
they're hungry.

MOTHER: I'm hungry.

ARTHUR: Shut up, Mother.

MOTHER: Arthur, get the dessert.

ARTHUR: For example, we are surrounded by people who eat
dessert at the end of every meal. Now, this isn't because
they *want* dessert, is it? Not every single one of them at
every single meal. It isn't because they're *hungry*. No!
In fact, my mother here is a very good example of what
I'm talking about. You heard her bring up the subject
of dessert? Well, the fact is, she hasn't eaten a dessert
in years! She's on a perpetual diet or something. She
never eats dessert. But can we have a meal here without
dessert? Not on your life! (*Sue laughs.*) Don't laugh!

SUE: I think it's funny.

ARTHUR: What's funny?

SUE: That your mother has this dessert compulsion. You
know, what you said.

ARTHUR: Are you laughing at my mother? You find my
mother funny? Is that it? Perhaps you would like to tell
us just which aspect of my mother it is that amuses you
so much. Yes?

MOTHER: Forget it, Arthur.

ARTHUR: It's insulting, Mother. She comes into this house,

your house, and then laughs at you as if you were stupid. Do you *like* being laughed at?

MOTHER: It doesn't matter.

SUE: I'm sorry, I really didn't mean to start anything.

MOTHER: You didn't start it.

SUE: I'd love to have some dessert.

ARTHUR (*laughs, rises to get dessert*): Sue, tell my mother about yourself. Start with your legs. Isn't it wonderful that you two have so much in common.

SUE: Why did you ask me over here, anyway?

ARTHUR: I felt sorry for you.

Break (*blackout*).

2.

Before dinner. The room is empty and dim. Arthur enters from outside. Mother speaks from her bedroom.

MOTHER (*off*): Is that you, Arthur?

ARTHUR: Who else, Mother?

MOTHER (*off*): Darling, I've heard the most wonderful news. Come kiss me.

ARTHUR: Just a minute, Mother.

MOTHER (*off*): What's wrong, baby?

ARTHUR: Nothing, Mother. I'm just a little tired. Wasn't Margaret here today?

MOTHER (*off*): Of course. That's what the wonderful news is about. We had a long talk.

ARTHUR: Mother, Margaret's a maid, not a companion.

MOTHER (*off*): I know, dear.

ARTHUR: She's paid to clean, not to listen to you. She doesn't like to listen to you. She complains to me. She says you won't let her get the work done. Whenever I point out something she hasn't done, she turns right around and says it's your fault. She says you follow her around and talk all the time.

MOTHER (*off*): I know, dear.

ARTHUR: I know, dear.

MOTHER (*off*): I know, dear, but this was an exception. She had something to tell me. Guess what.

ARTHUR: What?

MOTHER (*off*): She wanted my advice.

ARTHUR: What about?

MOTHER (*off*): Guess.

ARTHUR: I have no idea.

MOTHER (*off*): She's going to have a baby, that's what.
That's the news. Isn't it wonderful? Arthur?

Mother rolls onstage in a wheelchair.

ARTHUR: Excuse me . . . How have you been feeling today?

MOTHER: Oh, just fine. Why, I've hardly thought about
myself at all today. I've been so excited about Margaret
I just couldn't wait till you came home.

ARTHUR: What is it that excites you so?

MOTHER: I'm so excited that she's going to have a baby. I
just told you. Isn't it exciting? The miracle of concep-
tion, another life comes into being, another organism is
created from nothing into a person complete with all
the joys and woes, thoughts and feelings, fingernails and
kneecaps. Another creature that comes into being so
gradually, and then gradually becomes an independent
creature that has its own life to be protected and guarded
as it gradually grows into a human person. Isn't it exciting? Oh, how gloriously and gradually it springs from
the mysterious alchemy of the womb.

ARTHUR: Your legs aren't bothering you?

MOTHER: No, I feel fine.

ARTHUR: I'm sorry, Mother, but could you just leave me alone
for a little while. I'll be all right in a little while. Just
go and watch television or something for a little while,
would you do that for me?

MOTHER: Of course, Arthur. I shouldn't pester you when
you're tired. You must be worn out. I know you think
I'm insensitive. But I know how you feel. I know it
won't make you feel any different, any better, but I
always understand how you feel, so you don't ever have
to pretend with me. You don't have to put up with me
when you feel bad. Just tell me when I'm irritating to
you and I'll stay out of your way until you feel better

ARTHUR: Just a little while. Please, Mother, just go away for
a little while.

MOTHER: All right. I certainly wouldn't want to stay in the

room with you when I'm not appreciated. I told you that
I understood everything, and I do. I'll be in my room,
and you call me when you want me to come out.

She rolls off. The stage is almost dark. Pause.

ARTHUR: Oh, by the way, Mother, I've invited someone over
for dinner tonight. (*Pause.*) You're not dead, are you?
(*Pause.*)
MOTHER (*rolls onstage*): Feeling better?
ARTHUR: I've invited someone for dinner. A surprise.
MOTHER: Who is it?
ARTHUR: You don't know her. Let it be a surprise.

Break.

3.

*At dinner. Sue and Mother are seated. Arthur is getting
dessert.*

ARTHUR: I felt sorry for you. You can't walk right, nobody
ever asks you out, your hair is always a little messed up.
You know. Also, I thought it was time Mother had
some company. She talks to the maid a lot. Margaret.
But that's about all. Most of her friends are dead or
moved away or something. I don't know. You tell her,
Mother.
MOTHER: What he means is, he's trying to show me something. I'm not sure exactly what it is, not yet. You're a
surprise, and I'm genuinely impressed. I mean it, Arthur.
I don't know what it means, but it seems very imaginative. (*To Sue.*) As for the general thing of bringing
a girl home, he hasn't ever done it before. Did you
know? Since he's grown up, I mean. We have, shall I
say, occasional discussions about his . . . shyness. Isn't
that what we call it, Arthur, shyness?
ARTHUR: Cowardice. Terror. What did you call me?
MOTHER: So in a way this is very good. This first step.
ARTHUR: Thank you, Mother. *An edge of irony mocks his
meaning as he turns to his mother and says, "Thank
you, Mother. Thank you for the compliment. May I be*

worthy of it in the hours yet to come." She smiles
thinly, meeting him on his own guarded terms, and
says . . .

MOTHER: Indeed. May you indeed. I look forward to your
worthiness.

SUE: What about me?

ARTHUR: You're here, that's all.

SUE: Is this some family game?

ARTHUR: My father was killed.

SUE (to Mother): I'm sorry.

MOTHER: It's all right.

ARTHUR: Certain of us have survived him, however. We had
our names in the *Times*. "Survived by a son, Arthur,"
it said. Among other things.

MOTHER: Shut up, Arthur! (*To Sue.*) Something comes into
his tone of voice and gives him away.

ARTHUR: Let's talk about the jungle. (*Pause.*) All right, then,
we'll go on talking about Sue.

MOTHER: We've had almost enough of this.

ARTHUR: What about the hair? Do you want to tell us about
your hair?

MOTHER: Don't go too far. Arthur, you don't want to go too
far.

ARTHUR: Or we can talk about Mother's hair. Would you like
to feel it? Go ahead, she won't mind.

MOTHER: Stop now.

ARTHUR: Will your hair look like my mother's in a few years,
do you think? It's going thin at the part, you should
notice that. I like the bluish tint, too. They also come
in pink. Which do you prefer? Sue? Which do you
think you'll use, pink or bluish? If you don't use one or
the other, it goes yellowish. That's horrible. It looks all
dirty. Like those men with nicotine stains in their full
white mustaches. We don't have many of those in New
York, for some reason, but you must have seen one
someplace. Well, you can't have your hair looking like
that, now, can you? No, of course. Of course *not*,
meant. Ha ha. Pink or bluish?

MOTHER: Shall we have coffee in the living room?

ARTHUR: Damn it, Mother!

SUE: I think I must have come on the wrong night.

ARTHUR: I don't know. I don't know how wrong it is. Hov

can you say something like that before it's over? Did
you really want a perfectly dull dinner with Arthur
from the office and his mother? What a thing to look
forward to! What a memory that would make! Polite,
quiet, circumspect Arthur and his widowed mother who
turns out, what's more, to be confined to wheels. If this
is wrong, would that have been right?

SUE: I don't know.

MOTHER: Don't admit anything to him.

ARTHUR: What did you come here for tonight? What were
you looking for here?

SUE: I don't know.

MOTHER: He's looking for soft spots. Don't show them to
him.

ARTHUR: I'm trying to find out what time it is.

MOTHER: You're trying to trap Sue right now, right this
minute, and it's crude, it's unfair. You're a bully.

ARTHUR: All bullies are cowards, so it makes sense. You said
I'm a coward, you say I'm a bully. Logic.

MOTHER: Child's logic.

SUE: I can take care of myself.

ARTHUR: All right. (*Pause.*) It's time to talk about the
jungle.

MOTHER: No, this is enough now. (*She rolls over to the sofa
and pats the arm invitingly.*) Sue, come over here and
get comfortable and talk to me.

Break.

4.

*After dinner. A sheet completely covers Mother in her wheel-
chair. Sue is sitting on the sofa. Arthur is wandering with a
rifle in his hands.*

SUE: Had you planned to do that—when you invited me to
dinner, I mean?

ARTHUR: Oh no. I don't think so. It had entered my mind, of
course.

SUE: Were you planning it this afternoon at the office?

ARTHUR: I'm almost sure I wasn't. This isn't why I invited

you to dinner, if that's what you're getting at. It's a
pleasure to have you here and all that. I wouldn't like
to be alone. I welcome your support. But I hadn't
counted on it. No, I hadn't planned it this afternoon
at the office.

SUE: At the dinner table?

ARTHUR: I can barely remember the office. What about you?
Was it only this afternoon that we were in the office?
Don't talk about what we did at the dinner table. Don't
start reminiscing.

SUE: I'd better be going.

ARTHUR: No, certainly not. You certainly don't want to leave.
Don't try to tell me that.

SUE: Yes, I do.

ARTHUR: I don't believe you. I don't begin to believe you.

SUE: I think you're crazy.

ARTHUR: Do you?

SUE: I don't know what you might do next.

ARTHUR: Neither do I. I can do anything. It's easy. There's
nothing to stop me.

SUE: You'll get locked up.

ARTHUR: Don't talk to me about consequences. That's beside
the point. Obviously there are consequences. There are
always consequences—when you do nothing, when you
sleep, when everything you do is an imitation of something you did yesterday. So what? It's supposed to scare
people, and it works. You can go through a whole life
without inventing a single moment, a single act, without ever surprising yourself. That's what the system is
for, the whole setup. But Sue, look, it's nothing! There's
really nothing there! All you have to do is see through
it and it vanishes.

SUE: I want to go home.

ARTHUR: Well, you can't.

SUE: You're adorable when you do that.

ARTHUR: What?

SUE: Go on. I'll play with you. Go on talking. Do what
you have to do. Do whatever you like. I almost know
how you feel . . . No, of course I don't. How do you
feel?

ARTHUR: Sue, listen to me!

SUE: Do you know what you've done? Do you have any

idea? They're going to ask: did he know right from
wrong at that moment? And what can you tell them?
Is it legal insanity, Arthur? Do you know right from
wrong?

ARTHUR: I know right from left, that's enough. I know back
from front. I know inside from outside. What is this
nonsense?

SUE: That's what they ask: did you know right from wrong.

ARTHUR: Well I suppose the answer is yes. I knew something.
At that moment I certainly knew something. I knew
enough to pull the trigger. It didn't take much muscle
but it took something.

SUE: I think we should just go on chatting until you lose your
mind, and then the police can take care of everything.
It will be something to tell my grandchildren.

ARTHUR: What grandchildren? If you think you're going to
get grandchildren in the accounting department, you're
in for . . .

SUE: Lay off, my friend.

ARTHUR: Anyhow, it's a hell of a way of thinking. Do you
go out of your way to do things that will entertain
grandchildren? Do you wrap every experience in tissue
paper to save for two generations? I really do feel sorry
for you sometimes.

SUE: Please cut it out. I'm nothing at all like the kind of
person you take me for, and the longer you go on with
this corny image, the more embarrassed you're going to
be when you finally wake up . . . Now I'm doing it, the
same talk-talk-talk.

Break.

5.

Before dinner. Arthur and Mother.

MOTHER: I didn't know we were having anyone over for
dinner.

ARTHUR: I know you didn't. I said it's a surprise. What's
wrong? Did you have other plans?

MOTHER: What other plans?

ARTHUR: I don't know. Maybe *you*'re having someone over.

MOTHER: That's not at all funny.

ARTHUR: Maybe there's some television show you want to watch. That's all right. I can amuse myself with her.

MOTHER: Are you sure?

ARTHUR: What?

MOTHER: Anyway, that's not it.

ARTHUR: Oh, for God's sake, Mother! Will you please not make a scene, just this once. She's a nice girl, and we'll have a pleasant evening, and that's all there is to it.

MOTHER: I always have a pleasant evening.

ARTHUR: Stop it!

MOTHER: And what do you mean by "just this once"? You make it sound like you have a habit of bringing girls home. What's wrong? What is it, baby?

ARTHUR: Does it bother you to see people doing things you can't do any more?

MOTHER: No.

ARTHUR (*jumps in the air and kicks his heels together*): How about that?

MOTHER: You're not very good at it.

ARTHUR: You should see me in the high hurdles. You should see me on the escalator. This very afternoon. They get out of the way when they see me coming. You should see that! . . . I can dance, I can swim, I can play tennis. I could if I wanted to. For a couple of months one winter I walked up the stairs to the office every day instead of riding the elevator, just to keep in shape.

MOTHER: What do you need to keep in shape for?

ARTHUR: Just for you, to show you. I have legs like a race-horse. I could ride a bicycle ten miles.

MOTHER: Feel my biceps, then. I could roll ten blocks. I'm not so good on the stairs, I'll admit. Is it a contest you want?

ARTHUR: Look, Mother, we're obviously getting on each other's nerves tonight. It's my fault. Let's just say that I'm tired. Let's just stay out of each other's way until Sue gets here.

MOTHER: And then take it out on her . . .

ARTHUR: Let's stop. I've stopped.

MOTHER: Come on, don't stop! Coward! Chicken!

ARTHUR: Why don't you go freshen up, wash your face . . .

MOTHERS Don't I look nice? Don't I even look clean? Arthur,
I got fixed up specially tonight. You mean your old
mother doesn't . . . I've lost my looks, that's all there
is to it. It happens to everybody. Here I spend half
the afternoon fixing myself up, and my son tells me to
go wash my face. I must be getting old . . . So here I
am, Arthur, old. This is the way I look, and it's too late
to do a thing about it.

ARTHUR: I was joking, Mother. I said that without thinking.
You look beautiful. You look . . . elegant.

MOTHER (*Southern accent*): Why, thank you, sir, for such
a gentlemanly thought. I swear, chivalry has not quite
died out here on this lovely old plantation. A shy little
belle like me may have to fish a little, but in the long
run she gets what she's after.

ARTHUR: Let's be friends, Mother. Let's try as hard as we can.

MOTHER: Just friends? Why, I thought you meant . . .

ARTHUR: That's it. You really are my sweetheart after all
. . . Will you set the table for me? I'm going to get
cleaned up. Are you all right?

MOTHER: I'm fine.

Arthur goes off. Mother sets table. Pause.

MOTHER: What do you tell them at the office?

ARTHUR: What?

MOTHER: What do you tell the boys at the office? What do
you say over lunch? Is it crowded where you eat? How
many of the boys from the office sit with you while you
eat, and can you be overheard from the next table?
What do you say when by chance you find yourself
alone with one of them? Or are you careful? Do you
smile sympathetically at their confidences and sip water?

ARTHUR (*coming on*): What is it, Mother?

MOTHER: Do you talk about women? What do you say
about women, for example?

ARTHUR: Stop it please, Mother.

MOTHER: During the day I know you're busy and you have
certain obligations and distractions, and I'm here in
the evenings. But what do you do after I've gone to
bed, when you lock yourself in the bathroom? While
you're standing in the shower you can see yourself in
the full-length mirror. What do you see? When you're

in bed awake on a summer night and you've thrown
off the covers and the bed is hot with your body's heat,
if the subject of sexy women should cross your mind at
a moment like that, Arthur, what do you tell yourself?

ARTHUR: I don't think this is necessary.

MOTHER: Change yourself, Arthur.

ARTHUR: Change me.

MOTHER: Change yourself.

ARTHUR: Look at you . . .

MOTHER: Don't be stupid.

ARTHUR: Look at your hair, look at your eyes, look at your
cheeks, look at your pinched lips, look at your chin,
your neck, look at the dress hanging on your shoulders,
look . . .

MOTHER: Go on.

ARTHUR: Look at your . . . (*Pause.*)

MOTHER: Look at my breasts. Look at my breasts. I remember everything, Arthur. Once they were like yours, like
a little boy's. I remember that. And I remember when
they were heavy, and the nipples were full and dark,
and you sucked blindly in my arms. I remember looking
at them last night in the bathroom. I looked at them last
night for a long time. I know what they look like.

ARTHUR: No, stop now.

MOTHER: I am not fooling myself, not about my age or
about my breasts. I know what they look like. What
breasts do you know, Arthur? If you want to look at my
breasts you can. Would you like to look at my breasts?

ARTHUR: No.

MOTHER: Close your eyes at least and imagine them. Now.
Close your eyes. Imagine my breasts. They are flat. They
hang down. They are empty bags. They are extra flaps
of skin on my chest. Can you see them? . . . I wish
you'd realize, my dear son . . . that we have very little
in common. I am old. You are a coward.

ARTHUR: What do you want me to do?

MOTHER: It makes no difference.

ARTHUR: We go on and on like this.

MOTHER: I know.

ARTHUR: Don't just tell me you know, tell me *what* you know.

MOTHER: Stop expecting to be told things.

Break.

6.

*At dinner. Harold, a powerful middle-aged Negro man, enters
and rushes through the apartment. Arthur comes in behind
him carrying the rifle.*

HAROLD: Margaret! Margaret! I know you're here! I know
they're hiding you here somewhere! Make a sound, any
kind of sound, so I'll know where you are, so I can find
you! I came as fast as I could, as fast as they'd let me!
Where are you? Margaret! I *can't* be too late! No, no!
What kind of people are they to do a thing like this?
Margaret! Margaret? (*Pause, then raving.*) It is I who
am pregnant! I! I! Savaged by who called me savage.
It is I! And after that: the horror! The dread! Oh
devilish moans and weeping! Terror! You ask how I
come to be thus distraught. You cannot imagine. Just
think what you've done! Think! Your consciences creak
and groan from strain like elevators overloaded with
passengers of lead. Think then what you *might* have
done! The dreadful possibilities! You must sweat and
sigh. Is there no relief, relief nowhere? I am soiled with
your vulgarity! Look at each other that way if you must.
Go on exchanging those glances limp with ignorance.
What manner of man is this? I read you well. How dare
he burst into our evacuated life with his vile accusations,
abominations? Revelations! I know what you fear, believe me when I say it. Little people panting and gaping
before my immensity. Well, I am no longer interested
to shelter them in my hair. My curly, crinkly, *black* hair!
Or you could bake me, skewer me, baste and salt me,
time me and gobble me down. The heat is not stranger
than cold, not more painful than Africa—the sound is
always with me devouring and lusting. Oh my God!
Good grief! Where is my head! It's nice music. Before
you go . . . no, no . . . You are all striped, do you know?
Striped, striped. Blue and white, horizontal stripes. My
head spins and reels, my body pulsates in mighty heaves,
my eyes are foreign and wet with mistrust. Abandon,
rage, expose, forgive, forget. The feeling flattened me in

its wake and left me panting, spent like a nickel. What a fool am I! Cigarettes on the floor, don't get too upset. Avoid the music—don't listen. Don't! I'll get through this one day at least. The stripes! Jesus! The picture clears after all this. Sky spreads, blue and deep as eyes. Black as eyes at night. But don't ask my forgiveness, it's not to be given! You give birth so seldom. The thought occurs to me to offer you money. It is yours, not only mine. Give her back! Tell me what you've done! I implore, I humbly beg in my pale disbelief, snow-blind and tender-footed I beseech. A continent propels me and I am barely mighty to resist. You broke it purposelessly. Memories crush and smother me. Her face grows larger by the minute, it fills the room, bursts and fills the building, bursts, bursts. There is nothing but her face, nothing anywhere. No America, no Africa, no Asia. The seas are dry, the clouds are still. The music is muffled in these wads of flesh. God is crushed by her face. And the child is mine to bear, it is I who shall labor. May you touch no grief as dark as mine.

MOTHER: You must be Harold. I've heard so much about you.

HAROLD: Where is she?

MOTHER: Margaret left around five as usual. Is anything wrong?

HAROLD: Where is she?

MOTHER: Margaret told me the wonderful news. I'm so happy for you both.

HAROLD: You've shot her with the gun. I know! I'll see you pilloried, I'll see you damned! (*Arthur laughs. Harold turns on Sue.*) Who are you? You don't know these people. These people would do anyhting. Normal people don't answer the door carrying guns. I should have shot first.

ARTHUR: Do you have a gun?

HAROLD: No, I don't, not yet. (*Wild again.*) Margaret! Margaret! Come back to me, please, baby, come back to me! This is Harold calling to you! Come on back to me!

MOTHER: I'm afraid there's some mistake, Mr. . . . Harold. Margaret left here a little before five as usual.

ARTHUR: You're just in time for dessert.

MOTHER: Arthur! (*Sweetly, to Harold.*) She said something

about shopping. She was going to cook dinner for you. Chops, I think. I don't know what could have happened to her. Perhaps there's been an accident of some kind. Have you called the hospitals? Have you checked with the police?

HAROLD: No, no police!

MOTHER: If only you would tell me what's wrong, possibly I could help. I understand your being worried, but I can't think why you're blaming us. Now, there, there. Don't be upset. I'm sure there's a perfectly reasonable explanation. Just be patient, and everything will work out.

Harold looks at her blankly, then with a terrible groan rushes from the room. Break.

7.

Before dinner. Arthur and Mother.

ARTHUR: I'm responsible. I'm a responsible man.

MOTHER: It's an adolescent's idea of responsibility. You still don't know what it is to *exist*. You treat yourself like a piece of faulty equipment. Arthur, you weren't made in a factory.

ARTHUR: I don't know what you're talking about.

MOTHER: Pay more attention. You're still living in my life. And you act as though I'm part of yours. Well, I'm not. You're too old for that.

ARTHUR: Mother.

MOTHER: And too young. I live here. I have my things here. This is my place for memories. I'm not interested in you as a souvenir. And I don't see how you can be interested in me at all. Don't you know I'm going to die? I might die this very evening. And then what? What would you think about? This is a museum—a museum of my life and your childhood.

ARTHUR: Mother?

MOTHER: Oh, I know, it's very poignant. Yes, yes, I am your mother. Very well. Would you like me to take away your long pants and put you back in your pretty gray

Easter suit and Eton cap? I will shine your Oxfords and tie them for you and turn down the tops of your little white socks, and we will go out and walk together in the bright spring sunlight. You are a child, you have no past. The sun shines, and I bend down now and again to brush back the lock of hair the wind has pushed down across your forehead. Your hair was blond then. Would you like to have blond hair again?

ARTHUR: It would be embarrassing in the office.

MOTHER: Well, I'm glad you're taking me seriously. Come here, Arthur, let me look at your hands. Did you wash your hands? You mustn't come to the dinner table with dirty hands and dirty fingernails, Arthur. Come, come, let me look.

ARTHUR: My hands are dirty, Mother.

MOTHER: Your hands are dirty, my son.

ARTHUR: And my fingernails are broken. The cuticles are torn and painful to me.

MOTHER: You must soak them in warm soapy water and use an orange stick.

ARTHUR: I play in the sand, and the other little boys tease me.

MOTHER: Pay no attention to them. Sticks and stones, Arthur, sticks and stones.

ARTHUR: They say I'm too big to play in the sand.

MOTHER: You *are* too big to play in the sand.

ARTHUR: What will I do, Mommy? Mommy, Mommy, my fingernails are broken and the other boys are painful to me. I came to dinner with my hands dirty, I threw sticks and stones at the other boys, they threw sand at me, and we all screamed bad words. My mother was in the house and she told me to be anything I wanted to be.

MOTHER: That's right.

ARTHUR: All right, all right, I said, then tell them that I will be . . . tell them that Arthur will be . . . will grow up and be a grown-up and be a Daddy. Arthur is Daddy. All the other boys throw stones at Daddy, but Arthur hits them with sticks and rubs sand on them. It's all red. Daddy picks up little Arthur and carries him away on his shoulder. Daddy is tall and Arthur is light and easy to carry, and they go farther away than anyone can see them, and Daddy grows a long white beard and is old. Arthur is tall too now, and Daddy sits in the biggest chair and blinks at Arthur with his dim eyes and Daddy says, "Daddy dies now. Now Arthur must be Daddy. Bye bye, Daddy." The new Daddy cries and cries, and he puts the old Daddy in the ground under a big stone, and he walks out into everything. Here is Daddy, and he kills everybody he sees. He has a big stick and hits everybody and kills them. They all ask him, "Where is little Arthur?" "I am Arthur," he tells them, but they don't believe him, and he kills them all.

Pause.

MOTHER: And then?

ARTHUR: That's all.

MOTHER: Everyone is dead, and this Daddy is the only one there is. The whole earth is strewn with them, all knocked in the head with the big stick and dead, and Daddy walks around and around looking for more of them to hit and kill.

ARTHUR: What else can he do?

MOTHER: There are no more choices. They are all dead. Arthur-Daddy is taller than anybody. He has nobody to talk to, but he is taller than anybody, and he walks around and around. I'm going to leave now.

ARTHUR: Don't leave! Don't leave now, not now, not yet! (*Mother rolls into her room. Arthur is alone.*) I didn't mean that I should be alone. I know I killed everyone, but it was for the wrong reason. It wasn't because I hate them, or because they were bad. I *love* them. I used to love them. It was only because I hurt and they wouldn't listen . . . Let us say now that it is over, and they will all spring up from the ground and be alive without scars. Before the broken walls they will rise up and the sun will strike them with warm life. I did not intend their destruction, but I was in pain and could not speak. My words came as blows. There should have been an alternative . . . My father and my mother were not actually involved in this, but they too died, they were consumed as shamefully as the others. But let us say, please let us say that they too now arise and breathe again the soft air and are bemused by the movement of the grass. Let us say that. (*Pause. The lights have dimmed.*) Mine is the same as his! No: I am here and he is destroyed. (*He*

prowls.) My mother is a woman of rare powers, a woman who has lost none of her strength although now her body is weak. See how she suffers. See how, despite her handicap, she goes on cheerfully, reasonable and alert, her mind unimpaired, her energy intact. See how she judges men . . . I would have her spared. (*Pause.*) In the holocaust my father will be helpless and indefensible. He is a man of ordinary value, a man whose mind turns on and off like any other man's. His virtue is the doubt he permits himself, at times when he feels not too fragile, not too vulnerable. But there is no rock beneath his foot, no, and lightly he leaps back . . . Him too I would spare. (*Pause.*) It is only that they are mine. They are not special or of consequence. It is only that I love them. (*Pause.*) They now arise in the soft air and kiss one another as the light surrounds them. Transformed, they live again in light. The blows of my stick had but dazed them and they are made beautiful as in the mind. Our home is a place of light. We discover an extravagance of love. We always touch. (*Pause. Mother rolls in with the large rifle. She takes aim at Arthur. Arthur does not acknowledge her presence.*) Nonsense! No such thing! No such power is mine—I don't want it. All right, he said, let them live—just get them away from me. Take them away and have them washed. Rub them with the aromatic oils and have them cloaked in silks and then let them gather before our window and we shall bless them. Let their leaders come and kiss our ring. But have them washed and perfumed, their odor is beyond my power to endure. Good, he said, clapping his hands thrice. Now get out of here, all of you, and leave me to my meditations. Leave me in peace. Leave me alone. Let me be. All I ask is a moment's privacy. Have the goodness to permit me this little time. You know how full my days are, now that the trade mission has reached us. And they cannot stay beyond the equinox. Treaties must be concluded, gifts exchanged, bonds sworn, hostages presented. All in due course, my dear fellow, he said. (*Pause.*) So I die now. (*Pause.*) Say goodbye, then, Mother. You might kiss me, but I'd disarm you if I could. At least tell me goodbye.
MOTHER: Goodbye.

ARTHUR: Goodbye, she says. The gun trembles in her grasp, and a single tear trickles down her right cheek onto the stock, but her lips are firm, her jaw set.

MOTHER: Goodbye, son.

ARTHUR: Goodbye, son, she says. Well, Mother, he replies calmly, I guess this is it. I guess we've come to the end of the line, as they say. So, as the sun colored the end-papers of the day, she drew a steady bead and neatly shot him dead.

The doorbell rings. The lights come up. Arthur goes to Mother, takes the gun and puts it aside, and goes to the door, which is out of sight. Mother does not move. There is a long pause, during which some odd mechanical sounds are heard. Then Sue comes into view. She wears mechanical braces on both legs and uses two crutches to walk. Break.

8.

After dinner. Mother covered. Sue gets up from the sofa, no crutches, walks normally around it, and sits again in the same place.

SUE: Was that a surprise or wasn't it? I told you the crippled thing was all an act.

ARTHUR: I didn't believe you.

SUE: Well, now you know. (*She removes braces.*) And now I guess we're really in this together. I had no intention of doing that. I don't know why I picked you, but I did. Now you know.

ARTHUR: You think *I'm* crazy.

SUE: Skip it, Arthur. If you don't say I'm crazy, I won't say you're crazy. Now let's talk about something else.

ARTHUR: Let's go back. Sue, go back to your old self. Be poor little crippled Sue with the messy hair and the empty life.

SUE: What for?

ARTHUR: So I can like you. Just so I can like you. I don't even like you this way.

SUE: Wait till you get to know me . . . Now what about the body? What are we going to do with the body?

ARTHUR: But look, Sue, you can't just go around pretending to be crippled. It's not normal. It's not reasonable. It doesn't make any sense.

SUE: I mean, we can't just let it sit here.

ARTHUR: What are you trying to do to me?

SUE: Nothing. I'd like to see you finish what you've started, that's all.

ARTHUR: What do you want?

SUE: Nothing. You have surprised me better than I could possibly have expected.

ARTHUR: You mean you approve? You think I did the right thing?

SUE: On the whole, I think it's a bad idea to kill people, and especially one's parents, but that's just an opinion. I don't know what to say. I like thrills and chills and a little laughter. And some mystery. I hate most explanations. Can't we have some more shooting?

ARTHUR: Have you ever gone hunting?

SUE: No. I've been skeet shooting a few times.

ARTHUR: I was thinking of quail.

SUE: I've been fishing—in Colorado when I was a little girl, before my father was killed. We used to fish for rainbow trout, but we always caught something else. I can't remember what.

ARTHUR: How was he killed.

SUE: It's not relevant to anything.

ARTHUR: Do you want to know what happened to my father?

SUE: No.

ARTHUR: That's why I had to kill my mother.

SUE: It doesn't matter why you killed your mother. Except you're not finished. What are we going to do with the body? I repeat.

Break.

9.

At dinner. Mother is next to the sofa. Sue must get her crutches, which are out of reach. Arthur begins speaking and

ignores her. Sue shakes her head to decline Mother's help.
She lowers herself out of the chair onto the floor, lies down,
and reaches and gets the crutches. Then she laboriously raises
herself to a standing position, adjusts the braces, walks across
the room, and sits on the end of the sofa next to Mother's
wheelchair as the following speech ends.

ARTHUR: I have been told that no man can survive in soli-
tude. In the most beneficent jungle, in a constantly
temperate clime with fruits on the trees and an abundance of all the necessary means of sustenance—food
and shelter, pure air to breathe, water to drink, a balmi-
ness of the weather surpassing belief—with all this no
man could long survive alone. He would die not of
hunger or of thirst, not racked by disease or torn by
a savage beast of nature, no, but by his loneliness. He
would lose his mind and become dead. One becomes
dead in the same way that one becomes ill or becomes
hungry or becomes thirty-one . . . But I do not think it's
true. I do not believe that I would die. I could scramble
easily for the high coconuts. I could swim for my pleasure and exhilaration. I could carve a spear from some
heavy wood and hunt fish in the lagoon. I would leap
through the woods joyously in pursuit of animals to kill
and eat, or stalk the wary beast with Mohican silence.
Exposed and involved with the jungle I would be man
complete at last. The ghosts I fear would vanish at every
dawn and no mortal plague me in deed or thought
through the brilliant day. It would be a difficult and
perfect life . . . But perhaps not for others . . . Even the
hermit requires companionship, real or fantastic. The
city recluse may wait for the postman's step and be
comforted by that sound, or by noises creeping through
walls from neighboring rooms, or by the mere regularity
of whoever brings his food. One's companions, I suppose, can even consist of the absence of companions. If
Mother were somehow absent and I sat to dinner here,
in this chair, at this table, in this room, at this hour, then
her absence would certainly be palpable to me. It would
be many meals before I would be alone, haunted neither
by her presence nor her absence. I wonder how long . . .
In the jungle the two of you, even the two of you to-

gether, would of course be helpless. Which of you could climb to pick fruit? I mean, the problem would no longer be metaphysical. You're lucky to live in the city, aren't you. . . . If God has stricken your legs, are crutches not sacrilegious? . . . I would help you, but I don't want to blaspheme . . . I find this spectacle intolerable.

The lights change.

SUE (*to Mother*): Hello, honey, I'm home.
MOTHER: Good day at the office?
SUE: So-so. What's for dinner?
MOTHER: Guess.
SUE: I can't imagine.
MOTHER: Your favorite.
SUE: Ummm . . . I know! Braised boy!
MOTHER: Oh, you guessed it the first time.
SUE: Not . . . not . . . not Arthur! Not our boy!
MOTHER: Yes.
SUE: Oh, you are the bravest thing! Just think, only three months old.
MOTHER: Not even.
SUE: And you sacrificed him for me.

The lights change back.

ARTHUR (*to Sue*): Only metaphorically speaking, of course. No violence. Nothing direct, mind you. He died of a heart attack while fishing in the Adirondacks.
SUE: And when was that?
ARTHUR: Some years ago. Mother and I have been perfectly happy these past few years, haven't we, Mother?
MOTHER: I think you should go into psychoanalysis. I mean it.
ARTHUR: But it was really murder. She murdered him because she wanted me, of course.
MOTHER: I have you.
ARTHUR: You don't come near me.
SUE: We have an interesting group of people in my department. We get along with one another very well. Actually, we have a good time. It's not just boring the way it is for most people. You know, clock in the hours and pick up the check. We really enjoy it. I think I'd keep going

to the office even if they didn't pay me. And of course once you're there you might as well work. I'm not one of those girls who likes to sit around and gab all the time, not me. There's nothing I like better than having a job to do and doing it. Why, I can lose myself in work for hours. Like last week Miss Smith was four-seventy off in the receivables and couldn't find it by five o'clock on Friday, so what do I do? I come in on Saturday, unasked, unbidden. I drag myself in about eleven in the morning, send out for coffee, spread out the ledgers, and settle down to the big desk. The next thing I know it's getting dark. I found what she was looking for, of course—but that wasn't even the main thing. I was transported, you know? You know what I mean? I wasn't in that dreary office, I wasn't in this poor body, I was . . . I don't know . . . I was . . . you know? I was . . .

MOTHER: Arthur, could you open the window a little?

SUE: Another thing. I have this girl friend, see, she's a dancer. A modern dancer, you know? Well, and we talk about our, you know, problems a lot together. We haven't got the same ones, of course, but anyway, we got in the habit. So she tells me about this class she has. She's always talking about it. They lie on the floor part of the time and sort of writhe around. She showed me a couple of times. It's exciting. And so they had a big party in the studio one time and she was dancing with one of the boy dancers for a long time and it was hot and she felt this thing pressing against her stomach sort of. She's kind of short, and it was pressing into her sort of here, above the navel, and it was not very comfortable, especially when he squeezed her hardest and kept rubbing it into her, she said not even in time to the music. I never told that before to anybody in the whole world. What do you think?

MOTHER: Oh . . . well . . . it's very interesting. I thought it was an interesting story.

SUE: I mean, what do you think I should *do*?

MOTHER: Do?

SUE: Don't you think I should *tell* her? You can't just let things like that *happen*, can you? I have to do something. You know how those dancers are anyway, he's probably not even interested in girls. She may never see him again. I'm so confused I don't know what to say any more.

ARTHUR: Sue, what do you think you're doing?

SUE: Another thing I should tell you . . . Well, I don't know how well you think I know your son, but I'll tell you, I've been working in that office a long time now, and this isn't the first time he's talked to me. No sir. It *is* the first time he's asked me out, though.

MOTHER: He doesn't have many dates.

SUE: I didn't know whether to accept or not. You know, just out of the blue sky like that.

ARTHUR: Stop it! Both of you, stop this ridiculous . . .

SUE: You should warn him about doing things like that. How do you know what kind of a girl he might bring into your home? Into the bosom of the family, even. What's left of it. You don't know a thing about me, and neither does he. I could be a psychopathic killer and you might not ever realize it. You can't even be sure I'm crippled. Actually, it's nothing but an act. I can easily do a polka.

ARTHUR: Miss Smith, did you say?

SUE: That's right.

MOTHER: Oh, do you know her too, Arthur?

ARTHUR: I know everyone. I hired everyone. When I got the job I fired everyone and got an entirely new staff of people who would be loyal to me. Miss Smith apparently has less loyalty than I previously thought.

SUE: Oh no no no! I'd do anything not to get Miss Smith in trouble!

MOTHER: Would you sleep with Arthur?

SUE: What?

MOTHER: Would you let Arthur fuck you?

ARTHUR: I'll promise to forget you said anything about Miss Smith at all. How about it?

MOTHER: Surely the question is not so difficult. Think of it in units of value—dollars, say, or coconuts, or pelts. Anything will do.

ARTHUR: Never mind, Mother. She obviously doesn't understand. It's all she can do to balance the accounts receivable ledger.

SUE: Oh, I see. It's because of the business about my legs.

You're getting the upper hand again—or should I say the upper foot?

ARTHUR: Don't talk about legs and feet so much in front of my mother. I'd think you would have a little more delicacy. I'm more than slightly disappointed in this exhibition.

MOTHER: Don't say that, son. I don't mind at all.

The doorbell rings and continues ringing rhythmically to the end of the episode.

ARTHUR (*terrified*): Who is it? What do you think it is? Mother? (*To Sue.*) Does anyone know you're here?

SUE: No.

ARTHUR: Mother?

MOTHER: I don't know.

ARTHUR: It's a murderer, I recognize the ring. He's come to kill. He's come to stay. No one's in the mood for death and then he comes. You open the door and he's polite, indifferent to the terror in his host. He reaches out his hand. You forget your manners, you lose your style. Who am I now, facing his empty, neutral gaze, fixed by his lidless eyes? Who am I? I won't answer, I decide, and he'll go away.

SUE: You can't.

ARTHUR: Why not?

MOTHER: Answer the door, Arthur. People don't just go away. (*Pause.*)

ARTHUR: Whatever you say.

Arthur gets the rifle, checks that it's loaded, and goes out of sight to the door. Break.

10.

After dinner. Arthur and Sue; Mother covered.

ARTHUR: It was October, I think. The rough clothes. The color I think of is brown. Rain threatens all the time. We are entirely alone. My father taught me to shoot well.

SUE: You might have shot him.

ARTHUR: Yes, I might have.

SUE: But you didn't.

ARTHUR: No. I shot at the birds. I never hit one. I never
killed anything when we went hunting. My mind was
on something else. I have caught fish. I caught bass on
a later trip. No, I didn't kill him. We were out on the
lake fishing, and it was starting to rain. My father was
trying to start the outboard motor. He kept jerking on
the cord, again and again. I said I was cold and he gave
me his jacket. He went back to the motor, and then
stood still, and looked out across the lake, and just fell
over into the water.

SUE: Rain came in the window and I couldn't move from
the bed. I called out but the thunder drowned my voice.
I cried and the tears were endless. I tried not to think
about anything. The floor was covered with water. The
curtains were drenched. I squeezed the pillow against
my face, against my eyes. I covered my ears and cried
and could think of nothing but the rain.

ARTHUR: I have dreamt of the Ganges and the burning ghats.
I have spent nights on a barge anchored in the Nile at
the ruins of Antinoöpolis. No more remote mountains
exist than those of my mind. Tonight I will dream myself to forests of teak, even now I stride the decks with
Ishmael and swim with fish among the anemones along
the coral reef. Sails billow and the swell carries us
through the moonlight and the phosphorescent surf
booms in the distance on the beach. Penguins stroll
about in the perpetual light of summer on the ice. I
sing my grief to you . . . We are here, at this instant,
in this place. I have committed an act. I have lifted my
hand. I have taken a breath, said a few words, moved
one finger a fraction of an inch. No Eskimo was my
witness, no Brazilian pulled the trigger, no quail was
the target, no child's unsteadiness let the bullet go astray.

SUE: So at last that's settled.

ARTHUR: And what happens now will be the next thing.
Whatever it is. If police pound down the door and rush
me to jail or an asylum, it will be the next thing. If
your hair is a wig and you take it off and are a man, it
will be the next thing. If that sheet moves and Mothe

speaks again or a bomb drops here and now or we go
on talking and marry and have children and lead ordinary lives and die peacefully in each other's arms at 80,
it will be the next thing. Absolutely whatever happens.
And there *will be* a next thing. We can choose, or we
can just go on without choosing. We need not fear that
nothing will happen. Every moment until the moment
of our deaths will be matched by a next moment.

SUE: And what shall we do with your mother?

ARTHUR: Kiss her goodbye.

Break.

11.

At dinner.

MOTHER: Arthur, please close the door.

Arthur goes out, closes the door, and returns.

ARTHUR: There is a world of love. Beyond these motions the
currents are soft and swerve among lovers. The skin is
soft and so sensitive that every touch brings unbearable
delight. I might throw my arm carelessly about your
shoulders and we would take flight without effort, almost unaware. There is a freedom so complete that it
knows no cost or caution or passing time. There is a
world in which all speak as lovers. There as here, all are
lovers in desire, but in the world of love all are themselves and always at ease. I speak briefly. There is a
world of love in which my mother could not fear to die,
in which I would be neither coward nor bully, in which
your useless legs would count as little as my curly hair or
Harold's dark skin or Mother's age. We do not suffer
from our pains, nor from our pleasure. We permit ourselves and others every need and sentiment. To desire
is blessed. The best of men are those not afraid to want.

SUE: Truth is beside the point. The truth of my desires is
that . . . there is no hope. It is not a question of courage.
I am unafraid, but it counts for nothing. For you perhaps it would, but not for me. I open myself to kind-

ness. I am kind. I make the effort to amuse. I watched a camellia bloom and then it withered. What would you recommend? You speak of this world and believe it possible—but you do not take me there.

MOTHER: Both of you are right but I'm still sad.

Arthur gets the gun and points it at Mother.

ARTHUR: You speak the last words.

MOTHER: It is good if you desire it. (*The lights change.*) I despise apologies as vulgar. I am impatient and will speak of style. What with everything that happened, the meals, the laundry, what with your father's loud voice and dry skin, what with the coming and going of pain and pleasure, interests, friends, various kinds of love, what with the time I spent on my son, the time toward this moment, it was always touch and go whether I would find the opportunity for style. As a matter of fact, I *did* kill your father. I was part of his life and he died. How can you think it matters? One pays the price for individuality. Something like that . . . I hope you don't get caught. But I can't be serious about the future.

ARTHUR: Come on.

MOTHER: Oh don't wait for me. My mind is really on something else.

THE END

CHAS. DICKENS'
CHRISTMAS CAROL

*freely adapted from C. Dickens, D. Duck,
E. Phlegm, and others*

(BY SOREN AGENOUX

made for Joseph Cino and Bob Olivo
and dedicated to the one I love, Arnold Horton.

Chas. Dickens' Christmas Carol is an occasional play. It
was commissioned as a Christmas show for the Caffe
Cino and written and produced immediately. Soren
Agenoux probably set out to do a straightforward
adaptation of the Dickens story, but the play he wrote
is vastly more complex. The musty, literary reality of
the classic is relieved by gaudier flashes from Walt
Disney's Scrooge McDuck comics, interjections of
high test Lower East Side speed, and flourishes of
Agenoux's own ineffable imagination. The writing is
extraordinary, whole passages ranked like shelves of
crystal goblets shattering before they reach your ears.
Technically, the play achieves collage effects previously
known only on the silver screen. I directed the
production, which was a climax of collaboration.

M. S.

Chas. Dickens' Christmas Carol was first presented at the Caffe Cino on December 20, 1966. It was directed by Michael Smith with the following cast:

EBENEZER SCROOGE: Ondine
TIM CRATCHIT: Charles Stanley
BOB CRATCHIT: Arnold Horton
JACOB MARLEY: Donald Brooks
(followed by Robert Patrick)
GHOST OF CHRISTMAS PAST: Jacque Lynn Colton
GHOST OF CHRISTMAS PRESENT: JACOB MARLEY
GHOST OF CHRISTMAS YET TO COME: SEÑOR ORO
SEÑOR ORO: Charles Stanley
MRS. CRATCHIT: Soren Agenoux

The lighting was designed and performed by John P. Dodd.

Stage Manager: Christopher Diekman

OPPOSITE: Ondine (Scrooge) and Jacque Lynn Colton
(Spirit of Christmas Past) in *Chas. Dickens' Christmas Carol*
Photo: Billy Name

CHARACTERS

JACOB MARLEY (his ghost, his voice, and his various incarnations), "a spectre of Scrooge's former partner in business."

EBENEZER SCROOGE, "a grasping, covetous old man, the surviving partner of the firm of Scrooge & Marley."

TIM CRATCHIT ("Tiny Tim"), "a cripple, youngest son of Bob Cratchit."

BOB CRATCHIT, "clerk to Ebenezer Scrooge."

GHOST OF CHRISTMAS PAST, "a phantom showing things past."

GHOST OF CHRISTMAS PRESENT, "a spirit of a kind (but phlegmatic) nature" (played by JACOB MARLEY).

GHOST OF CHRISTMAS YET TO COME (played by SEÑOR ORO).

SEÑOR ORO, an amnesiac, compulsive entertainer, and fund raiser.

MRS. CRATCHIT, "wife of Bob Cratchit."

VOICE OF A BOY IN THE STREET, teen-ager whom Scrooge hails on Christmas Morn.

Lights dim up on interior of Scrooge & Marley's clerical office. Bob Cratchit's desk and high stool upstage.

Marley, Scrooge, Tiny Tim, and Bob Cratchit stand in file forestage.

MARLEY: Hod carriers are very dull! I'm dead! (*He exits.*)

SCROOGE: Everyone wants to be me, so Christmas is what it is to me.

TINY TIM: This play is dedicated to Scrooge!

Bob Cratchit goes upstage and enters office late. Scrooge shoves a clock in Bob's face and puts his hand out under Bob's nose. Cratchit sets a coin in it.

MARLEY'S VOICE (*mechanically repeats ten times*):
Detach—Distract
detach—distract
detach—distract
detach—distract
detach—distract
detach—distract
detach—distract
detach—distract
detach—distract
Etc.

BOB CRATCHIT: Marley's dead.

SCROOGE: I solemnized the funeral with an undoubted bargain.

TINY TIM (*still downstage*): If we were not perfectly convinced that Hamlet's father died before the play began . . . there would be nothing more remarkable in his taking a stroll at night—

BOB CRATCHIT: —in an easterly wind—

TINY TIM: upon his ramparts, than there would be in any other middle-aged gentleman rashly turning out after dark in a breezy spot.

Scrooge seats Tiny Tim at the side of his father's desk, takes his crutches from him, and hangs them next to his cane and hat on the wall.

CRATCHIT (*to Tim*): He carries his own low temperature always about with him; he ices this office in the dog days, and doesn't thaw it one degree at Christmas.
TINY TIM: Foul weather doesn't know where to have him.
CRATCHIT: Heaviest rain,
   and snow,
   and hail,
   and sleet can boast
   of an advantage over Mr. Scrooge in one respect:
   They often "come down" handsomely.
TINY TIM: And Mr. S. never does.

Scrooge throws a bag of money into a corner. The phone rings on the desk. He picks up the receiver.

SCROOGE: Scrooge (*quacks*) McDuck speaking!
   What can I do for you?
MARLEY'S VOICE: You can listen to THIS, McDuck!
PHONE: BU-Z-z-z-z-z—Z
SCROOGE (*setting down receiver*): I'm . . . I'm all rattled! WHERE am I? (*Reaches top hat and cane off wall, glances in mirror, then in Tiny's eyes. Muttering.*) I've never seen THIS PLACE before! (*To mirror.*) Mister, can you tell me where I am? (*To Cratchit.*) You—you're not a person! You're a reflection of ME! (*Muttering.*) That guy ME? . . . a stuffed old bird I never SAW before! (*Clasping hat to head, and running out.*) This is awful! I don't WHERE I am, or WHO I am! I only know I want to go to the DISMAL SWAMP!
TINY TIM: Nobody ever stops him in the street to say, with gladsome looks—
CRATCHIT (*jumping to a stand off stool*): "My dear Scrooge, how are you? When will you come see me?"

Lights up on downstage street scene, Scrooge runs on, halting at a Gromyko-like figure (Marley).

SCROOGE: I'm confused, mister!
   I don't remember this city,
   and I don't remember ME!
MARLEY (*to himself*): Heh! He got the message, all right! (*To Scrooge.*) I can tell you ALL you need to know, Señor! I am your SECRETARY, COPILOT NOGGEN

SHINE KY! You wish to go to the DISMAL SWAMP!
I'll help you go there right away!

SCROOGE: You sure MUST know me! Am I glad YOU, Señor
Noggen, came along!

TINY TIM (*limping down the street on crutches dressed as
Donald Duck*):
Hi! Uncle Scrooge!
You're late for our dinner date. . . .

SCROOGE: ?Huh? I don't remember a date for dinner!?
And I don't remember YOU,
laddie! Never-saw-you-before-in-my-life!

MARLEY (*severe*): You've mistaken Señor Pato for someone
else! So Good Darkening, sir!

SCROOGE (*correcting*): Evening.

MARLEY: Good Evening, Sir!

TINY TIM (*to Cratchit at his desk*): For a SENOR, that old
duck sure had a SCOTCH accent like Uncle Scrooge!
Well, Uncle Scrooge must still be in his Money Bin!
I'll go see what's delaying him! (*Limps off.*)

Two gongs sound.

CRATCHIT (*head alert up from desk*): The city clocks—

MARLEY'S VOICE (*mechanically repeats ten times*):
Detach-Distract
detach-distract
detach-distract
Etc.

CRATCHIT (*continuing over voice*): —have only just gone—

Another gong sounds.

—three, but it is quite dark already . . .

MARLEY'S VOICE: It has not been light all day . . .

CRATCHIT: —and candles are flaring in the windows of the
neighboring offices—

TINY TIM (*back on—on his crutches. Mocking tone*): —like
ruddy smears upon the palpable brown air.

CRATCHIT (*taking from far darkness of top desk drawer a copy
of* Theatre Arts, *then reading from it*): "There should
be a law that makes grace mandatory for all crippled
creatures. . . . The world has no one to blame but Sarah
Bernhardt for starting traditions that result in Barbra
Streisands—"

Tiny Tim lights a candle, sets it on desk; Cratchit warms his hands over it.

SCROOGE (*offstage*): Scrooge has a very small fire, but the clerk's fire is so very much smaller that it looks like one coal.

Then he comes rushing past on downstage street.

TINY TIM: A merry Christmas, Uncle! God sav you!
SCROOGE: Bah!—

He is joined by Tim and Cratchit:

HUMBUG!

CRATCHIT (*entreating*): He has so heated himself
with rapid walking in the fog
and frost, that he is all in
a glow; his face—

Scrooge halts to listen.

—is ruddy, and handsome;
his eyes sparkle, and his breath
smokes again . . .

SCROOGE (*sputtering*): Artifice-cheating-deceit-deception-dis-honesty-treachery-treason-trick, you fuckin' faggot! MERRY CHRISTMAS! What right have you to be merry? What reason have you to be merry? You're poor enough!

TINY TIM (*arbitrating*): Come then, what right have you to be DISMAL? What reason have you to be morose? You're rich enough!

SCROOGE: Merry CHRISTMAS!? How can you get away with it? What's Christmas-time to you and your clerk-father-and-family but a time for paying more bills without the M-O-NEY; a time for finding yourself a year older, and an old trick, but not one hour richer, or better-laid? If I could (*sudden accent*) voik my vill, ev'ry idiot who goes about with "Merry Christmas" on his lips should be boiled with some kid's peyote, and buried with a steak of horsemeat through his heart.

MARLEY'S VOICE: Stake of holly through his heart, Señor!

SCROOGE: But I am sure I have always thought of Christmas-time, when it has come around——apart from the veneration due to its sacred name and origin, IF ANYTHING BELONGING TO IT CAN BE APART FROM THAT—as a bad time. (*Phone rings. He picks up receiver.*) Yes—(*Quacks.*)

PHONE: BU-Z-z-z-z-z-z-ZZZZ

SCROOGE: HURRY, Hurry, secretary! I have the wildest DESIRE to get going to the swamp!

PHONE (*Marley's voice*): That's the old spirit! (*To himself.*) McDuck is the most eager EXILE I ever hauled into the land of nevermore! *Hyaaaaaa!*

SCROOGE (*to mirror*): Who's that, again? Who am I? Where —? oh . . . (*Explaining tone.*) Cino no longer does this and makes himself unavailable for quiet conversations about creative Things; I told 'im when MARLEY died I planned to do nothing and withdraw into a year of mourning . . . (*Rushes off.*)

A billet-doux falls to the floor out of his passing wind. Tiny Tim limps over to pick billet up, reads it aloud.

TINY TIM: "*In March I will be able to work again with those who help me to feel free and refreshed about life and work; preconceptions and negative attitudes are death to the kind of things I do.*"

CRATCHIT: Wha—? Tiny, baby, that old duck you met—you *sure* he didn't know you?

TINY TIM: I'm sure, Dad!

Besides the guy with him called him *Signor Pazzo!*
Look, if Uncle Scrooge doesn't show up by morning, we'll drop a nickel on the sidewalk!

CRATCHIT: Good boy!

THAT will bring him running—
Unless

TINY TIM: UNLESS he CAN'T run!

Fade out.

Lights up on Scrooge inside airliner.

SCROOGE: Uh—hello, sir!

Who are you?

SEÑOR ORO: My SECRETARY, THERE—(*pointing to Marley standing in a corner*)—tells me I'm Señor Oro, but all I know is that I'm a guy with a wild compulsion to go to the DISMAL SWAMP!

Scrooge snuggles down in seat beside him.

Another thing, Señor—

SCROOGE: I think it's *Best-tah?*

SEÑOR ORO: Another thing, Señor Basta, I know also that I, ORO, am, in extent and conscious sense, aware that I am part of a little group—well, to get to the small of the back of it, tomorrow's Christmas, isn't it true? Mira, NAVIDADES, correct me if I'm wrong—

SCROOGE: Sure enough, then, this is Christmas Eve, and where—WHERE is it we should be?—

SEÑOR ORO (*encouraged*): DISZ-MAL SVAMPP, where else? Besides, then, that certain central applecore of encircling Apple-Want of my eye, I mean, I am, we are, endeavoring to raise a fund to buy The Poor some meat and drink, and means of warmth, you know. We choose this time because it is a time, of all others—

Music: Donovan's "Mellow Yellow."

—when Want, not to mention Apple-Want, is keenly felt, and—(*Thumps Scrooge on back.*) Abundance rejoices. What-shall-I-put-you-down-for? (*Waving pen in air.*)

SCROOGE (*jumping to his feet*): Nothing!

SEÑOR ORO: You wish to be anonymous, such as Jack-y Ken-dy?

SCROOGE (*waving parachute in air*): I wish to be left alone, since you ask me what I wish, er, Señor, this is my answer. (*Waves parachute.*) I don't make merry myself at Christmas and I can't afford to make idle people merry. My clerk is, at this very moment, a bug at my business— He is Poor, since he will not raise himself to my wasp, yet as he intends to make tomorrow merry for himself and family, he *will* do so, and well knows it, out of his own unweighty pockets; I help to support certain establishments, certain recognized charities—*The Girls of Chelsea Amphetamindell*—THE VELVET UNDERGRINDLE—young people digging out from premature burial by overriding freeways, and so forth, they cost enough, and those who are badly off must go to these.

SEÑOR ORO (*waving picture of Pat Nixon in the air*): MANY can't go to these; and many would rather die.

SCROOGE: If they would rather die—(*He pulls a card out of parachute.*) Señor, if they—what's this? Your identification, my good man, it reads: SENOR ORO, alias C. FRANCIS SPELLMANO—are you a prince of your church, sir?

SEÑOR ORO (*snatching card away from Scrooge*): Ask Gen. Ky, our secretary . . .

SCROOGE (*pulling parachute out from behind Oro's back*): *This* one is mine—Where was I—? (I am *not* going to a phone call's swamp for Christmas, that's adamant!) (*Drops other parachute into Oro's lap.*) And yours, no doubt of it— Where was I—where's the door—? (*Turning in circles.*) Where's the emergency windows—? Where was I? (*Suddenly subduing himself.*) Oh . . . if they would rather die, those you warned of, they had better do it and decrease the surplus population— Besides, excuse me, I don't know your people—I'm not interested in politics, yours, my clerk's, his crippled son's, or your unfortunate secretary's.

SEÑOR ORO: But you might be—should you stumble on the Ghost of Christmas Yet to Come, who knows, I know, believe me!

SCROOGE (*frantic*): It's NOT MY BUSINESS! It's enough for a man to understand his own troubles, financial, whatever, and not to interfere with other people's: mine occupy me unrelentingly. Good afternoon, MONsignore!

Blackout.

Lights quick up on Scrooge back in office; Cratchit, his pen scratching, at work; Tiny Tim asleep in the chair. Afternoon dim light. Telephone rings. Scrooge picks up receiver abruptly.

PHONE: B-U-Z-Z-z-z-z-z-Z-Z

Blackout.

Lights up on Scrooge seated back in plane; a docile expression as he turns to Señor Oro beside him.

SCROOGE: Señor Oro, I have a strong feeling that THIS is where I should land!

SEÑOR ORO: *I* have the same feeling, Señor *Path-cha*—that this is the spot!

MARLEY (*from corner*): You are right, señores! This is where
you belong—the *middle* of the DISMAL SWAMP!

SCROOGE (*looking out window—gasps*): But there's no AIR-
FIELD! How do we LAND?

MARLEY (*tossing parachutes to both*): You use PARA-
CHUTES—like you always do! But THESE, not
THOSE! Don't you remember?

SEÑOR ORO: I don't remember EVER having jumped before,
but I've got a *feeling* that I MUST!
Well,
here
goes. (*Parachutes out.*)

SCROOGE: I'll be right behind you, Señor Oro! (*Parachutes
out.*)

Blackout.

SCENE 2

*In stage darkness sound of echoing winds through a deserted
house. Slow, slow dim up of ghostly light to reveal an enor-
mous door knocker nearly covering back stage wall.*

*The face of Marley plainly, but not too plainly, being the
shape of the knocker. Scrooge wanders in in nightdress, holding above his head one small, lit taper.*

SCROOGE: This is not good. (*Looks, with a squint, at face on
knocker.*) Humph! Darkness is cheap, and I like it!
(*Muttering.*) Why do we have words?

MARLEY'S GHOST: What evidence would you have of my
reality beyond that of your senses?

SCROOGE: Are you serious? Marley, aren't you a Red Spy, or
a severe Right Indochink?

MARLEY'S GHOST: I am the ghost of your partner, Jacob,
newly dead. Why do you doubt your senses, Ebenezer?

SCROOGE: Because (*he puts out his taper, and relights it again
at once*) a little thing affects them. (*Muttering.*) Para-
chuting into the sewaged center of a god-forsaken
swamp . . . (*Aloud.*) —A slight disorder of the stomach
makes them cheats. If you're dead and reliving, old
friend, you are probably an undigested bit of beef I ate,

a blot of mustard, a crumb of cheesemeat. There's more
of gravy about you than of grave, whatever you are . . .
now.

MARLEY'S GHOST (*the bloody bandages binding his head now
appearing clearly*): Man of the worldly mind, do you
believe in me or not?

SCROOGE: What are you that I must give you credence,
though you stand acknowledged? The stains death
broke over your head I, of course, have no knowledge
of . . .

MARLEY'S GHOST: I am not Marley now, and it's not Marley
who must warn you so badly he sees you unbeckoned,
Scrooge. The spirit within that man who died, and *all*
creatures of his two-footedness, too, must have somewhere, or for separate whiles, gone forth in life to meet
people as they sit inside furless hides, in whatever booth
or corner of sidewalk, and interior, café-times at whatever quality of table clothed in lace or plastic fashion.
I am that spirit and am restless for more places than
Marley could get to in his days because of your whip-
rulers, successful businessman! We must get out—please
don't whisper that *you* won't have to—you know, we
must get out, and must take in, not merely to watch,
but sit on the bad bubbles of the unlucky, shut up the
beggings for bread with whole loaves, or at least some
stack of slices of the stuff; otherwise, WE WILL BE
CONDEMNED TO DO SO AFTER DEATH.

SCROOGE: Oh, Marley, Marley, skirt of our midst, I'm here
now. Can't you even relieve your shapelessness where I
am in some unconscious gristle under my surface-skin?

MARLEY'S GHOST: If I wanted to, how could I satisfy what's
left to float of Jacob once-friend that you have been
shaken or cautioned enough?

SCROOGE: Don't be hard upon me,
Don't be flowery, for Christ's sake.
But you yourself were always
a good man of business, Jacob Marley, don't forget . . .

MARLEY'S GHOST: Look, don't you dare step back,
I'm moven towardwell your taper,
can you see my plastic saranwrappings?

SCROOGE: This is too much!
You can't scare simpering you seem so damn silly!

MARLEY'S GHOST: Horrible, if you weren't so mean,
    you'd see, however you see, that
    these petty translucencies (called "Baggies")
    are inextricable from what I now am.
    And why—they were sutured to me daily, or
    nearly daily, during the life of our partnership
    in making deals, and great deals of money.
    No office lunches, you ruled, for either,
    easy for you 'cause you couldn't want them,
    so these plastickings of my wind-weighty movements
    were the containers of the sordid unhappy sandwiches
    you forced me to bring and eat at my desk to *economize*
    on office expenses that even you couldn't count larger
    than pennies . . .

    How is it that I appear before you, as
    you live, in a shape that this close up you now can see, how
    you won't know in any time that passes, old man,
    you can see me, right?
SCROOGE: Yes . . . yes . . .
MARLEY'S GHOST: Yet do you know
    I have sat invisible—
BOB CRATCHIT'S VOICE: beside you in the office
    many
    and
    many a day . . .?
SCROOGE (*at the end of stamina*): I am awake still I may be
    speaking to answer some dream, Spirit of Marley, if that's
    your name, can I tell you you knew too little of me,
    as well?
    I have a regard for persons,
    more I've been before we met in our young years, much
    more than a respecter of them, of us, I've been too
    totally to talk about it, can't you see, and too coldly,
    that is, in a coldish light because touching people for
    warmth darkens my brain, and they turn terribly unim-
    portant to me if there is nothing to apply to them that
    clarifies their ways, that's clear, you see, I've gone out
    to them, fairly forbiddenly as the marbles roll, but
    really they've been my flock many, many reckless people,
    so don't tell me,
    if you don't know, that my flock consists of human

beings of any sort—
homosexuals,
junkies, thieves, criminals, the rejected by society. That's
who I'm Pope
for—the few who really care . . .
Come in closer to me, Marley, and confess.
You know the cameras are rolling.
This is a new kind of confession—it's called True Con-
fessions!

Both of them are shaken by laughter.

MARLEY'S GHOST: Let me warn you,
I still can though I admit we're both pretty silly, Scrooge,
you will be haunted by three spirits, stay in bed, if that
is the congenial advice I can give, pretend you're asleep
under extreme exasperation of tight-shut eyelids, whatever you'll see, my warning is only that you will be
haunted by three spirits—
SCROOGE: Like you?
MARLEY'S GHOST: What would yes to that say?
SCROOGE: Couldn't I take 'em all at once?
MARLEY'S GHOST: Don't know what it'll be in form or order
or confused mistakes of anxious fright, but you'll be
haunted by three before the dawn of Christmas Day
pushes up sunlight.

Marley's Ghost dematerializes cogently.

Scrooge goes straight to bed.

*Lights—demisemistagedarkness. Sound—twelve gongs or
church chimes.*

MARLEY'S VOICE (*mechanically repeating ten times*):
Detach-Distract
detach-distract
detach-distract
detach-distract
Etc.

Scrooge wanders on, rubbing eyes, yawning.

SCROOGE: It can't be—did I hear twelve—?
It can't be noon of Christmas Day . . .
The bells're wrong . . . guess an icicle

must have got stuck in their works . . .
I did hear at least eleven—

He yawns—pause of five beats.

One gong sounds.

MARLEY'S VOICE (*mechanically repeating twice*):
Detach-Distract
detach-distract

*The figure of a woman appears to Scrooge before he has
a chance to go back to bed. She carries a sprig of holly
with bright red berries on it; she blends in and out of
alternately blue and green unearthly lights. A tall orange
flame shoots straight up out of the top of her bonnet.*

SCROOGE (*half-amused*): Now a head without a body;
then a torso with a single arm flapping at its side;
Now with two arms floating up light as silk streamers
yellow and green colors of May Day . . . o-o-o-oh-h-h-h!

He shivers uncontrollably momentarily.

GHOSTS OF CHRISTMAS PAST (*a Kathryn Grayson clarity and
emptiness of tone*):
Je suis Mélisande and Mary Garden,
Ellen Terry and Ellen Stewart,
Gene Tierney and LaThui Nu,
Mistah Scrooge, Eben, spelled E-b-o-n when you were
     black and seventeen, I am Billie Holiday,
Mae Marsh, Contessa da Robilant,
and Miss Teed, Miss Brockman, Mrs. Jayne round faced
piled with platinum hair, Miss Will who gave you Proust
and Valéry, Valerie Bettis and Bette Davis, your
actresses, teachers, lady-loves, flush-filled man who
tucked in ladys' mounds without muscle . . . *Bei
Männern
     Mädchen liebe stage* . . .
Candy spun like webs above the sky tacked and stitched
by threads to a hangar escaped from and finally swal-
lowed by swollen rows of dirt . . .
     passion dirt . . .
"*I'm fat as a hog
Stuck in a bog, Bottom* . . ."

S-C-R-OOOO-G-E!

SCROOGE: Oh, go away!

GHOST OF CHRISTMAS PAST: Really go away? Sissy going on sixty! I'm burning up remembering you at seventeen and twenty. Where is seventeen and twenty today? I'm on fire, Eben chief, can't you see my Pawnee bonnet's conflagrating . . . no . . . no . . . don't touch . . . If you're burned, it will still prove nothing. Nothing can stop it anyway so late . . . gone like a couple of ponies are Seventeen and Twenty . . . You lit me, or your class-arsonist, don't recall which, with the branding iron you seared their horsey rumps with so they'd holler, yell, and run off and away, way past the mesa, past the joshua, past the ochre prairie . . .

SCROOGE: You don't recall . . . but you'd blame me 'cause those erotic blame-badges, ceremony by ceremony, all came to be mine. I can't be responsible for that burning cap—it doesn't continue getting its fuel from the mal-substance of your filmy ninny spirit-self, so shut up, and just get lost . . . there were, I can recall, Seventeens who were bad mares, Twenties who were born to be hens . . . how would they run out and be free? Pumas would enjoy the mares tibula by fibula, fairly put; chicken-hawks raise the flecked swoop of a lazy wing and probe into the mashy, gritty heartsores of the scrambling escaped hens, facileness applied of locks picked with a girl's hairpin . . .

Mélisande or Jacqueline Bon-Bon, girls are nowhere nowadays to Ebenezer Scrooge, can't afford their care, procrastination, and upkeep. Boys can comb down any grown man's rumpelstiltskin, sexy and chunky . . . sweet. What's the black difference in the Lone Ranger jeans or in Stones' skyblue widewales and heely boots when you had some of each and all of them children . . .?

GHOST OF CHRISTMAS PAST: You can't reject me, sir, or make me ashamed to pull you back toward the boy in your buried past . . . if not for him, I couldn't possibly fly . . . and if not for him, I'd walk around and about every-where to go oblivious to all that is male not placed in flagstone or concrete . . . what a lot to miss when you're spiritually concerned with the madness of maleness, like

me . . . you can't make me sad, simply can't, though
I'd know the meaning of the sad-word when uttered,
don't underrate me, can't make me sad, you can't. Don't
know lineage of spooks you intimately have laid, but
not in ignorance or rank and file do I say: I, I am a
Spirit, don't know who else you expect, though won't
be anyone more surely a spirit in the sense of esprit than
me! Foolish Eben, seven and ten, do you anticipate a
visit from your Special Friend, Present? Your Present,
whatever her corpus configures for friend, is some in-
finitely repeatable drink of a moment pumped sometime in . . . 1854 . . . that's just a guess. The real past is
your boyhood, a time in your lifetime, going on prov-
ably in as infinite a manner as your fancied preference
plucked from a past earthbound to no body made on
earth reasonably recently. I enjoy the fresh-mown nostalgia, not soggy, not longing, of recalling that December ices jungle-gyms and moistens to the point of neglect
and loneliness broad rows of calisthenic mattresses where
sports teams in sweat suits gray below blond and shiney
brown heads sprinted and rose in semesters that have
inevitably passed through long waists out of skittish
black cottony nests of initial pubic hair . . . it's a
pleasure knowing I'm a stone to the cold and so effort-
lessly savor the yellow and pink-tissuey sweet-pea auras
deposited unknowing in these firmly packed tickings by
long leg muscles and big-boned limbs of the boy, newly
big, now gone on to Seventeen and Twenty, a few freely
humping the undersized, increasingly deprived, haggard
Kundry of last wilderness, and more gone to grave war
or sucked up in Manhattan sky funnels suspended, yet
never at peace, or sexed with purpose sufficiently to skip
off the sills of windows, anyway, that undisguisedly op-
erate as walls of glass and never, never open, so to stop
shaving their edgy young organs through suit pants
puffingly stuffed with razor-licking frustrations on the
rise, bleeding from these abrasions little but cruelly,
naturally set right by a deft stroke or two of one of a
dozen masturbatory-sensational styptic pencils . . . I
watch lots of young men you'll never be knowing, but I
don't care where they go, ever, or if that's where I
should be going . . .

SCROOGE: Who told you you were modern, class dame of the moment, taffeta spine of the hour, like that! Really! If you were female, as you gloat to me that you're being, you wouldn't sound like Rupert Brooke napping under a counterpane of love for blue china. Pathetic Pocahontas Burning Bonnet, sex-happy spirit, if you were living with your leggy burden below the belt, I'm sure there'd be no mooning over passions temporary as milkweeds sailing on the skim of the down-soil, soil forty years later crusty and holding up structures heavier than all-hell Egypt. What are you shaking your stick at, if not at me? What I loved where you come from, a peaceable kingdom possible only collected to this place or that place in time, the details of raincoats, galoshes, Sunday suppers, rolls in the hay all alike and, as memories, soft as bunnies, universally lovable, and cosmically inane. I was visited by a ghost before going to bed tonight, and though he resembled, and in many ways conveyed to me the man I knew him to be during his life, I was eventually convinced that he still, or some part of him, was lasting out so that I might not be forced to, when laid down for good. You accuse me of being a bruiser in bed at a time when certain bed words couldn't anywhere be heard. Are you sorry? Did you find the legion of boys you prey in the air around under a Christmas tree?

GHOST OF CHRISTMAS PAST: Under a love apple, I'd say! If you knew how thoroughly you do love me, Eben, we would go shopping and stop on the way to sing in the streets.

SCROOGE: SWEET . . . sweet . . . I'm so tired of trying to tell you, dear featherweight Lady Dread, that you and I definitely agree that you are, indeed, *sweet*—!

GHOST OF CHRISTMAS PAST: IN WHAT WISP
 endures of lots of former loves
 All the love there is in the world that's released its hold,
 hovered briefly chiefly in solely public affairs, gone beyond radar, and then been forgotten . . .
 Boys are not fat cat to me,
 Who am I, where is there in me
 a person-place, a mole on a synapse,
 or even a crack in a knuckle

to whom boys refer purrs
and ask to be scratched, comforted,
and swell? There are no preferences
where there are no "me's"—I tell you, Mr. S.,
at best I can make do, or, rather, what can be made do
is made do that can be since there is no "me" that can
do, can make, can rather—"that is" . . . "You see" . . .
"This is what is more heaven in the way I can see best
      heavens for me."
Boys?
Girls?
I could tell you about girls' brassieres and how tender
they are at the age some brunettes get them to wear,
or, how I like to detect the trace of a young girl's body
that will stay behind, when she's been all toweled down,
in the steam lifting gradually on vagrant currents to the
ceiling, the trace in the steam after a long, hot bath—
lines are drawn sloping like the outlines of curbstones in
the fog of sidewalks across round shoulders—a line, a
broken hair of a line with split ends, is all, and neither
a scent or presence denser than the wisps of a line . . .
sometimes suggesting a perfect cross running between a
suggestion of breasts that somehow suggest the nest of
a navel that they rise superiorly above like puffer pigeons,
or waddling round capons (if capons could fly), the
perfect cross running, for all purposes, like a kite's tail
from the height at which a suggestion of tits fly, trailing
all down to the steam's porcelain source of emanation,
the perfect cross whose arms come right in certain
feminine adolescent postures delineating themselves
clearly through good rich glycerine soapings past counting, habits begun before babies learn to count, arms of
an imaginary cross fitting in among provided delinea-
tions (also imaginary though somehow quite certain
since any epidermis trades vapors with the surrounding
temperatures it warms itself to measure up to, as com-
pared to the shape of cross which is a line when you
know inside yourself the probability of its appearing
there, though not drawn, and appearing in a geometry
based in steam!). The perfect geometrically probable
cross has arms that hypotenuse at a crucial spot so they
seem to slip under both tits' bottoms—

It matters little, any of it. To you, very little, Mr.
Scrooge.

SCROOGE: I'm afraid my attention wandered to a suggestion
of sleep, and from there to a spectral pair of spectacles
that slipped in through those stinking turpentine louvers
in my bedroom, though hardly there at all, and princi-
pally half-made, their lenses continuing to be ground
while they taxied to the whatnot shelf where they met
their dates, forty winks.

GHOST OF CHRISTMAS PAST: For you, it's all but over, I sense,
so rather than guessing what now, my love, you can say
anything. (*Titters.*) You were on the first day a lover.
Now another love has displaced that morning love.

SCROOGE (*with an acute dryness*): Naturally.

GHOST OF CHRISTMAS PAST: Never mind, you can still be gay,
losing heart while you dodder
between tea caddies and your toffies,
as if the Old were Old, no more,
no less,
the way the Young are Young,
and only young.

SCROOGE: What love has replaced the one that's enlisted your
worries?

GHOST OF CHRISTMAS PAST: In your case, Eben, Love of
Gold—

SCROOGE (*with the Cool that passeth understanding*):
You come even-handed, Miss *Thing*,
dealing, like the world of living
times and creatures passing, even-
handedly, don't you?

Let me tell you:
THERE IS NOTHING ON WHICH THE WORLD
IS SO HARD AS POVERTY; AND THERE IS
NOTHING IT PROFESSES TO CONDEMN WITH
SUCH SEVERITY AS THE PURSUIT OF
WEALTH!

GHOST OF CHRISTMAS PAST: Well, that's a problem made for
you, if not of your own making, isn't it, poor man—
your wealth?

SCROOGE: Want me to begin throwing a few things your way,
Miss Sweet *Thing*?

Get out!
Which is commonly among the fleshly taken
to wither the Social Contract, that, please listen:
I'm asking you,
Will you *please* leave—

GHOST OF CHRISTMAS PAST: Eben, hear me out to where I can
take thought to escaping in my self-effacing tinkle—

SCROOGE: *I was once a boy,*
And that's my last tinkle!
I'm going to bed—
Take all Christmasses hitherto and yon
cooked up to peeve me for the next thousand,
and more, years, out with you in a finely wrought titter
or two, when you get outside in the plain-faced December
streets, tricked out for the morrow, like you, darling,
plainly to BORE—

GHOST OF CHRISTMAS PAST: Hear a word through my leave-
taking motion
from one lady who loves you for one and every
other orange autumn since—this longong of
hers has trapped her and left her the whole
lack of human wherewithal on that sand bar
you stranded her upon so's to keep her, without
worse toxin, at bay . . .

SCROOGE: Name?—her name?

GHOST OF THE CHRISTMAS PAST: Naomi.

SCROOGE: Does she weep like her nanny Niobe?
I MUST be talking to myself—there
doesn't actually seem to be such a
thing as a meaning for the word WEEP,
anymore, don't you know!
Won't you let me *sleep?*
You *are* aware of the pure grass-roots
Romance involved in sleeping, going
without questioning, and surrendering
as if there were no answer besides surrendering,
going to, fast to
sleep.
It's the most basically humane adventure in Nature!

GHOST OF CHRISTMAS PAST: It's just an attitude
to say that your pancakes are like caves—

Making conversation:
Let's say "Butter's got fingers
when it hasn't got knives."

While Naomi's wailing—Eben—just listen:

"IT FULFILLS MY IDENTITY AS A WOMAN,
Without which I would be completely
out of touch with the natural rhythms of life:
like watching suns lop over edges and molten lapis
lazuli—

SCROOGE (*reading letter over Ghost's cold shoulder, as if he wouldn't have one know he knows it by heart*):
"—*molten lapis lazuli spinning out on tide beaches,*

GHOST OF CHRISTMAS PAST (*vehemently taking next line to mean something personal*): "—*the cracking up in autumn of golds—*

SCROOGE: "—*the despair of winter*—(*aside.*) "Must have been written on St. Bah-Humbug's Day!

GHOST OF CHRISTMAS PAST (*in a taxing rapture*):
"the blumph
bloomiatingly
of spring, etc.

a raindrop exploding on my eye:
natural
and a kiss."

Scrooge grabs a glass of water and throws it in Ghost's face. Without a Twinkle, a Titter, or a Tinkle, the Ghost of Christmas Past dissolves into the air we breathe.

SCROOGE (*surpassing glee*):
Bloomiatingly
and
Good-bye!

Scrooge with a noticeable speed goes back to bed.

Blackout.

SCENE 3

Gong strikes once.

MARLEY'S VOICE (*repeating mechanically twice*):

Detach-Distract
detach-distract

Lights up on Scrooge coming onto set from his bed.
Lights separate into three or four unusual pools, which
reveal nothing on set, but in themselves promise much.
Scrooge waits, wanders in and out and/or "inspects"
these pools. Like a stack of cards these pools black out,
one by one, and Scrooge is left in total stage darkness.

A pause of five beats.

The Ghost of Marley appears carrying a lit flashlight.
Marley is dressed as the Ghost of Christmas Present—
as vinyl/mod as possible.

MARLEY: I am the Ghost of Christmas Present.

SCROOGE: Humph! Look like Marley to me.

MARLEY: If we went into all the things the Spirit of Marley
could enter or get to be, you'd be chanting a shopping
list instead of caroling on Christmas Day.

SCROOGE: A Spirit who never met me, a ghost who didn't
know my ways, might keep me from sleeping tonight,
but, Marley, you—

MARLEY: All Spirits know you, man,
and too many wish you a carp
or gamelan that stayed in life
like jack-o'-lanterns held over
to decorate Christmas windows
rather than a snakeskin slipper
that can never be shed.

I am the Ghost of this Christmas and because Marley
died in the year that belongs to this Christmas, I look
like Jacob Marley.

Marley turns flashlight on upstage wall. Flashlight goes
off when a hazy spot dims up sufficiently to reveal Bob
Cratchit's desk, while the silent figures of Bob Cratchit,
Mrs. Cratchit, and Tiny Tim, humming faintly and at
an extremely slow tempo "Joy To The World," busy
themselves noiselessly turning Cratchit's desk into a holi-
day table and scene of Christmas Day celebration as
Marley and Scrooge remain downstage in darkness, con-
versing.

SCROOGE: Is there a genial shadowing forth of all this day's dinners and the progress of their cooking in the peculiar flavor of what you sprinkle from your flashlight—?

MARLEY: THERE is. My own.

SCROOGE: Would it apply to any kind of dinner given on this day?

MARLEY: To any dinner kindly given. To a poor one most of all.

SCROOGE: Why to a poor one most?

MARLEY: Because it needs me most!

Upstage scene continues and reaches a climax as Bob Cratchit brings on a platter of food, a bowl of punch, or some such other obvious symbol of Christmas plenty. Family's humming becomes downright singing, tempo up, but not boisterous.

....*Lights as cheerful as a warm morning on a lake. Crepe paper streamers, red and green, fall as a drape over desk.*

CRATCHIT: Mama, and Tim, and Me!
All here but one!

MRS. CRATCHIT: Who, Bob, who isn't here?

TINY TIM (*raising one crutch in a gesture of hanging it on wall, puts on Donald Duck mask*): I know who it is!

CRATCHIT: Who, Smartee?

TINY TIM (*quacks*): Uncle Scro-o-o-g-ge!

CRATCHIT: And is he a cinnamon bear?

TINY TIM: Maybe a polar bear?

MRS. CRATCHIT: He was scratching at the door last night, I dreamed, I called in my sleep, "Who's scratching?"—he answered: "Christopher Crinkle!"—"Bob knows none!" I yelled. "Too bad,!" he chuckled, "I see him coming across the street to visit you . . ." I ran out of bed in my gown to the front door, flung it open, and there was Scrooge turned into a big white bear and he was eating Santa Claus!

CRATCHIT: So he is a joke—poor, lost bear—
We don't care, not even a little more,
on Christmas Day . . .

MRS. CRATCHIT: Well, without your job, Mr. Cratchit, what kind of Christmas would this be?

CRATCHIT: Mr. Scrooge *has* given us plenty of merriment,

I'm sure—and it would be ungrateful not
to drink his health, wherever he is—

MRS. CRATCHIT: He didn't return again to the office on
Christmas Eve?
Oh, Bob!

CRATCHIT: I locked up myself for once, my darling!

TINY TIM: A creepy phone call summoned him several
times to foreign cities before he was gone, Mom!

CRATCHIT: Well, here is a glass of mulled wine ready to toast
with,
and I say: to UNCLE SCROOGE!

They lift glasses; Tiny Tim lifts devil shake.

SCROOGE (*from downstage*): Their girl
was sent away with rickets—
and Timmy, the boy, has never
known what it's like not to be crippled.
Spirit, whose children are theirs,
since they can't take care of them?

MARLEY: As you know, old man, they are that man's only.
Your man's.

SCROOGE: I will pay the clerk more soon's 1968's recession
ends—people will start buying as many cars as they do
in the current boom that'll bust in spring, I hear. As I
see it, Detroit determines when raises are effected.

MARLEY: Did you reply to his last appeal for a raise?

SCROOGE: Indeed did the man who acquitted himself by
dying? Did you?

MARLEY: I allowed him half of my extra b.l.t. sandwiches
every Tuesday and Thursday for a month before I died—

SCROOGE: A bit safe, wasn't that? The Cancer Clinic gave you
little more than a month to go, *Marley!*

MARLEY: But I replied, in my way,
and kept out of the way of the real boss . . .
At least, I didn't invoke Detroit.
Don't worry your warts, they think of you
in spite of everything. They have a portion
for you of their love because Christmas would
quince them without spreading it thin—

But good will from Christmas Present, old frugal,
watch out tomorrow or the day after for that boy

Tim—he's simple, but sadder than you think;
I see under his curls a writing that reads: DOOM.
SCROOGE: Surely must be some resources, Marley.
Can't they appeal to some Charity?
MARLEY: Lasers to repack Tim's crumbling bones?
SCROOGE: I mind my business.
If my doctor can take a charity-patient now and again,
I do my best to keep the thing hushed up.
MARLEY: Oh, get back to bed!

*Marley pops a paper bag over Scrooge's head—upstage
scene is blacked out—Scrooge runs off to bed.*

SCENE 4

*Slow dim up lights on Scrooge lying on stage floor center,
sleeping.*

VOICE OF CHRISTMAS YET TO COME (*distant, but distinct*):
You're coming,
McDuck, you're coming, not dreaming, you can't be
dreaming,
I'm not dreaming . . .

Scrooge tosses, but does not awake.

There is a city over your head,
we scarcely seem to be entering that city,
the city, rather, seems to be springing
up about us, encompassing us there, over, over your head,
by some action of its own, the city is encompassing us . . .

Scrooge sleeps on.

VOICE OFF: It's goin' to be a cheap one, a bide-a-wee funeral,
you can bet on it, I really don't know of anybody's
goin'.
ANOTHER VOICE OFF: I don't mind going if lunch is provided.
SCROOGE (*only half-awake, dreamily*): I know these men perfectly,
businessmen, terrifically wealthy, and of
real importance. I don't who that funeral is for . . .

VOICE OF CHRISTMAS YET TO COME: Oh, you know!
   Think back, did you parachute
   when your Secretary thought you ought . . . ?
SCROOGE: My Secretary's not my clerk,
   My clerk is not in Sessue or Tokyrama,
   Bustamente Vegas has a secretary he can lend me . . .
VOICE OF CHRISTMAS YET TO COME: Did your secretary
   jump in parachute, did you parachute?
                           Did you parachute?
                           Did you parachute?
SCROOGE (*rising defiantly from floor, not moving*): I en-
   tertained troops in DISMAL SWAMP, I'll have you
   know!
SEÑOR ORO (*striding in, colliding with Scrooge as he rises*):
   I entertained troops
   in DISMAL SWAMP!

   (*As Ghost of Christmas Yet to Come*): Didn't you avoid
      war, by the way?
   And sight of war, and *future* war, and why
   did you rush back to your office in plenty
   of time . . .?
SCROOGE (*pacing, wringing hands*): I don't know,
   I don't know, what spirit are you? (*Turns in circles.*)
MARLEY'S VOICE (*repeating mechanically ten times*):
   Detach-Distract
   detach-distract
   detach-distract
   detach-distract
   Etc.
SEÑOR ORO (*tone, Sinatra-proud*): I'm the spirit closest to
   Christmas, so you'd better listen, I'm the Christmas all-
   expected, and all-delivered, I'm the goods from now on
   . . . awesome, absolutely awesome how totally I'm recol-
   lected and exactly reenacted. Advise you, man, to take
   out a checklist!
SCROOGE (*counting on fingers*): What else, let's see:
   1. More money to Bob Cratchit.
   2. More money Benevolent Bankrupters Association
      Funeral Fund.
   3. More money to mark Marley's grave.
   4. More money to all media.

SEÑOR ORO: Give the Future something to count on—good man! (*Fades off.*)

SCROOGE (*calling*): Men's courses will foreshadow certain ends, to which, if persevered in, they must lead— (*Louder.*) But if the courses be departed from, the ends will change.

TINY TIM (*voice of Christmas Yet to Come—dressed as Donald Duck—Donald Duck mask—limps on, intoxicated*): I'm Christmas Future, Phewww!
I'm wobbly, 'cause I'm so slightly
just any old thing, at all . . . (*Staggers off.*)

SCROOGE: Seems to be no order
to these latter visions
that it's a gravestone,
and the letters carved on it make up my name—
Ghosts are all about deaths
and uniformly simple, useless, and silly—

TINY TIM (*voice of Christmas Yet to Come, staggers on again, a black wreath around his little neck*): How silly? (*Removes Donald Duck mask—falls to the floor, and dies.*)

Blackout on Scrooge and dead Tim.

SCENE 5

Dim up quick on scene of Mrs. Cratchit knitting, with Marley standing by, back to her. Mrs. Cratchit sets work aside, puts one hand up to her face.

MRS. CRATCHIT: The color hurts my eyes!

MARLEY (*turning to her*): The color? Ah, poor Tiny Tim!

MRS. CRATCHIT (*hand to lap*): They're better now again. Been bad since our boy died. I don't want to show weak eyes to Bob when he comes home, for the world. He should be home soon, what time is it?

MARLEY: Past time.
However, I do think he has walked
a little slower than he used to,
these last few evenings, Mrs. Cratchit.

MRS. CRATCHIT: We're no poorer,
No richer, surely,

but no poorer. (*Pause.*) I have known him to walk with
. . . I have known him to walk with Tiny Tim upon his
shoulder, very fast indeed.

MARLEY: And so have I!

MRS. CRATCHIT: But he was very light to carry,
and his father loved him so,
that it was no trouble: (*Knitting again.*) No trouble,
and *there* is his father at the door! (*She rises.*)

Enter Bob Cratchit.

MARLEY: Tim was not so light as all that. (*To Bob, clapping
him on shoulder.*) Sorry, Bob, since your son died in
avoidance of service to his country—

CRATCHIT: He was crippled—

MARLEY: And Ebenezer Scrooge was queer,
and too old a duck. But you, Señor,
fall between the new conscription age of 28–36.

CRATCHIT: I'm thirty-four.

MRS. CRATCHIT: Where's he to be sent?

Lights dim out.

SCROOGE (*answering*): DISMAL SWAMP!

SCENE 6

*Bright lights full up. Sounds of caroling, jingle bells, laughter
in the snow, snatches of "Swan Lake" (for sentiment). Enter
Scrooge in nightdress, cartwheeling.*

SCROOGE: I'm here—It's Christmas! (*Stands on head.*) It's
here—I'm Christmas! (*Looks out window.*)

BOY'S VOICE FROM STREET: Wha—?

SCROOGE: What's today, young man?

BOY'S VOICE FROM STREET: Today! Ah, CHRISTMAS DAY!

SCROOGE: It's Christmas Day—I *haven't* missed it!
The Spirits have done it all in one night.
They can do anything they like. Of course
they can. Of course they can. Merry
Christmas, young man!

BOY'S VOICE FROM STREET (*trailing off—*): Mer-ry Christ-
mass—

Scrooge runs into downstage street, finds Tiny Tim.

TINY TIM: Hi, Uncle Scrooge!
You're late for our dinner date!
SCROOGE (*taking him up on his shoulders*): Not too late—I
hope.
Merry Christmas, my man,
Merry Christmas!

They enter office. Bob Cratchit enters shortly after them.

(*Scrooge sets Tiny Tim in chair.*) What do you mean
by coming here at this time of day?
CRATCHIT: I'm very sorry, sir, I am late.
SCROOGE: Now, I tell you what, my friend,
I am not going to stand for this
sort of thing any longer. And
so—I'm about to raise your salary—
More money to you, Bob, begin the new year!
CRATCHIT: It'll save Tim, sir.
SCROOGE: It'll save his father, Mr. Cratchit—
with a son on the Christmas side of the grave—
disabled, though improved he may be,
still disabled—you both—and all of us—
can avoid the draft!
TINY TIM: God bless us, Every One!

*Sound of cheers, sparkling snow tinkling underfoot, ring-
ing voices, and no dread.*

THE END

MUSHROOMS

a play

(BY DONALD KVARES

For Judith G. and Renata

Mushrooms, for all its formal modesty, resonates spookily
with more than one familiar and urgent concern.
These are times that twist men's minds. Donald Kvares
makes it just clear enough what he is writing about—
the technocracy of death, manipulative sex, thought
surgery, and other varieties of civilized barbarism—but
not so clear that the play becomes preachment. The
real actions are between the lines, implicit, even offstage.
The characters are too busy dealing with each other
to actually touch, and what we see is their urbane,
terrifying mutual rapacity. Even the victims are not so
much innocent as unfortunately in the way. On the
surface the play is conventional naturalism with
unsettling gaps in it; by the end it rises to the
protosurrealism of Grand Guignol.

M. S.

Mushrooms was presented by the Mannhardt Theatre Foundation, 542 La Guardia Place, New York, on December 3, 1967. It was directed by John Chace with the following cast:

AURETHIA ROLAND: Jane Macleod
BUDDY: Stephen Mark Weyte
JOYCE CLARK: Etain O'Malley
SOPHIE: Margaret Steel
GEORGE ROLAND: Bob Sonderskov
ROCHELLE: Frank Wilson

Music: John Herbert McDowell
Set: Maxine Klein
Lighting: Brahm Cohen

OPPOSITE: Jane Macleod (Aurethia) and Etain O'Malley (Joyce) in *Mushrooms*

CHARACTERS

AURETHIA ROLAND, a cool and elegant woman
GEORGE ROLAND, her husband, an eloquent humanist
BUDDY, an American zealot, nephew of Aurethia
SOPHIE, an Irish cook
ROCHELLE, a very rich homosexual, Negro
JOYCE CLARK, a sane, sweet American girl

*The sitting room and work parlor of the Roland Home and
Corporation, somewhere in California. A great, translucent,
corrugated window serves as a partition between Buddy's
room and the parlor. The walls are stucco. Downstage right,
below the partition, we find a record player which hangs from
gold chains, plus a transistor, a portable bar and barstool in
white vinyl and a white vinyl hassock; downstage left, we find
a stucco bookcase, an amoeba-shaped desk and low-slung deck
chairs, the lounging variety, and just above the bookcase,
toward upstage left, a tape recorder set inside a large white
box, with circular holes cut in it through which a sickly green
light pours. Upstage left is an exit to the back of the house.
Upstage right the front door of the house. The set is in
various tones of brown, cream, green, and white and creates
a warm, sunny, open feeling.*

TIME: Where we are right now.

*At rise, Buddy is at his desk, typing. Aurethia is at tape re-
corder, dictating.*

AURETHIA: Letter to Otway Corporation. (*Picks up letterhead
and refers to address.*) 341 Cotter Drive, Redwood, California, 94064. Attention—Joyce Clark. Dear Miss Clark.
We received your letter today with much interest and
shall look into the matter of foreign surplus as soon as
it is possible to do so. Paragraph. Mr. Roland has been
extremely busy for the past few days and has not gotten
around to calling you in regard to the above. However,
I can tell you right off that napalm is hard to come by.
Explosives of this kind are in small commodity in the
U.S. right now and according to statistical reports there
will not be another crop until late May or early June.
Paragraph. As you know, the summer months are slow
ones in Vietnam. There isn't much fighting there during
late July, and I for a fact know that in August, a lot of
sleeping is done in the rice fields. In any event, do keep in
touch and we will try to help you as soon as sufficient
napalm becomes available. Our chemical laboratories are
working on a process called Annihilation 5, which con-

sists of a highly portable form of nitroglycerin and TNT, compacted in small, silver vials for instant use. Yours sincerely, Aurethia Roland, Assistant Secretary, Roland Corporation. The usual envelope, Buddy.

Loud.

Here's a tape you can start on.

BUDDY: I have a date at six.

AURETHIA: Wonderful.

BUDDY: Will George be home tonight?

AURETHIA: He said he would be.

She returns to tape recorder. Pause. Turns on tape. Begins new letter.

Letter to . . . Horizon's, Inc., 224 Orange Grove South, Fort Lauderdale, Florida, 33315, Attention, Mr. Tai Shen, President, Committee of Aid to the Southeast Liberation Front. Dear Mr. Shen. We are most happy to inform you that a large shipment of napalm has been forwarded to us from our Denver distributors. Could you kindly send us your specifications. We will make sure that a goodly sum of napalm is in your possession inside of a week. As to your inquiries about Annihilation 5, I don't know where you could have learned of this, as it is a standing joke with us which is used specifically for our American cousins, when they get too difficult about shipments of napalm. In any event, please keep in touch. I remain, as always, etc., etc., etc.

Aurethia rises, as Joyce enters through front door. The first sight of Joyce is rather startling to her.

AURETHIA: Yes. May I help you . . .

JOYCE: Is Mr. Roland in?

AURETHIA: Not right at the moment.

JOYCE: Oh. When do you expect him to be in?

AURETHIA: Is there something you wanted?

JOYCE: I had to discuss something with him.

AURETHIA: I see. Well, all I can do is tell him that you called.

JOYCE: Never mind. I'll try back later.

AURETHIA: Who are you?

JOYCE: It's not important.

AURETHIA: I'm Mrs. Roland.

JOYCE: Oh.

AURETHIA: And you are?

JOYCE: Joyce!

AURETHIA: Joyce! (*Thinking.*) I don't believe George has ever mentioned you.

JOYCE: We only met once, at Redwood. (*Pause. Somewhat sadly.*) It was only last week.

AURETHIA: Do you intend to stand there till he comes?

JOYCE: No. I'll leave, and come back later.

AURETHIA: Sit down a while. We can talk about it.

JOYCE: I'll come back later. (*Joyce runs off.*)

AURETHIA: But . . . young lady . . . !

BUDDY (*sharply*): Who was it, Aurethia?

AURETHIA: I don't know. A young girl. Nobody important.

BUDDY: It must've been somebody.

AURETHIA: Just a crank, a crank call. They happen.

BUDDY: Often?

AURETHIA: Not often. But they happen.

BUDDY: I'm using the back room on the second floor later.

AURETHIA: I don't see why you can't.

BUDDY: Neither do I. It's a stiff date.

AURETHIA: May I have a cigarette?

BUDDY: You're shaking.

AURETHIA: Am I? How strange.

They glare at each other quietly.

BUDDY: Sit down. Relax.

AURETHIA: You're very pleasant today.

BUDDY: Thank you.

AURETHIA: What's this one like?

BUDDY: He's very nice.

AURETHIA: Is he wealthy, or just one of those poor ones again.

BUDDY: He has attributes.

AURETHIA: Can he help you . . . ?

BUDDY: You mean, can he help us . . . ?

AURETHIA: Of course. Can he?

BUDDY: There's an opening.

AURETHIA (*chuckling*): I would imagine.

Buddy rises, walks to Aurethia. Kisses her. Then he pulls away.

BUDDY: What do the letters say?

AURETHIA: Listen to them. You'll find out.

BUDDY: I intend to.

AURETHIA (*humorously*): Don't you trust me?

BUDDY: It depends on what you say in the letters.

AURETHIA: I always say the right and proper thing.

BUDDY: If I wasn't so interested in George, I might make a play for you.

AURETHIA: You have me!

BUDDY: I do?

AURETHIA: Would you like to me to prove it to you?

BUDDY: Let me listen to the tape, and then I'll tell you.

AURETHIA: Why don't you finish your typing?

Goes back to tape. Dictates.

Letter to Marian Farley, Oak Drive, Canton, Ohio. Dear Marian. George is out of town at the moment, but he should be coming back some time today. When he returns I'll make sure he gets right on the phone and calls you immediately. How's Fred? Is he getting on well? A common cold can be extremely difficult this time of year, and especially a malingering one. Please make sure that Fred gets a checkup as soon as he is better, because no one would really want this to develop into cancer. Paragraph. Please, Marian, don't ask about Buddy. He's all right. I made sure you got those thousand dollar checks on time every month and you have no reason to complain, and believe me . . . I will not welcome the idea of your coming here . . . !

She stops tape, replays "no reason to complain," erases the rest and continues.

I would so love to have you here, Marian, but we've been extremely busy the past few months and we have practically no time for social engagements. Too much is happening in the world, and too much time is being taken up by work for that very reason. However, I am sure we will have some free time near the end of July, and we will look forward to seeing you then. I'll sign off for now, but keep in touch. (*She stops the tape. To Buddy.*) I might as well see what cook is doing.

BUDDY: Tell her to save me a big piece of duck.

AURETHIA: How do you know we have duck for dinner?

BUDDY: I know.

AURETHIA: You spied in the kitchen.

BUDDY: Cook and I get on well.

AURETHIA: I would imagine so. You brought her here.

BUDDY: Don't you like cook?

AURETHIA: Oh, come on. I love Sophie. She's fiery.

BUDDY: She's icy too.

Aurethia exits to the kitchen. Through a scrim we see Sophie, sitting on a high stool in front of a chopping table, playing chess with various vegetables.

AURETHIA: How's it coming?

SOPHIE (*a sinister mountain of horror*): Get out of here.

AURETHIA: Don't you like me anymore, Sophie?

SOPHIE: Not right now. I'm trying to play chess. (*Pause.*) Is his Royal Highness expected home tonight?

AURETHIA: You know he is.

SOPHIE: Sometimes he don't show. (*She holds the cleaver up, in a warning position.*)

AURETHIA: He'll materialize before six.

SOPHIE: Okee. Just askin'. Now get out. (*Laughs voluminously, as Aurethia exits.*)

AURETHIA: Cook is such fun. What are you reading?

BUDDY: *The Jungle*. By Upton Sinclair.

AURETHIA: Why are you reading that?

BUDDY: I decided to give you a little treat.

AURETHIA: I love treats. Is it one of those man's-inhumanity-to-man things?

BUDDY: May I read it to you?

AURETHIA: If you wish.

BUDDY (*starting to read*): ". . . There would be meat stored in great piles in rooms; and the water from leaky roofs would drip over it, and thousands of rats would race about on it . . . A man could run his hands over these piles of meat and sweep off handfuls of the dried dung of rats. . . . The packers would put poisoned bread out for them, they would die, and then, rats, bread and meat would all go into the hoppers together."

This is no fairy tale and no joke.

". . . . The meat would be shoveled into carts, and the man who did the shoveling would not trouble to lift out a rat even when he saw one. There was no place for the men to wash their hands before they ate their dinner . . . so they made a practice of washing them in the water that was to be ladled into the sausages. There were the butt ends of smoked meat, and the scraps of corned beef, and all the odds and ends of the waste of the plants, that would be dumped into old barrels in the cellar and left there . . . and in the barrels would be dirt and rust and old nails and stale water—and . . . it would be taken up and dumped into the hoppers with fresh meat, and sent out to the public's breakfast. Some of it they would make into smoked sausage—but as the smoking took time and was therefore expensive, they would call upon their chemistry department, and preserve it with borax and color it with gelatine to make it brown. All of their sausage came out of the same bowl, but when they came to wrap it, they would stamp some of it 'special,' and for this they would charge two cents more a pound." (*He closes the book.*)

AURETHIA: He must've been one of us . . . Do you need any money for tonight.

BUDDY: Not with this date.

AURETHIA: You have a nice smile, you should smile more often.

BUDDY: There isn't much to smile about, you must admit.

AURETHIA: You're right. There isn't. (*Pause.*) Your mother is such a hysteric. Every time Fred has the slightest tic she writes us a letter for more money. I almost told her what I thought of her today.

BUDDY: Why didn't you?

AURETHIA: Because it would make her think it bothered me, and it doesn't bother me in the least. But if she thought it bothered me, God, the gush of sentimentality.

BUDDY: Don't get all balled up in explanations, Aunt Aurethia.

AURETHIA: Aunt Aurethia?

BUDDY: I mean, Aurethia.

AURETHIA: That's better. For a minute you scared me.

BUDDY: I know. I scared myself.

AURETHIA (*looks at the partition*): I love those corrugated
  windows. You can't really see the sun through them.
  They shelter it from your eyes.
BUDDY: It's getting dark out.
AURETHIA: Good.

There is a knock at the door.

BUDDY: Shall I answer?
AURETHIA (*rises and walks to the door. She opens it*): George.
  Don't you have a key?

*Her voice trails off. She looks out into the dusk. There
is no one there.*

BUDDY: Wasn't it George?
AURETHIA: No.
BUDDY: Who was it then?
AURETHIA: I don't know. (*Pause.*) Could it have been your
  date?
BUDDY: He would have come round the back way!
AURETHIA: Oh yes. Of course.
BUDDY: Didn't you see anything out there . . . ?
AURETHIA: No. Nothing. How very strange. The sun was
  setting, and the walk was filled with gleaming lemon
  trees.
BUDDY: Is that strange?
AURETHIA: Yes.
BUDDY: I guess it is.
AURETHIA: May I have another cigarette?
BUDDY: Help yourself.
AURETHIA: Stop typing, Buddy. I told you not to work.

*He stops typing. She sits down again. She picks up the
book and thumbs through it.*

BUDDY: There's another interesting section. He tells you how
  the hogs were trimmed. They had ankle chains they
  used to clap around the hogs' legs, and they would pick
  up the poor things by the legs, and sometimes the legs
  would snap, and the beasts would squeal in terrible
  agony, and a long chain would hoist them up, and they
  would be sent through a shearing machine which stripped
  them of their skins, and there would be men waiting on

a long line, and one would slit the hog's throat, and another would . . .

AURETHIA: The walk was filled with lemon trees.

BUDDY: You're not concentrating.

AURETHIA: They were planted a year ago. The gardener came, and he showed me this seed. It was just ordinary look-ing seed, but he said it would grow into lemon trees. I thought that might be nice, and I told him to go right on and plant them.

BUDDY: And now they're here.

AURETHIA: Perhaps it was the gardener. Perhaps he wanted to blind me with more lemon trees.

BUDDY: Then why didn't he come in?

AURETHIA: I don't know.

BUDDY: Were you expecting anybody else . . . ?

AURETHIA: No. (*Rasping sound.*) Wait! Ah, it was the *back* door. (*Aurethia starts off.*)

BUDDY: Where are you going? It's my date.

AURETHIA: I just want to meet him.

BUDDY: Let me introduce you?

AURETHIA: I can introduce myself, thank you.

BUDDY: Now wait a minute!

They both exit out back.

George enters. He is a very handsome man, but his face has a mournful, half-dead expression. George gets him-self settled in the room. Joyce darts in through front door.

JOYCE: George! (*He turns quickly.*)

GEORGE: Joyce. Good God. You frightened me . . . !

JOYCE: I'm sorry . . . I . . . !

GEORGE: I don't understand. What are you doing here . . . ? (*She embraces him. He responds jerkily.*) How did you get here . . . ?

JOYCE: A friend left me at the end of the woods. I walked the rest of the way.

GEORGE: This is no place for you!

JOYCE: I had to see you. (*Slight pause. George seems dis-tracted.*) You left so quickly. You hung me up so much. I haven't been able to rest . . . !

GEORGE: I can't talk here. (*She tries to embrace him again. He holds her away.*) Please, if you could come back later, we can talk. I just have to get a bit settled. It's hard to adjust. I'm a bit slow. (*Sees her hurt face.*) Please don't think . . . I'm not . . . I'm just very slow.

Pause.

JOYCE: When should I come back?

GEORGE: I don't know . . . I . . . !

JOYCE: A half hour . . . ?

GEORGE: I guess. Yes, that would be good enough. A half hour. (*Pause.*) An hour would be better.

JOYCE: Why are you doing this? . . . You're not the same person I knew in Redwood. That man was young and full of hope . . . !

GEORGE: You don't know me. I never showed you anything.

JOYCE: What happened to all our plans, George? Don't you remember anything that you said? I thought we were going to do so many things. I thought you really cared. You came on like you did, like you knew where everything was at! You had this giant broadsword and you were going to slice away all the barnacles, all the warts, all the ingrown leeches, everything that's sapping the strength from our country. You were really heroic, George, because you cared.

GEORGE: I still care.

JOYCE: Why this change then? (*Pause. Silence.*) You built our hopes up. Don't pretend you didn't care. I know what you're like. I know you, George. The man in Redwood was full of youth and spirit, he loved life. He was warm, and close, and strong. And I . . . !

She almost kisses him. George pulls away.

GEORGE: I can't function right now!

JOYCE: Don't ask me to stay away an hour. It's getting dark, I don't like the dark in the country. You can't see anything at all.

GEORGE: A half hour.

JOYCE: All right. Where can I wait?

GEORGE: The woods.

JOYCE: No, George, no. It's getting dark. I won't go into those woods.

GEORGE: You could . . . You could . . . !

JOYCE: What? I could what . . . ? (*She stares at him for a moment. He seems to be straining to think.*) George, what's the matter?

GEORGE: Nothing. (*Sound of Buddy and Aurethia, returning.*) Go into the woodshed, behind the house. Go on now.

She runs off. He walks quickly over toward the tape recorder. At that moment, Aurethia and Buddy enter. George stops. Buddy laughs.

BUDDY: How do you like that? It was only George . . . ! Hello, George.

AURETHIA: Did you see anybody outside?

GEORGE: No.

AURETHIA: That's funny. How long have you been here?

GEORGE: I just got here.

AURETHIA: Then it's you.

George looks at them strangely.

AURETHIA: How was your trip?

GEORGE: I stopped over in Redwood.

AURETHIA: What were you doing in Redwood?

GEORGE: Admiring the sunset!

AURETHIA: How fitting! There's a stain on your suit.

GEORGE: I picked a lemon.

They gaze at each other. George sees some warmth in her face and begins to smile.

AURETHIA: That's funny. We were just talking about the lemon trees.

GEORGE: Were you?

BUDDY: She was just mentioning they were there.

GEORGE: Of course they were there. They've always been there.

AURETHIA: I know. But I just made a statement to Buddy that they were there.

GEORGE (*after a pause*): Are you all right . . . ?

AURETHIA: What . . . ?

GEORGE: Are you . . . (*with emphasis*) . . . all right?

AURETHIA: Of course.

GEORGE: I'm glad . . . !

BUDDY: Aurethia and I have a surprise for you tonight. We
have your favorite dinner dish. Sophie prepared it herself with her own lily white hands, and *her special meat
cleaver.*

GEORGE: Oh did she.

BUDDY: Yes. She was just chopping away all afternoon.
Sophie loves to chop. It's her favorite pastime. I think,
quite frankly, she would be much more at home as an
ax murderess, or even a butcheress, than just as a simple
cook.

GEORGE: I'm sure.

BUDDY: How was Denver?

GEORGE: Very interesting.

BUDDY: Was much accomplished?

GEORGE: Oh . . . oh yes. Quite a bit. It was a very rewarding
experience.

BUDDY: Then you must have some letters to dictate?

GEORGE: Oh . . . oh yes. Quite a few.

BUDDY: I see. Well, go ahead. If you have work to do, don't
let me stop you.

GEORGE: Do you mind if I relax for a few minutes . . . ?

BUDDY: No. Not at all. Relax if you want to. It's your
house . . . !

Rasping sound.

That's my date. (*Buddy exits.*)

AURETHIA: I wrote to Marian today.

GEORGE: Never mind that now.

*George goes to tape recorder, starts dictating. Aurethia
gets herself a drink.*

GEORGE: Letter to Joplin Industries, Joplin, Missouri, Attention John Frey. Dear John. Heard about your son's bap-
tism, but could not manage to get down to Joplin to
watch it. Sorry about that, old man. It's not every time
in his life that a fellow gets himself baptized. How's
Bertha, and little Mary? Do love them so. John. I'm
desperate!

*Aurethia, upon hearing this, turns and watches George
throughout speech.*

I know you will listen, even though you can't really

help me with it . . . ! You are of that special race that understands this sort of thing, and can well imagine what I am going through. Paragraph. Please don't think I am blubbering. I never blubber. It is one of my traits that my eyes are always dry. Tears are gone from my eyes, and if anything in this letter seems tearful to you, just count it down as one of those rare instances in contemporary society where matter triumphs over mind! I am sick at heart, John. I just came back from Denver, from the National Alliance for Retaliatory Action, and the level of discussion carried on there was most disturbing.

We sat in a big conference room with a great map of the world behind us. The map was all in blinking lights, and the lights went off and on every time a trouble spot somewhere on Earth was flaring up. Which means, quite simply, that the lights went off and on quite a good deal. The men in the room were, well, I can't begin to tell you how they were, or were not, so to speak. Their lips were parched and gray, and their faces, white. And their hands were folded very stubbornly in their laps. And they didn't flinch. When they spoke, a small line of air issued from their mouths and filled the dimness with reality. Nothing new was stated, no new plans were made. But one man said, in a very calm voice, "What are we to do with Ashtabula?" and then he sat there, his hands folded in his lap, and waited for an answer. Of course, there was none, yet I seemed to be the only one gaping at that table. No one stirred. The others merely remained silent, but I was gaping. Do you realize what that meant, John? I hope you can, as you are understanding, and have deep feelings about small towns, just as I do. Ashtabula. I meant to say something. I meant to say, "Leave Ashtabula alone, it never did you any harm. It's just there, and has always been there, and there's nothing to be done about it." But I didn't. I was straining. I felt myself pulling at the chair anxious to lunge forward and tear these human computers to pieces. But I couldn't. Fear froze me. The greatest fear I've ever felt in my whole life. Of course, I could never imagine that you would feel such fear, or know its origins or explain exactly what caused it. But

I must explain because I have never felt an icy fear grip me. And this leads directly to my explanation, and my letter and my deep need to communicate what Denver and the N.A.R.A. were all about.

AURETHIA *(in utter coldness)*: Why are you telling me this?

GEORGE: What . . . ? *(Pause.)*

AURETHIA: Why are you . . . ?

GEORGE: I . . . I'm sorry.

AURETHIA: There's no need to be sorry.

GEORGE: But I am.

AURETHIA: And I said there's no need to be. Just strike the letter, will you please? *(Pause.)* Strike the letter . . . *Strike the letter!*

They sit there in total silence. George does not respond. He crosses to bar. Sits on stool. Aurethia moves over toward him and makes a sexual advance to him. He does not respond.

AURETHIA: I wish you would stop looking so grim, George.

GEORGE: What should I do?

AURETHIA: You could inquire into how I spent my time while you were away. People talk about such things occasionally.

GEORGE: What did you do?

AURETHIA: I played Scrabble for a while. I won ten dollars from Buddy.

GEORGE: Anything else?

AURETHIA: I played chess with cook.

GEORGE: Cook? Who's that?

AURETHIA: Sophie!

GEORGE: Oh yes! Good old Sophie! Did you win?

AURETHIA: Of course not. Do you think I'd insult Sophie?

GEORGE: She does get insulted.

AURETHIA: Dinner should be ready soon. I'd better tell her her not to cook it too well. All the juices drain out. *(Aurethia exits.)*

GEORGE *(back to the machine, briefly)*: John. I'd like to say a few more things. I'd like to say that . . . I'm not a free agent. I'm not my own man. I want to get away. I want to get some real good oatmeal. I want to go back to Ashtabula.

"Anchors Aweigh" comes on the tape.

Buddy enters with Rochelle, a rich Negro queen.

BUDDY: George. This is Rochelle.

ROCHELLE: So you're Georgie.

GEORGE: Yes. I am.

ROCHELLE: I met your nephew in a bar downtown. He was so impatient.

GEORGE: Yes. Buddy is sometimes impatient.

ROCHELLE: I'll teach him patience. I've got lots of money, and I have openings. He can learn a lot if he sticks with me. Don't you think that's true, Buddy?

BUDDY: Rochelle's a very sweet girl.

ROCHELLE: I'm not a girl but we'll let that pass.

BUDDY: I was only being funny.

ROCHELLE: I don't like that kind of humor. You have a very nice house, Georgie. Tax free?

GEORGE: Just about. (*Chuckles slightly, to himself.*)

ROCHELLE: You must've paid a lot for it. I pay a lot for everything.

AURETHIA (*emerges from the kitchen*): Dinner is almost ready. Hello.

ROCHELLE: Hello there. Are you Buddy's aunt?

AURETHIA: You must be Buddy's date.

ROCHELLE: Yes I am. I'm Rochelle.

AURETHIA: How marvelous? Would that be a Cardin Original?

ROCHELLE: Not at all. I have my own very special couturiere. She's a lovable dyke and we've balled each other a few times. She keeps the money I give her tucked under her bodice or in a little bag in her crotch. And nobody ever sees it. She's the shrewdest little cunt I've ever met. Oh, by the way. I'll have a scotch and water if you're serving.

AURETHIA: Oh. Of course. Will you be staying for dinner?

ROCHELLE: I have dinner waiting at Carlo's.

BUDDY: Yes. We're going to Carlo's.

AURETHIA: Wonderful. I love their shredded beef.

ROCHELLE: Ropa vieja is my dish. But I'm not too worried about food. I have enough food to last me the whole night.

AURETHIA: What a very funny person, Buddy.

ROCHELLE: Thank you.

BUDDY: We have to go now.

ROCHELLE: Are you embarrassed?

BUDDY: No. Not at all. I just want to get out of here, that's all.

ROCHELLE: Don't you like it here?

BUDDY: Dinner will be getting cold.

ROCHELLE: I just said I wasn't hungry.

BUDDY: Well, I'm starved.

ROCHELLE: Oh, that's too bad about you, Buddy boy. Starve awhile. I'm paying for this shebang.

Aurethia turns on record player.

BUDDY: I know that, Rochelle.

ROCHELLE: Call me Rocky. My friends do.

BUDDY: Okay, Rocky.

ROCHELLE: Oh, Aurethia. You're a real swinger.

She starts to dance sensuously.

ROCHELLE: Oh let's. That should be marvy poo. (*They start to dance.*) Come on, Georgie.

AURETHIA (*turns off record*): Never mind about George.

ROCHELLE: All right. Never mind about George. Huh Martha.

AURETHIA: My name is Aurethia.

ROCHELLE: I know, baby poo.

AURETHIA: I'm glad you know.

ROCHELLE: Forgive my raunchiness, but since people know me as the raunchiest lay in town, I have to give them what they want.

AURETHIA: I'm sure.

ROCHELLE: Don't be so sure, my sweet, you'll live longer. I've got lots of money to burn. I invested it all in M-104's and now I'm the richest thing around hereabouts. Isn't that right? Buddy-boy . . .?

AURETHIA: Are you in M-104's?

ROCHELLE: Right as rain, my sweet!

AURETHIA: George, did you hear that?

GEORGE: I did.

AURETHIA: We could use M-104's. Couldn't we, George?

GEORGE: What? Oh, yes. We could.

ROCHELLE: Get your own, baby. Hey, you know, you're very cute, too. I mean, you're a little older than Buddy-boy over here, but you're a living doll.

(*Buddy shows a surgical needle to Aurethia. They smile at each other.*)

GEORGE: Thanks.

ROCHELLE: Look. He's blushing.

BUDDY: Come on, Shelly.

ROCHELLE: Rocky!

BUDDY: You've had enough for one night.

ROCHELLE: Have I now? Who's paying for this? Tell me! Who's paying for this?

BUDDY: You will!

ROCHELLE: Okay. Then shut your lips tight.

GEORGE: Lips shut tight.

ROCHELLE: What . . .?

GEORGE: Nothing. (*Pause.*)

ROCHELLE: Oh, look at Georgie. He's all sad and runny. He looks like he wanted to crawl into a corner and turn into water.

GEORGE: Forgive me.

AURETHIA: What's the matter, George?

GEORGE: Nothing.

BUDDY (*to Rochelle*): Can we go?

ROCHELLE: Is Buby embarrassed?

Rochelle walks off majestically; Buddy follows with needle.

AURETHIA: What's the matter, George?

GEORGE: Nothing.

AURETHIA: George, what's wrong?

GEORGE: Nothing.

AURETHIA: I said . . . !

GEORGE: Nothing. (*Pause.*) I'm very much in need of a bowel movement, if it's all right with you.

AURETHIA: Oh George.

GEORGE: Is it all right . . .?

AURETHIA: Go to the bathroom, will you?

George leaves. Aurethia goes to the tape and turns it on.

"John. I'd like to say a few more things. I'd like to say that I'm not a free agent. I'm not my own man. I want to get some real good oatmeal. I want to go back to Ashtabula."

The tape ends. It runs on a while silently, as Aurethia listens. There is some modern music, fading in briefly. Joyce enters. She hides behind partition when she sees Aurethia.

BUDDY ON TAPE: Hey, this is a good one. A song about Mother.

Aurethia stops the tape and exits, turning out the lights. Joyce walks toward the tape recorder and turns it on again.

M is for the million times she had me.
O means that she's over 21.
T is for her teeth that gave me hickeys.
H is for her hairpins in the bed.
E is for her earthiness it sends me.
R means ripe and ripe she'll always be.
Put them all together they spell MOTHER,
The girl nobody loves, but me.

(*Speaking*) How do you like that, Aurethia? Isn't it funny?

AURETHIA ON TAPE: I don't like it, Buddy. And I wish you'd stop calling me Aurethia.

BUDDY ON TAPE (*joking*): Don't you understand? That's what's happening, baby. Get with it, Aunt Aurethia. Move into it.

AURETHIA ON TAPE: What would Uncle George say?

BUDDY ON TAPE: He'll go along with it. He's always loved catastrophe.

AURETHIA ON TAPE: Only from a distance.

BUDDY ON TAPE: You have beautiful lips. Close your eyes.

AURETHIA ON TAPE: Why?

BUDDY ON TAPE: I want you to relax.

AURETHIA ON TAPE: Yes . . . !

BUDDY ON TAPE: See the lake outside the window. It's calm. It's serene. The water is crystal clear. See the bottom of the lake. See the round, brown, heavy stones, resting there through ages and ages. You feel heavy, very heavy, you are the stones, resting there, heavy, very heavy, heavy, heavy . . .!

AURETHIA ON TAPE: Buddy. What are you doing?

BUDDY ON TAPE: Nothing.

AURETHIA ON TAPE: I can hardly see you.

BUDDY ON TAPE: I'm here. Close to you.

AURETHIA ON TAPE: I'm so tired. I want you close . . . close . . . !

(Cut to another part of tape.)

BUDDY ON TAPE: And that's what's happening. There's a great breakdown in American life. Nothing is the way it used to be. Nothing is normal, or right. It never has been. We've corrupted the truth with religion and politics. The real truth, the real need, is for self-concern. You long for the sun, don't you, Aurethia . . . ?

AURETHIA ON TAPE: Yes, yes I do.

BUDDY ON TAPE: You love the lemon trees, don't you . . . ?

AURETHIA ON TAPE: Yes.

BUDDY ON TAPE: What else do you love . . . ? What else . . . ?

AURETHIA ON TAPE: I . . . I . . . !

BUDDY ON TAPE: You love me. Don't you? You want me.

AURETHIA ON TAPE: I . . . !

BUDDY ON TAPE: Say it. I'm young . . . I'm young and strong and handsome.

AURETHIA ON TAPE: Yes. I want you. I want you. I want a child. Yes. Come take me. Take me.

The tape skips again. Uncle George is playing "Clementine" on the piano. We hear his singing for a moment, and then he stops. There is a slight rustling.

GEORGE ON TAPE: Is that you, Buddy?

BUDDY ON TAPE: Yes.

GEORGE ON TAPE: Do you want to talk to me?

BUDDY ON TAPE: No, George. Keep on playing, that sounded great.

He continues to play. In the middle of the song he stops again. There is a scream of agony. There is much scuffling, and then nothing.

AURETHIA ON TAPE *(low)*: No!

BUDDY ON TAPE: Don't worry, Aurethia. *(Pause.)* It's nothing. He's unconscious now, but he'll be out of it in a moment, and then we'll be able to work.

AURETHIA ON TAPE: What are you doing?

BUDDY ON TAPE: Don't get hysterical. Hold his head. I'm

going to perform a slight operation. I'm inserting a surgical needle, through his eye, into the frontal lobe . . . It's all over now. He didn't feel anything.

AURETHIA ON TAPE: What if he doesn't respond?

BUDDY ON TAPE: He'll respond.

At this very point, Aurethia enters and turns on lights. Joyce turns swiftly, and seeing Aurethia, starts to run, but trips and falls. Aurethia turns off tape.

AURETHIA: Are you hurt?

JOYCE: No. No, it's all right.

AURETHIA: That was quite a fall.

Joyce gets up.

AURETHIA: Mr. Roland arrived about a half hour ago. He'll be out in a minute.

JOYCE: Oh . . . yes . . . !

AURETHIA: Why don't you sit down and rest yourself? Go ahead. It won't bite.

Joyce glares at Aurethia for a moment; Aurethia is smiling warmly. Joyce sits down in the chair. Aurethia sits opposite her. They look at each other for a long time, Aurethia still smiling.

I guess you're very tired.

JOYCE: Oh . . . yes, I am.

AURETHIA: I would imagine. Redwood is a long way from here!

JOYCE: How did you know I . . . ?

AURETHIA: You said so before. (*Pause.*) Anyway, I knew.

JOYCE: What do you mean?

AURETHIA: You can tell me about it, if you want to . . . !

JOYCE: I'd rather speak to Mr. Roland.

AURETHIA: He can't tell you anything more than what I could . . . !

JOYCE: I don't know about that.

AURETHIA: Did he say anything to you before?

JOYCE: What?

AURETHIA: Did he tell you anything . . . ?

JOYCE: No he didn't. He didn't say anything.

AURETHIA: Then what makes you think he has something to say?

JOYCE: It's not important.

AURETHIA: I wish you would confide in me. Joyce, is it . . . ?

JOYCE: Yes, Joyce.

AURETHIA: You'll find I'm sympathetic. Really. You will.

JOYCE: I don't know.

AURETHIA: Why don't you try me out? I'm not such a bad egg.

JOYCE: I never said you were.

AURETHIA: Perhaps not. But every time I extend myself to you, you pull away. That's not exactly a sign of trust . . . !

JOYCE: It has nothing to do with that, Mrs. Roland . . . !

AURETHIA: Then what does it have to do with . . . ?

JOYCE: It's not easy to explain. I mean . . . !

AURETHIA: What . . . ?

JOYCE: I don't know how to say . . . !

AURETHIA: Don't worry about that. Just say it as it comes to you.

JOYCE: I . . . I . . . well, he came to see me in Redwood.

AURETHIA: I know that much.

JOYCE: He said he had something to talk about. It was very urgent. I met him for lunch. He was very pleasant, and we talked for a long while. I brought up the subject of napalm shipments, and why you've been so laggard.

AURETHIA: Oh, I see. Then you are Joyce Clark.

JOYCE: Yes. I'm from Otway's. Didn't you know that?

AURETHIA: No. I didn't. But it's all right. Go on.

JOYCE: Well . . . he said he had something to tell me, and then, when the time came to speak about it, he couldn't speak, he just sat there and said nothing, but he was straining to say it . . . and I felt so sorry for him . . . I don't know . . . this feeling of sorrow came over me . . .

AURETHIA: What could he tell you . . . ?

JOYCE: It was something important. At least, it was important to him, I know that much. If I'd had another five minutes with him, I'd have known what it was. But he had to leave . . . !

AURETHIA: And that was the last time you saw him . . . ?

JOYCE: No. We went to dinner. We went to a show. (*Pause.*) And always, he seemed to be on the verge of pouring himself out to me, but . . . !

AURETHIA (*smiling wryly*): He copped out again!

JOYCE: Well, it wasn't for want of trying not to.

AURETHIA: George always tries not to. (*Sharpening sound from kitchen.*)

JOYCE: I feel he could say what he wanted, if only people gave him the chance to . . . I feel there's more in George than anyone gives him credit for . . . !

There is a pause. Joyce looks almost pleadingly at Aurethia. Aurethia just stares back, expressionlessly. Sound of sharpening.

What's that . . . ?

AURETHIA: What? Oh. It's just the cook. Why don't you stay for dinner? We can all discuss this over roast duck.

JOYCE: All right!

AURETHIA: How did you get down here? By train or . . . !

JOYCE: No. A friend gave me a lift. (*Stop. Sharpening sound.*)

AURETHIA: It was very sweet of him to do that for you! (*Joyce nods.*) Is your friend in town . . . ?

JOYCE: No. He was going on to Los Angeles, and he dropped me off. It's my vacation.

AURETHIA: The company means a lot to you, doesn't it . . . ?

JOYCE: Everything means a lot to me, Mrs. Roland.

AURETHIA: You seem so young, I mean . . . too young to be holding such an important position at Otway's.

JOYCE: I'm not that important. I just handle napalm shipments. I could be doing so much more . . . !

AURETHIA: *Just* napalm shipments? What qualified you for such a position?

JOYCE: I worked three years with the Peace Corps.

AURETHIA: Well, that's very impressive . . . !

JOYCE: I really don't know much about it. I mean, about all this. But I know it's helping the country and that's all that interests me. I want to be of service in some way!

AURETHIA: Of course. All of us do. Our cook is Irish, you know?

JOYCE: Really?

AURETHIA: Yes. Sophie's ultra-patriotic.

JOYCE: Most Irish are. I'm part Irish myself.

She removes her red, white and blue bandana and places it on the table.

AURETHIA: I thought so.

JOYCE: What made you think so?
AURETHIA: The nose. The eyes. (*Pause.*) Sophie's got a ruddy face and a hearty laugh, and she's big and buxom. And she makes marvelous roast duck.
JOYCE: She sounds wonderful.
AURETHIA: She is wonderful. (*Pause.*) Would you like to meet her?
JOYCE: I'd love to.
AURETHIA: Come on. You'll meet Sophie, and then Mr. Roland will be out, and we'll all have a pleasant dinner.

She opens the door of the kitchen and gently nudges Joyce inside. Smiling innocently, Joyce enters the kitchen. Aurethia introduces Joyce to Sophie, and then Joyce, noticing Sophie's chessboard, lowers her head to look at the chess pieces. Sophie raises her cleaver and lowers it down on Joyce's head as the lights go out on the kitchen and up again on the living room. Joyce's brief scream is the only sound that is heard. Aurethia exits coolly from the kitchen and walks to the desk, starts to look at letters again. George enters from bathroom, pulling at his pants. He walks straight to the bar and begins to pour himself a drink.

AURETHIA: I thought you finished the letter to John Frey.
GEORGE: I did.
AURETHIA: I heard some more of it.
GEORGE: What more?
AURETHIA: The more about Ashtabula.
GEORGE (*impulsively*): I know what I said.
AURETHIA (*bitchy*): All right. I'll just erase the whole tape. We can start from scratch tomorrow.
GEORGE: You can start right now. (*Glares at her.*)
AURETHIA: No. I'll do it tomorrow.

George picks up scarf.

GEORGE: What's this?
AURETHIA: Huh!
GEORGE (*pointedly*): Whose scarf is this?

Enter Buddy. He shows Aurethia the needle. She sees it out of the corner of her eye.

AURETHIA: I bought a scarf today.

GEORGE: I've seen it before.

AURETHIA: Of course. It's been here all the time.

GEORGE (*long pause*): It's . . . a very beautiful scarf.

AURETHIA: I know.

> *Aurethia starts to take it from George's hand. But Buddy pulls it away. He puts the scarf on Aurethia. Aurethia crosses to bar, slowly. Picks up plate of raw ginger. Walks back to George.*

AURETHIA: Have some raw ginger. It's excellent.

> *Offers it to George. Buddy takes plate from her hand, holds it in front of George. He slowly extends his hands, as though in ritual, until plate of ginger is practically under George's nose. Sniffing at it, George takes a piece of ginger off plate and eats it.*

> *Lights down slowly.*

THE END

GORILLA QUEEN

a play

[BY RONALD TAVEL

With patience, to the unpracticing
We dedicate the natural thing.

Gorilla Queen is one of the most insane plays I've ever
seen, even counting other works by Ronald Tavel.
Crammed into the camp form of a movie musical is a
farcical treatment of ultraserious themes. Two whole
civilizations, the scum of the jungle and the cream of
Hollywood, are tossed about in a whirlpool of philosophy.
Beast and movie star couple in grubby lust. Purity is
despoiled by a mad male nun. Transformation leads to
transformation with vertiginous extravagance. All the
climaxes are in the wrong places, and dualisms multiply
until the tragic ending is only a pretext for another
happy, or at least manic, beginning. Meanwhile the
language never ceases its headlong punning, beyond
vulgarity, beyond criticism, beyond belief.

M. S.

Gorilla Queen was presented by the Judson Poets' Theatre at Judson Memorial Church, 55 Washington Square South, New York City, on March 10, 1967. The production was subsequently transferred Off-Broadway to the Martinique Theatre, where it was presented by Paul Libin. It was directed by Lawrence Kornfeld with the following cast:

VENUS FLY TRAP: Jo Ann Forman
BRUTE: George Harris II
LIGHTING GIRL: Deborah Lee
GLITZ IONAS: Adrienne de Antonio
        Mary Duke
        Norman R. Glick
        John Harrill
        George Harris III
        Dick Lipkin
        Norman Soifer
MAIS OUI: Selena Williams
KARMA: Paula Shaw
CLYDE BATTY: James Hilbrandt
TAHARAHNUGI WHITE WOMAN: Quinn Halford
CHIMNEY SWEEP: David Kerry Heefner
SISTER CARRIES: Eddie McCarty
PAULET: Barbara Ann Camp
QUEEN KONG: Norman Thomas Marshall
INTERN: Cal Thorpe

Set: Jerry Joyner
Costumes: Linda Sampson
Music: Robert Cosmos Savage and Al Carmines
Lighting: John P. Dodd
Production Stage Manager: Roland Turner

James Hilbrandt (Clyde Batty) and Norman Thomas Marshall (Queen Kong) in *Gorilla Queen*

Characters

BRUTE	QUEEN KONG
GLITZ IONAS (nine or more)	CLINIC INTERN
CLYDE BATTY	VENUS FLY TRAP
TAHARAHNUGI WHITE WOMAN	MAIS OUI
CHIMNEY SWEEP	KARMA MIRANDA
SISTER CARRIES	PAULET COLBERT

Note on Pronunciation

Unless otherwise indicated, foreign words and names are pronounced correctly and not Anglicized.

Taharahnugi is pronounced with equal emphasis on each syllable.

Dark stage; then a traveling spotlight, beneath which Brute, a sluggish but amiable gibbon, comes ambling across the apron. He is dressed in a tacky ape-hair outfit with ill-fitting gibbon mask. A bare arm, ankle, ear, etc., sloppily exposed. He pauses and speaks the prologue.

BRUTE (*with very heavy Brooklyn accent*): Ladies and gentlemen of every genus: When I was a kid my Daddy used to say, "I'll explain it to ya when ya get older." Now in order that daddies no longer have to explain anythin' to their kids, we are presentin' dis play. Dis here play don't leave nothin' to the imagination. After all, most people ain't got any. Hit it, Maestro!

The overture music, a bongo-heavy, rapid marching beat, strikes up at a deafening pitch. Then just as suddenly, it loses all enthusiasm and peters out into ambling nonsense chords as the members of the Glitz Ionas, a tribe of gibbons, enter from various directions. They are costumed in played-out ape-hair outfits, bras and skirts of long fur and mat that have seen better days, ape masks alternately silly and grim, etc.; here and there naked midriffs, arms, legs, necks, toes, etc., very obviously exposed. Spotlights follow the chaotic entrance of the Glitz Ionas: each crawls about, grunts, adjusts his costume—some put their costumes on right there on stage; sounds of "Ooo-ou-oop," "Gubba-mubba," "Get dis garter, will ya!" etc. They all carry bananas.

Gradually, the set becomes visible: upstage center is a huge fireplace with grate, over which rises a wide, long chimney. Downstage right is a seven-foot-high bamboo cage, almost completely camouflaged with jungle foliage. Before the cage stands the immobile figure of the Venus Fly Trap. She is dressed in form-fitting green tights with reddish-pink face, hands, and feet. Long forbidding needles corona her face, hands, and feet. She is slender and graceful, like a mime.

Downstage left is a rattan table on which are tall drinks and a flower basket containing acacia blossoms, bulrushes, carnations, daisies, ivy, myrtle, and grape vines. Two rattan wicker chairs.

183

Between the fireplace and the cage and between the fire-
place and the table, and against the backdrop and the
wings, is built a row of shelves, several feet above the
floor, forming a very distinct semicircle. The stage is
decorated, here and there, with potted plants and flowers,
preferably any which would not be found in a jungle;
the symbolic growths of the flower basket are noticeably
repeated at key points about the stage.

Several of the Glitz Ionas jump up and take a place on
the shelf. More and more Glitz Ionas arrive, grunting
and bickering, their cacophony of sounds reaching a
feverish pitch as the last mischievous one takes his place,
squatting, on the shelf. Then, suddenly, the deafening
bongo-heavy overture resumes, and they all break out
into song, an irregular collection of voices to be sure, but
not to the point where the words become indistinct.
Flickering lights illuminate the long, semicircular row of
their face masks; they scratch their crotches with little
apparent relief.

Just before the overture ends, Mais Oui, carrying a cus-
pidor, arrives in time to sing the last two lines, in timid
high soprano before jumping daintily up on the shelf
between the fireplace and cage. Mais Oui is one of the
Glitz Ionas, played by an actress; but she should appear
to the audience to be an actor, very effeminate in word
and gesture. Throughout the play the other characters
will refer to and respond to Mais Oui as if she were
actually an effete, effeminate male.

GLITZ IONAS (*singing*):
    Hear Barbaric Overture
    Overhearers hold a bore,
    Though our toying each his fore
    Overseers more deplore:—
    Human, vomit, let it pour,
    If your nausea upward soar;
    Know, though toilet fill galore,
    What you heave you but restore
    To our stomachs sickened more:—
    We be all a single corps!

    Still, who stay and do not snore,

They that share our common lore,
Swing ahead to years of yore
When to humor sophomore
Jungles rang with raucous roar.
Now our throats are straining sore
So we'll stretch no furthermore
This Barbaric Overture!

MAIS OUI (*hurrying in, singing with mock obsequiousness*):
Please to use the cuspidor
For opinions—not the floor!

*The overture music ends with a loud crash upon which
the lights on the Glitzes go out—and a strong spot immediately goes up on the rattan table downstage left.*

*In the chair nearest to the left wing is seated Clyde
Batty, very short and very thin, hair slicked back in a
bogus 1930's style, costumed as the animal trainer his
name recalls. In the chair closest to center stage is seated
Karma Miranda, a very huge, very heavy woman, got up
like a lovely rococo shepherdess made of porcelain; her
skin is powder white; her buckled shoes, bonnet, and
shepherdess's crook are gilt; Belgian lace covers her
shoulders and leggings; a purple rose neatly catches up
her wide bell skirt. Sequestered from these two, and
languishing on the floor in front of the table is Taharahnugi White Woman, a brownskin male actor, ravishing
in a tight white sarong and wig of long raven hair; bare
footed with ankle bracelets, huge round falsies, thick
lipstick, and long lashes.*

*When the spotlight goes up on them, the conversation
begins without a second's pause, as if it has been in
progress for some time. Clyde's voice inclines to the
squeak, Karma's to an alto pitch.*

CLYDE: And so finally, Miss Karma, the theatre is superior to
cinema because whereas in cinema everything is mis-
placed, in theatre the four corners of the stage are the
four corners of the earth.

KARMA: But that still doesn't explain why people walk out
in the middle of a play.

CLYDE: Oh, them, they're just trying to get into the papers.

KARMA: Well, I'll be a monkey's uncle, I never thought of that! But I sure am glad you told me, Clyde, 'cause this sure is better than a movie.

CLYDE: What is better than a movie?

KARMA: Sitting out here on the canopied verandah of the old plantation, sipping cool mint juleps, being enamored of the pagan emir of this forbidden tropical paradise and its primitive untamed dangers. And here, here in Egypt, where adventure lives and romance rules, here—

CLYDE: Here, where?

KARMA: Where? In Egypt.

CLYDE: This ain't Egypt. I wouldn't dream of planting a plantation in Egypt, Miss Karma.

KARMA: But why not, Clyde, Clyde Batty, since you're actually an animal trainer?

CLYDE: Because while Egypt is an interesting country, it is, on the whole, a bit disappointing historically.

KARMA: I sure can sympathize with you on that point. But where, then, are we?

CLYDE: In Nigeria, of course, Miss Karma. You see, if we're in Nigeria, we can sympathize with the whole British nation. Nigeria, after all, was Britain's showcase in Africa.

KARMA: Quite. Listen, Clyde, have you heard tell anything about a certain . . . Queen Kong?

CLYDE: Queen Kong? Why, no—are you she?

KARMA: Not likely—nor like her. I assume Queen Kong is a great ape.

CLYDE: Sounds likely, but it's not likely. Someone who is queen around here is more likely to be a woman than a great ape, don't you think? A great woman. And you, my dear Miss Karma, are as great a woman as ever I hope to—

At this point, Taharahnugi White Woman begins squirming along the floor toward Clyde's boots. He will speak throughout with a heavy Caribbean accent.

TAHARAH: Show cause! Show cause!

CLYDE: What?

TAHARAH: Show cause!

CLYDE: What for?

TAHARAH (*sexy*): Show cause! Show cause why theez show shouldn't be clozed down!

CLYDE (*bending over toward Taharah*): And what is your identity, little one?

TAHARAH (*sizzling*): I am Taharahnugi White Woman! Men are attracted to me and men who are attracted to me soon crack up!

CLYDE (*fingering the falsies bulging out of the top of Taharah's sarong*): I can believe it—that's a real crack up front you've got there, Taharahnugi!

TAHARAH: Some-sing de matter wit you?

CLYDE: Perhaps, but the matter is in good hands.

TAHARAH: Good hands?? They look like effete white whiteman's hands to me. Don't reach for more than you can grab, Bwana Clyde!

KARMA: Well, well, this play and interplay is rather dull, after all. Gargoyle, l'addition, s'il-vous plaît.

TAHARAH: Eet is too hot for you out here, Mem-sab?

KARMA (*ignoring him*): Gargoyle, l'addition, s'il vous plaît, I say.

CLYDE: You'll never get the check asking for it in that tone of Swahili. Waiter, the abacus, please!

TAHARAH (*squirming up the table leg and sitting square on the table top*): I am the waiter.

CLYDE (*with roaming fingers*): Can you wait for me?

TAHARAH (*ignoring his familiarities*): Will there be anything else?

CLYDE: Will there?

TAHARAH: Oh, don't be so fresh! Theez ain't one of doz places where de waitresses are topless, de entertainers bottomless, and de audience brainless, and therefore you can be free to say anything you damn please!

KARMA: The check, please.

TAHARAH: Did you haf the high-priced spread on your table?

KARMA (*regarding his rear*): No, indeed! Nor was the egg-drop soup very high priced either.

TAHARAH: How do you mean?

KARMA: The egg was doubtless dropped into it, but apparently removed shortly thereafter.

TAHARAH: How obscene! And you a woman!

CLYDE: Garçon!

TAHARAH: Oh, mais ou!

KARMA: Mais Oui?—who's that?

CLYDE: She's that real small gibbon you sometimes see swing-

ing with the rest of the pack at the edge of the plantation.

MAIS OUI (*from her position on the shelf*): Oh! how exciting—he has an eye out for me.

KARMA (*disgusted*): He'll have an eye *knocked* out for you!

TAHARAH (*picking up the challenge posed by Karma and
suddenly switching his attitude toward Clyde*): I am the
waiter. Can I wait for you?

CLYDE (*hampered because Karma is there*): I, er, I—if it's
part of your job, I mean if your job entails—

TAHARAH (*sizzling*): Yeez . . . tails. I weel wait for you by
the Venus Fly Trap plant. The beeg one. . . . You know
where 'tis, yeez, Bwana Clyde? (*Chucking Clyde under
the chin.*)

CLYDE (*fumbling, suddenly no longer the aggressor*): Er
—er—one fly trap looks pretty much like another to
me.

KARMA (*sarcastic*): They're all Greek to him.

TAHARAH: Do not slander his manhood so, Mem-sab. (*Winking.*) In Greek is called Aphrodite Fly Trap. You weel
fin' it . . . If you don't fin' it, it fin' you. If it don't fin'
you, it *de*fine you.

KARMA (*sarcastic*): Well, that's just fine.

*Taharah takes a long, hot walk across the stage till he
reaches the Venus Fly Trap, at whose feet he immediately throws himself, languishing as if under a palm,
legs sensuously planing along the floor as if in heat.
Clyde adjusts his leather belt.*

CLYDE: Oh, Miss Karma, will you excuse me, I wanna call
Sister Carries.

KARMA: What do you wanna call him?

CLYDE: A fruit.

KARMA: I disagree with you, he's not a fruit.

CLYDE: Well, disagree without me for two minutes, will you,
I really do have to call him about a trip to Hollywood.

KARMA (*suddenly sexy*): Holly *would*?? —Holly *did*!!

CLYDE: Er, I'm trying to get a booking for my animal act out
there. I wanna be discovered.

KARMA: But you're leaving without paying the check.

CLYDE: I always leave restaurants without paying the check—
that's cause I crave that thrilling ice-blue hole tha

hollows out your back when you're slipping away and
still within apprehending distance of the waiter.

KARMA: Oh, yeah? There's something going between you and
that waiter that slipping away without paying the check
won't help you to slip out of.

CLYDE: Look, I hate to be callous—

KARMA (*angry*): You ain't—you're callow. Go—go! You and
your animal act! Go, beast, go!

*Clyde braces his narrow shoulders, then struts across
the stage like a peacock toward Taharah. At that moment a Chimney Sweep hops out of the left wing and
lands precisely beside Karma. He is quite tall, quite
skinny in form-fitting black tights, with a stovepipe hat
roofing his porcelain face; he is as clean and neat as any
other man, "for it was only make-believe that he was a
sweep; the china-workers might just as well have made
a prince of him, if they had been so minded." The
Chimney Sweep carries a large emerald-green plantain.
A quartet scene ensues, carefully integrated and counterpointed; do not employ the "freeze" technique during
this four-corner interlude.*

SWEEP: Beg your pardon, Miss, what time do you have?

KARMA: Anytime. (*Looking at her wristwatch and giving him
the exact time it reads at that moment.*) But right now,
it's exactly———.

SWEEP (*suddenly placing the tip of the plantain on Karma's
inner elbow and speaking like a hardened criminal*):
That where ya shoot it, baby?!

KARMA (*indignant*): I beg your pardon!—and ruin my lily-
white arms?!

*Sweep helps himself to a generous sampling of her lily-
white and lovely arms.*

CLYDE (*bending over with his hand touching Taharah's
thigh*): What a delightful contrast must be between the
inner pink and outer dark . . .

TAHARAH: Ooooooooooo . . . you found the right place. Did
you follow the brain wave I astro-projected to direct you
here?

CLYDE (*lifting Taharah in his arms*): . .No, I just followed
the heat wave.

KARMA: Ain't it hot enough without your hands all over me?

TAHARAH (*on his feet, turning his back to Clyde and leaning against him as if he were a palm tree*): Ooooooooo, Bwana Muskels! What manner of labor do you do to haf developed such beeg muskels?

CLYDE (*nibbling on Taharah's neck*): I don't have to labor: I have a private income.

TAHARAH: Perhaps Bwana could be induced to share it?

CLYDE: I said it was private.

KARMA: Yer a chimney sweep, ain't cha?

SWEEP (*kissing her between her fingers*): How can you tell?

KARMA: By your skin-tight tights.

SWEEP: You like skin-tight tights, do you?

KARMA (*giving him the "screw-you" finger*): No, just skin—tight!!

TAHARAH: Perhaps Bwana haf income from some other activity, which he could be induced to share?

CLYDE: At the least, I could be induced to share the activity—you see, I'm a pataphysician. (*Patting Taharah's falsies and worming his hands into the top of the sarong.*)

TAHARAH: Ooooooooooo, a pataphysician; you must haf studied at beeg college—like Barnyard or somethink.

SWEEP (*quickly, making time*): But I'm more than just a simple chimney sweep; I'm also a May-son, a Taurian, one who uses words like *completely, totally, always, forever,* and so on—a May-son, a brick layer to you.

KARMA: Or a rock dropper, but I wouldn't know about that; you see, I abide in a very small grassass shack.

SWEEP (*suggestively*): Well, I'd like to enlarge your place.

KARMA: All ya have to do is get one foot in the door.

TAHARAH: College is de door to de inner life.

CLYDE: A nose for news could smell it from without.

SWEEP: What's yer name, toots?

KARMA: Karma.

SWEEP: Karma what?

KARMA: Karma Miranda.

SWEEP (*brandishing the plantain*): Karma Miranda, the Brazilian Fly-Fortress! You married?

KARMA: I haven't the right time to be married—I have too many affairs of state.

SWEEP (*pulling away and coming downstage for an elaborate aside*): Affairs of state—I thought so! That broad don'

pull this boy's third leg—she ain't Karma Miranda—
she's Queen Kong! And not married—what a break! If
I can make her to the altar I'll be sable to shit the de-
grating job of chimney sweep and be King for a lay!

*He returns to manhandling Karma, who has quietly fol-
lowed him downstage with an auditor's curiosity.*

TAHARAH: Is the Mem-sab Bwana Muskels' wife?

CLYDE: Who, Karma? Hell, no, Karma's jist my fiancée.

TAHARAH: Then perhaps Taharahnugi White Woman can be
Bwana's financée.

CLYDE: How much are ya willin' to lay out, Too-hairy-noogi?

TAHARAH: For Bwana, I weel put up all my spangles . . .

SWEEP (*smacking Karma's face*): A smack in time saves nine.

KARMA (*stunned*): Hey! what dja do that for?

SWEEP: Cause I'm more than just a simple bricklayer or May-
son if you like—I'm also a smacking thief.

KARMA (*rubbing her cheek*): A smacking thief?

SWEEP (*stealing, unnoticed, the purple rose that catches up
her bell skirt*): Yeah, pretty romantic, huh?

KARMA: Watch it, sonny mae, watch it. You're playing with
fire.

SWEEP: But of course, cause I'm more than just a smacking
thief—I'm also a chimney sweep.

KARMA (*perceiving her outermost skirt slowly falling to its
full length now that it is no longer caught up by the
rose*): How self-reliant is my chaperone skirt: it draws,
unaided, the veil across my lips.

TAHARAH: Taharahnugi White Woman do not want Bwana
Muskels to beleef that she haf only money on her mind.
Taharahnugi is well to do in her own right.

CLYDE (*obscenely smacking his lips, his hand now completely
up Taharah's sarong*): I'll bet you're well to do, Too-
hairy-noogi. And you're pretty well bushed, too, aren't
you?

TAHARAH: Taharahnugi very, very bushed. She know some
thick seluzive bushes where she and Bwana can rest *up*.

CLYDE: Well let's not wait till the cows come milk.

TAHARAH: Bwana Muskels not afraid of getting lost in the
bush?

CLYDE: I know my way around the country.

TAHARAH: Then follow my scent, O strong one!

CLYDE: I'm followin' with a long one.

> *Taharah, seeming suddenly very tall, breaks into the elegant Watusi ceremonial dance and glides back and forth across the stage, head swirling, arms winging, Watusi bongo accompaniment. Clyde follows awkwardly behind trying to imitate the dance, and they work their way upstage while Karma gives her speech; as Karma finishes speaking, Taharah and Clyde exit behind the huge cage at right, and the music ends.*

KARMA (*removing her bonnet*): I shall never forgive Clyde Batty for Watusiing away into the wold with that Taharahnugi White Woman waiter. It is inhuman to forgive—on the one appendage, one inflicts self-harm by retaining the offense and not equalizing it; and on the other appendage, one inflicts harm on the offender, for by letting him go unscathed, one is donating him liberty to harm oneself and others again, and thus to damn yet once more his eternal hole.

SWEEP (*debonair*): Never let the jungle sun set on your jealousy.

KARMA: Who's jealous? After all, what does a mere native girl have over a half-breed?

SWEEP: She has Clyde Batty over her, for one appendage. But tell me, I never knew that you were a half-breed.

KARMA: Certainly, I am. I'm half native, half Brazilian. Don't I look it?

SWEEP: At second peek, I guess you do. It's written all over your porcelain-pale complexion. Listen, Miss Miranda, have you heard tell anything about a certain . . . Queen Kong?

KARMA: Why, sure. Hasn't everyone? It's printed in the program credits.

SWEEP: Not everyone can read. And it isn't everyone who reads words. But speak, my dear, could . . . (*very cautious*) it be . . . that you . . . in the ineffable complexity of your womanliness, conceal the fact . . . that you . . . are . . . this mysterious . . . Queen Kong? You're certainly big enough to be.

KARMA: Ha—ha! Long may you wonder but never know the truth, for the jungle keeps well its unrevealable secrets!

SWEEP: But surely you could proffer some impertinent information anent this curious queen called Kong?

KARMA (*Portuguese accent*): You likes Brazilian music?

SWEEP: Here in Angola, who dare not?

KARMA (*Portuguese accent*): You likes it, you got it!

The music begins with great dash and flare as Karma tosses the flora out of the basket on the table; the basket has a bandanna attached to the bottom of it: Karma secures the bandanna under her chin, thus securing the empty basket on top of her head as a hat; and begins to dance in little Miranda steps out toward center stage. The music for the song is "South American Way," except for the chorus, which is sung to the children's rhyme, "One Banana, Two Banana." As Karma starts her song and dance, the Glitzes jump off the shelves and accompany her as if they were a Latin chorus line à la 1940's Hollywood. During the "Bwana" chorus, each Glitz glides by Karma and tosses a banana into her basket as she quickly calls out the numbers. Karma dances about briefly with huge smile during the short introductory music, then whips into her song.

KARMA (*singing*): I Yi! I Yi!
Efer learn to lust in a freak show,
Lose your easy queasiness
Wiz zee sleasiest
Man Gargantuan Girl?

I Yi! I Yi!
Efer drop your civilized mores,
Kiss a rare and hairylike
Sort of scarylike
Man Gargantuan Girl?

KARMA AND GLITZES (*all singing, Karma pointing to the following parts of her body to heavy bongo accompaniment, and the Glitzes tossing bananas into her basket-hat*):

(*to her nose*)	One bwana,
(*to her mouth*)	Two bwana,
(*to her ears*)	Three bwana, four,
(*to one breast*)	Five bwana,
(*to other breast*)	Six bwana,
(*to rear and lap*)	Seven bwana, more!

KARMA: I Yi! I Yi!
    Efer try to mate wiz a monster,
    In zee jungles vapoury
    Rim an apery
    Man Gargantuan Girl?

    I Yi! I Yi!
    Efer lick a lap wasn't human,
    Eat a unitarian
    Sex barbarian
    Man Gargantuan Girl?

KARMA AND GLITZES (*Karma pointing to the following parts to heavy, rapid bongo accompaniment*):
(*to her cheek*)	One red,
(*to other cheek*)	Two red,
(*to her breasts*)	Three white, four,
(*to her rear*)	Five blue,
(*to her lap*)	Six blue,
(*shrugging shoulders*)	Who takes more?

The music goes into the minor bridge and Karma sings and now dances more ornately with the Glitzes. [Delete major bridge.]

KARMA: I Yi! I Yi!
    O, zee Man Gargantuan Girl!
GLITZES: I Yi! I Yi!
    I Yi! I Yi!
KARMA AND GLITZES: O, zee Man Gargantuan Girl!
    O, zee Man Gargantuan Girl!
KARMA: I Yi! I Yi!
    Efer long to sire zee children
    Of zee deva cleavable
    Inconceivable
    Man Gargantuan Girl?

    I Yi! I Yi!
    Efer beat your meat for zee bestial,
    Dip your tricky dicky-hot
    In zee sticky spot

    (*Pause.*)

    —Of zee Man Gargantuan Girl?

—Of zee Man Gargantuan Girl?

KARMA AND GLITZES (*Karma pointing to the following parts of her body to heavy, rapid bongo accompaniment; Glitzes tossing bananas in basket*):

(*to her nose*)	One bwana,
(*to her mouth*)	Two bwana,
(*to her ears*)	Three bwana, four,
(*to one breast*)	Five bwana,
(*to other breast*)	Six bwana,
(*to her rear*)	Seven bwana—

(*throwing wide her arms, and the Sweep tossing his plantain into the basket-hat*):

KARMA AND SWEEP: MORE!!!

The song ends with a loud pound on the bongos and the dancers freezing. Then the Glitzes scamper back to their positions on the shelves, and Sweep applauds Karma's performance.

SWEEP: Very, very delicate, Señorita Karma, and very poetic!

KARMA: But was it in good taste?

SWEEP: Farce is seldom in good taste—but genitals always are. Soap and scenters see to that.

KARMA: I take it, then, that you like my little act?

SWEEP: More than you can conceive—although the information it offered concerning the nature of Queen Kong did not exactly identify her as yourself.

KARMA: How could it?—I'm not Queen Kong. How many times do I have to render that particular exposition?

SWEEP: But are you positive, and thinking positive, when you say you're not Queen Kong?

KARMA: How could I be? First of all, a queen is a human male; and second of all, anyone called Kong must be an animal—a giant ape. It's a contradiction in terms.

SWEEP: Naturally, because it's terms. Male! man! female! king! queen! human! animal! ape!—what are these terms except expedient, comforting designations?

KARMA: But you don't mean to—

SWEEP: Would you predicate your existence on a *legal* definition?

MAIS OUI: The point is what ya go for or ya don't go for. And that chimney sweep is jist too skinny for me.

BRUTE: I ain't so skinny.

MAIS OUI: I been noticin', hon, I been noticin'.

SWEEP: I go for you, Miss Señorita, more than you've conned—

KARMA: But, Señor Sweep, you hardly know me.

SWEEP: I know that you can dance as well as Salomé, and (*making for her bosom*) that you're solid—

KARMA (*evading his grasp*): Yeah, solid as Lot's wife.

SWEEP: And those are the only two important things in a girl.

KARMA (*puffing out her bosom*): What are the only two important things?

SWEEP: One, that you're not Queen Kong, and two, that you won't become her. Your mentality certifies as much. Now listen, why don't you forget that rake, Clyde Batty, and take up with me?

KARMA: Take up where, a chimney?

SWEEP: I'll show you a chimney you ain't even dreamed existed, baby!

KARMA: I can't wait. Set up a trysting place.

SWEEP (*thinking*): A twisting place? Let me see . . .

KARMA: Got your stinking cap on, don't ya?

SWEEP: I've got it! Know the layout on this stage pretty well?

KARMA: Well as any Nigerian might.

SWEEP: Great, since this is Angola! Tell ya what, meet me under the Venus Fly Trap.

KARMA: What time?

SWEEP (*looking at his wristwatch*): Let me see, it's——— (*saying the exact time*) now;—how about 10:30?

KARMA: Suits me. See ya then, Señor Chimney Sweep.

SWEEP (*walking upstage toward Mais Oui*): See ya, Big Girl!

MAIS OUI: Hey, how come ya still wanna make time with her, I mean now that yer sure she ain't Queeny Kong?

SWEEP (*holding the purple rose up to Mais Oui*): The dick has its directions that *the* Direction knows not of.

Sweep ostentatiously drops the purple rose into the cuspidor that Mais Qui has placed beside herself on the shelf. A chorus of "Man Gargantuan Girl" plays softly as if to mark the end of the scene, and ends as Karma settles herself into a bored theatre spectator in the chair closest to the left wing, Clyde's previous seat.

Then eery, surrealistic mime music begins as Sweep dances slow mime steps toward Venus Fly Trap who slowly comes alive, moving arms and one leg in graceful mime movements. The two figures in tights seem now suddenly alike, Gemini-like. Sweep dances around and dangerously close to Venus. By now all the lights have dimmed, except for a purple spot on these two. Sweep stops and stares at Venus, then smacks her face.

VENUS: I the Venus Fly Trap am,
    Who you are don't mean a damn,
    Sexy Barker, Auntie Sam,
    Buster Crabbe or other ham!
    Motionless I stand in sham
    Waiting till an actor jam
    Dick into my diaphragm:
    Then on dick I sudden slam
    In my snapping snatch to cram,
    Closing up as cruelest clam—
    You don't need no diagram!

SWEEP (*looking all about her, brushing his obvious crotch up against her side*): You've nothing to be robbed of—not even virtue—so shut your trap!

VENUS: Snap!!!

One arm extends quickly and clamps on his crotch.

SWEEP: Aie! Mama-meeee!!!

He struggles to free himself but cannot.

VENUS: When from female man can't rob
    Womanhood, she'll nab his lob!
    Snap!!!

Her other arm darts out, her fingers clamping his neck.

SWEEP: And me someone who always avoided starched collars, despite my stovepipe—hat!

VENUS: One good smack deserves another Snap!!!

Her left leg shoots out and then around his thighs.

SWEEP: I don't mind a petticoat legging, but a fig leaf cov . . .

He is pulled close up against her, his words muffled.

VENUS: Snap-snap!!!

She snaps him tightly against her and clamps onto his whole body as if she were an iron vise.

SWEEP (*gasping, his voice being crushed out of him*): Gasp! Gasp! . . . mmmmmmmmmm . . . au Secours . . . gasp! . . . mumbo-jumbo . . . mmmmmmmmmm . . .

The eery, surrealistic music slowly peters out with the Chimney Sweep's breath. The purple spot on the two blinks out.

Lights softly brighten on stage left, and from the left wing, just in front of the rattan table, a bicycle built for two rides awkwardly out onto the stage.

Sister Carries, a witch doctor, is nervously steering the bike. A male actor, he is dressed in a grass skirt with shoes, socks, garters, and wears a nun's headdress; arm bands, ankle bracelets, voodoo charms; a gorilla tattoo on his chest; he is quite fierce looking (in a ludicrous way), bloody fangs protruding from the corners of his mouth. In the back seat, her hands tied behind her back, looking very 1930's, is Paulet Colbert. She has bobbed hair, is scantily attired in torn, transparent drapery, appears, in fact, to be nearly nude. The Glitzes become quite agitated when they perceive the approach of the bicycle.

MAIS OUI: Oh, look, regard, see where from the left wing, Sister Carries, apporting the latest sacrificial maiden, on his bicycle built for two comes riding!

CARRIES: Boy, if that ain't as obvious an identification line as any I fear to hear! Come here this instant, Miss Mais Oui, and help me off with tonight's sacrificial cutey.

MAIS OUI (*humming, fluttering daintly off her shelf and toward the bike*): Tra-la, tra-la, tra-la, bananas that zoom in the ring, tra-la!

CARRIES (*dismounting, humming*): But I'll be king if I'll be killed on a bicycle built for two . . .

MAIS OUI (*to Paulet*): Well, aren't you the juicy one!

PAULET (*to Mais Oui*): Don't you dare paw me, you hairy ape!

MAIS OUI: Hairy ape!—who do you think I am, William Bendix?

CARRIES: Some finesse, don't paw her, will you! A damaged sacrificial maiden is as gross an insult to the great God Kong as the fruit of the ground was to an earlier God.

PAULET *(staring at Mais Oui's peroxide gibbon headdress)*: What a situation! Hey, are you a real gibbon?

MAIS OUI: That's my God-gibbon destiny, dearie.

PAULET: Oh, yeah, if you're really a gibbon, then how come you got blond hair?

MAIS OUI: Well, I decided that I have only one life to live.

KARMA: Call that mustard-yellow lamb-shit, blond hair?

CARRIES: Lug her over here, Miss Oui *(motioning to center stage)* and aid me to pull this asbestos bikini on her.

PAULET: What a situation. Asbestos bikini?—what's that for?

CARRIES: You shall burn all the slower with an asbestos bikini on, my soon-to-be-late lovely, the more's the sacrificial fun that way. Heh, heh, heh!

MAIS OUI *(helping the resistant Paulet into the bikini)*: What's your name, dearie?

PAULET: Ona.

MAIS OUI: Ona what?

PAULET: Ona mujer.

CARRIES: Oh, he means your maiden name, silly.

KARMA: *Maiden* name?—boy, some of the people you can fool all of the time!

PAULET: My maiden name is Paulet Colbert. *(Pronounced as it would be correctly in French.)*

MAIS OUI: Paulet Colbert?—anyone would feel cold bare.

CARRIES: Yes, but she won't for long;—this stunning asbestos creation is a perfect tropical fit!

PAULET: But it itches. And ya could practically see my pyramids.

KARMA: Even a bit of your Nile.

CARRIES: Shut up, you bitches, both of you shut up!

MAIS OUI: If your name is really Paulet Colbert, you must be an actress.

PAULET *(heavy, exotic accent)*: Yez, dat is true—I haf played in many dramas, and serious tragedies.

MAIS OUI: Yeah?—name one.

PAULET: *Ben Hur.*

MAIS OUI: *Ben Hur*—shouldn't it of been *Ben Him?*

PAULET *(heavy, exotic accent)*: Certainly not—it vas the life story of Ben Gay.

CARRIES (*putting the final adjustments on the bikini and discarding the transparent drapery*): Well, you're about to play in the life story of Ben-gory-him. There, that's categorically superlative! viz., it's just so-o-o you, Paulet, and what man could ask for anything more!

PAULET: Drop dead!

KARMA: Hey, Carries, was that bikini hard to come by?

CARRIES: Not at all, I creamed in my grass skirt the second I spotted it in the store window.

MAIS OUI (*to Karma*): Wish you could whinny into something so svelte, don't cha, sour sow?

KARMA: You scheming queen!

CARRIES (*suddenly ecstatic*): Queen! Queen! The grand Queen Kong! Our gigantic god awaits the goodies! Come, the time for the offering is hard in hand, at hand!(*Turning to the shelves of Glitzes.*) O grubby Glitz Ionas, brazen brownnosers of the glamorous Conglomerate Kong, wait ye no more, but pouncing down from your precarious perches, draw ye now all around for all is in rotten readiness!

The Glitzes leap moronically from the shelves and hop about, scampering toward and around the center trio; they call out, "Ooo-ou-oop!" "Ooga-booga," "Uggerbugger," etc.

MAIS OUI: Steady, steady, girls, do not prelibate the juiciness!

CARRIES (*being bumped into*): Down, down, you dogs! Down, away, keep your distance, you ungrateful Glitz Ionas!

KARMA: Glitz Ionas?—what are they?

CARRIES: Why, don't you know?

KARMA: No.

CARRIES: Well, a Glitz is the same thing as a Fub.

KARMA: And what's a Fub?

MAIS OUI: A Fub is someone who goes around smelling bicycle seats.

GLITZES: Ooo-ou-oop! Lumper-humper! Mogombo! etc.

CARRIES (*to Karma*): You just sit on, in your box, Madame, and mind your own Modess, if you don't mind.

The Glitzes are now bounding about and grunting in free-lance confusion. Mais Oui opportunes the chaos to flirt with Brute.

MAIS OUI: Oh, you big bad furnace-fuller! How's your bulb?

BRUTE (*permitting the inspection*): Fine; how's yer socket?

CARRIES: Silence! Silence! O, gregarious Glitz Ionas! Cease off your Edenish-innocent frolicking and licking! (*The Glitzes come quickly to order.*) That's more preferable. Let us kneel now and pray together ensemble, and summon the presence of the ever-popular pagan god— QUEEN KONG!!

GLITZES: Queen Kong! Queen Kong! Queen Kong! Kong Queen!

MAIS OUI: Princess Gibbon! Princess Gibbon! Gibbon Princess!

They all kneel in a perfect semicircle about the standing Paulet, all facing the right wing, except for Mais Oui who kneels facing the audience, trying to steal the scene.

PAULET (*the essence of her thickness*): Gee, it's all kinda exciting. What a situation comedy.

MAIS OUI: Ain't excitin' for me: I seen this play before.

KARMA: You did?—what happens?

MAIS OUI: Oh, she dies in the end.

KARMA: Really? Well, at least that solves the existential problem of how to choose one's death—you end your days when they *have* to get rid of you.

CARRIES (*with astonishing solemnity; prayfully and even*):
O, matted-hair Inhuman Queen,
Best excuse for Brilliantine
That the theatre's ever seen—
We will fry in margarine
Paulet à la Mandarin—
(*thoughtfully*)
Better make it French cuisine:
She's not kosher, she's unclean.
Deus ex machina, Ape Queen!
Now upon our set convene,
Since we're but the go-between
In this 'forties flick routine . . .

MAIS OUI (*softly, pondering*): The go-between what? . . . wonder what that means? . . .

BRUTE: The go-between yer opened seam.

A preposterously loud and impressibly awkward flourish:
enter Clyde from left wing behind the table, got up with
a sun helmet with a huge feather boa, and armed with
a pistol. He fires the pistol: Mais Oui starts to her feet
and then falls in a faint.

MAIS OUI: Oh! my hairy heart!

CLYDE: Abort this sacrifice at once, you hostile Hurons!

BRUTE: Eeeeeeeeeeeeeeek! ! ! Prince Kong!

CARRIES (*furious*): What are you—an American?

CLYDE: No, I'm a New Yorker, and I've been appointed
district commissioner of this district to oversee that
plausible law and northwestern order is strictly enforced,
and I have come to stop this wanton human sacrifice and
pointless, needless spilling of human blood and bring
peace to the people!

CARRIES: Fires of de fate! The fateful grow ever laxer! The
offerings fewer and further between! Kong grows more
implacably insistent—she *demands* more female human
sacrifices! !

CLYDE: Not in my district, sister!

PAULET: Oh, my handsome interlocutory interloper!—another
two minutes and you'd have come too late!

KARMA: Yeah, how come you're so late?

CLYDE: The avant garde is always late. Did the curtain go up
at precisely 8:30, or did it not? Besides, that California
deal fell through.

KARMA: Why, weren't you discovered in Hollywood?

CLYDE: I was indeed. And brought to the city limits and
warned not to return.

CARRIES: This ceremony shall proceed as proscribed, with or
without you, Commissioner, you must adjust to your en-
vironment and the typographical peculiarities therein!

CLYDE: I must persist to insist, but this rite shan't proceed.

CARRIES (*foreign spy accent*): I am afraid, Commissar, that
in this district, you vill nefer adjust.

CLYDE: Who are you, O power-monger?

CARRIES (*pridefully*): I am Sister Carries, distinguished witch-
doctress of the Glitz Ionas.

CLYDE: Sister Carries?—are you called that because of the
indigenes traditional bad teeth?

BRUTE: Oh, no, he's called dat cause he carries syphilis.

(bending over Mais Oui.) Mae, Mae baby, get up, yer
missin' the interruption.

CLYDE: Witch doctress, eh? Well for your uptodation, Sister
Carries, and for the uptodation of all you Glitz Ionas,
the day of the witch doctress is done. All that mumbo-
jumbo bloodthirsty juju is over—gone with the Dark
Ages to which it belongs.

CARRIES: The day of the witch doctress shall never be done!
The witch doctress is possessed of Absolute Presence, he
dates from prehistoric times, he of the cavemen, he as
the cave painter, alone of the cavemen, services us today.
His magic can never diminish, he is the cynosure of
centuries, his spirit haunts and edifies generations as yet
untold. All ye others pass into nothingness, but the inde-
finable mystical emanations from the ineluctable Presence of the witch doctress defy mere eternity, they gyrate
in the completion and deletion, the yin and yang of
cosmological incomprehensibil—

CLYDE: Shut your trap, Carries, I don't buy you any more
than self-styled poet Robert Frost. I demand to know
the charge against this girl that spellbinds the lot of you
to this spot to exterminate her!

CARRIES: The charge is that she was caught stealing morphine
—and then *more* pheen!

CLYDE: Such a crime does not merit so cruel and unusual a
penalty. Your criminal code seems to lack all standard.

CARRIES: Junkel law is swift yet just. It does have a standard:
we reward the worthy and punish the dumb.

PAULET: Really! What nerve! I may not be as smart as a
porpoise, but I can spit in that cuspidor from here! And
besides, I'm still growin'.

MAIS OUI *(reviving)*: What are ya growin'?

PAULET: Tits.

CARRIES *(throwing up both arms, singing to the Marseillaise)*:
Aux arms, mes Glitz Ion!
Faites vos battions!
Seize him! Give the white fool the bums' rush! Seize
him, squeeze him, and disarm him!

*The Glitzes, who have been cowering behind Carries,
arise en masse and clumsily stampede toward Clyde with
cocked pistol.*

CLYDE: Stand back, you beasts, or I'll shoot your hirsute faces off! Back, back!

The Glitzes freeze where they are, a mountain of fur.

CARRIES: On, drive on! Who the hell wants to look at your backs! Don't be intimidated, I say! This ain't the hunting season—he dare not shoot!
MAIS OUI: Carries is correct! Drive on! Drive in!
BRUTE: Grab 'im! Grope 'im! Stamp on his pizzle!

The Glitzes surge forward; Mais Oui leaps onto Clyde, kissing, pinching him feverishly; Brute grabs his pistol, which goes off in the struggle; Mais Oui starts back at the boom and faints again.

MAIS OUI: Ooooooooooooooo!—he got me which is more than I got . . .
KARMA: Gee, it's jist like in the movies. The "B" features.
1ST GLITZ (*sitting on Clyde who has been thrown to the floor*): Gracious, yer quite a piece: now that I'm on top of you, you'll never get up!
CLYDE: With a stomach like that, it's small wonder. Release me, release me, I say, or you will curse the evil August dog-day you were born!
CARRIES: O flunky foreign imperialist, no one is here to obey you! You see, my brave Commissioner, these are not the servile tenants of your allotted district—they are Kong's fateful brownnosers, good and glorious Glitz Ionas down to the last lousy gibbon amongst 'em!
CLYDE: If you persist in this, Sister Carries, the Governor will send his men to take you. It's an unfriendly act and rank insubstantiation . . . Oooo—don't sit on that!
2ND GLITZ: What d'ya wanna do wit 'im?
CARRIES: Fetter him for now. I'll think up something suitable after our heathen rite. We'll plant him in concrete, or dump him in the quagmire out on the moody moor.
CLYDE (*being fetterd*): Now, now Carries, dont be too hasty.
CARRIES: Hastiness in creation is at the core of camp. We'll homogenize this hetero yet!
MAIS OUI (*reviving with a joyful bounce*): And now let us resume our raucous revels at the point at which we were so dashingly deterred. Places, everybody, places!

The Glitzes place Clyde, hands fettered to feet behind him, on his stomach nearly at the shoes of Karma. Then they hasten to resume their previous kneeling positions about Paulet.

KARMA (*to Clyde*): Comfy, hetero-hero?

CLYDE: I've got an itch.

KARMA: An itch to lech, you mean! Suffer in silence. Sic semper dirty old men.

PAULET: Lest aught snatch me from death's jaw, doom's my lot!

CLYDE: How do you feel about theatre now, Miss Karma?

KARMA (*yawning*): I'll tell ya, it's a drag. Bores my bubbies. I feel like nodding right out.

GLITZES (*screaming*): QUEEN KONG!! APPEAR!— DEAR!!!

A deafening clap of thunder and bongo-banging; the lights go out suddenly; the entire cast shrieks frighteningly in the dark. Then lights flash on/off with disorganized psychedelic effects.

Queen Kong appears in a sudden blinding spotlight at the back of the theatre, standing amidst a clump of foliage, apparent now for the first time. Queen Kong is played by a male actor of huge dimensions, dressed completely in the gorilla outfit so dear to Hollywood's heart; long shabby hair, fierce face, etc.; rhinestone tiara and pretty little rambling roses fixed on his head; emerald and ruby rings on his fingers and toes.

Kong, growling and roaring, pounds his chest; then the fierceness peters out into a very effeminate gesture with his hand: a broken wrist, the "violet limp wrist." Immediately, he resumes his menacing manner and menaces his way through the audience, fearfully preposterous all the way up to the stage.

At this point, a Clinic Intern, dressed in white intern's outfit, inexplicably emerges from within the audience carrying a quart jar of what appears to be a yellowish liquid. As Kong rampages his way toward the stage, the Intern begins soliciting the audience with cries of "Void a specimen! Void a specimen, please! Hurry up now!

Void a specimen!" Then the Intern also works his
way through the audience toward the stage.

*The singing and dancing of the Glitzes begins some time
before Kong and the Intern can reach the stage, creating
thereby three disorganized and chaotic effects upon the
audience at once.*

*For the stanzas beginning "Keen-prong" and "Ding-
dong" use the music for "A Bicycle Built for Two";
original music should be provided for all the other
stanzas.*

GLITZES (*singing together and dancing in a frenzy*):
    Keen-prong Queen Kong, ride on our rumpers' fat,
    Where grillas sit, there they have never shat;
      Our rear ends are soft and comfy
      And you can have a Humpfrey
        Which uses more
        Posterior
    Than a bike on whose seat you sat.
HALF OF THE GLITZES (*making a dash for the bicycle*):
    Howe'er he love feet
    No ape is complete
    Till he learn how sweet
    A bicycle seat
    Is to the elite!
KONG (*singing and gamboling in the midst of the musical
    confusion in all his immense glory*):
    The scent-quenching treat
    Of a bicycle seat!
    Grab a bicycle seat!
    Smell a bicycle seat!
OTHER HALF OF GLITZES (*rushing to the bicycle and attempt-
    ing to get at the seats which the others have removed
    from the bicycle and are busy sniffing with delirium*):
    A bicycle seat!
    It makes obsolete
    All savory meat,
    Finds roses effete
    And perfumes deceit!
BRUTE (*going into a forties tap-dance routine*):

Subtle the odor
From shy exploder.

MAIS OUI (*joining the tap-dance*):
Keen she who knoweth
What silent outgoeth.

PAULET (*high hysterical alto*):
Save me! Save me!
Army or navy!

1ST GLITZ (*going into forties jazz steps; the tap-dancers
moving off from center, but continuing to dance*):
Carbonate juices
Lacking excuses
Garner abuses!

2ND GLITZ (*joining the bebop steps, swinging with 1st
Glitz*):
How oft with looseness
Wanton profuseness
Ends in recluseness!

PAULET (*uneven hysterical alto shriek*):
Save me, O some savior!
I'll improve my behavior!

INTERN AND 3RD GLITZ (*going into Rockette leg-high-over-
head business*):
Naive to think beast
Or flipped-out artiste
Alone can find feast
In festering yeast.

4TH AND 5TH GLITZES (*joining the Rockette steps, the pre-
vious duos continuing their individual routines*):
Condemn not who may
Unwary bewray
A throne with bouquet
Of buns' exposé.

GLITZES (*half of them bounding in a circle about Kong, the
other half in a circle about the struggling Paulet*):
Ding-dong Queen Kong, sit on our faces please,
We just want to taste where we can not squeeze;
Our motives are not too naughty
Rear lips are tight and tauty,
So we'll just lick
Your toothless quick

And our appetites thus appease!

PAULET (*a cracked alto, desperate as several Glitzes begin to lay hands on her*):
Save me! Save me!
Oh, he's a knave, he
Lets me be gravy;
Bosom so sav'ry
    In a tropic oven
    There by gibbons shoven!

KONG (*rising to his gigantic height, arms benedictory, singing basso profundo with electrifying solemnity*):
Glitz and Fubs, how We adore
Praise of Our fortissimo
Fleeing leaky black-eye store:
Hence for fruit and brute we'll blow
Out Our crown posterior
Mildew where it's apropos.
Air from regal portico
On thine bike seats We'll bestow.

Kong bends his rear toward the bicycle seats appropriately placed by 1st and 2nd Glitzes; others begin to drag Paulet, terrified and screaming, toward the fireplace; the remainder dance in heathen hotness around Carries; Mais Oui makes as if to follow the instructions in Carries' lyrics, trembling tenor.

CARRIES: Strike your Ronson lighter, lass!
Quick! ignite the royal gas!
Then put torches to the flame
And we'll burn this Colbert dame:
Col' her hole and earthen heart,
Yet the spark from regal fart
Shall consume her to a cinder,
She'll go up like female tinder
Smelling to the scentless sky,
Half-completing till she die—i yi yi! . . .

Aghast, looking toward the fireplace.

I yi yi! ! !

Looking bewildered all about the stage.

STOP! ! ! Every Damn Body Stop! ! !

*The music curtails bluntly and all freeze. The Glitzes
holding Paulet drop her to the floor with a thump.
Karma, who has been sleeping since Kong's entrance,
awakens.*

CARRIES: *Where is the Chimney Sweep?!*

KONG (*after belching loudly*): Funny, didn't even miss the
creep.

INTERN (*offering the jar*): Void a specimen, Your Majesty?

KONG: Anytime.

*Taking the jar and turning around, making gestures
as if he were urinating into it; several Glitzes watch.*

BRUTE: Yeah, how about dat—where *is* da Chimney Sweep?

CARRIES: You sightless imbeciles! Where is he?

1ST AND 2ND GLITZES (*rhythmically*): We don't go. We
don't blow. Nor know. Nor know.

CARRIES: Twin tarts! What do you mean you don't know!
Hasn't he been summoned? Hasn't anyone seen him?

MAIS OUI: I might have, but he's so nowhere I wouldn't even
see him if I did.

CARRIES (*angry*): Whose deputed was it to subpoena him?

BRUTE: I don' understan' dat kinda talk.

CARRIES (*furious*): Oxymoronic slaves! ye all shall suffer the
sniffer's death save he be made instantly apparent! ! !

MAIS OUI: No, no, not the *sniffer's* death! not the *sniffer's*
death! I could never keep my tongue still for that long!

BRUTE: I'll drop sometin' heavy on it for ya, dat oughta help.

KONG (*back still turned*): The Brute is considerate.

KARMA: What's the defuculty, Sister Carries? Why did you
quit just when things were warming up?

CARRIES: What do *you* know about traditional religions? How
can we complete the mysteries without the Chimney
Sweep?

KARMA: But what do you need him for?

CARRIES: What do we need him for? ! ! Did ye all hark that
female fool? ! How can we consume Paulet Colbert in
yon fiery furnace sans a Chimney Sweep's first sweeping
the chimney clean? (*Going to the fireplace and examining it contemptuously.*) Just look at this, will you! Sotten
with soot! Crammed with ashes! Debauched with debris!
Awful with offal!

KARMA: So fancy it doesn't have to be. After all, it's the sentiment that really counts.

INTERN (*taking the filled jar from Kong*): Ridiculous! Ridiculous and dangerous! Dangerous and unhealthy! Do you know what the smut-smog level is around here?

KARMA: Sorry, I don't.

INTERN: It's 99 per cent.

CLYDE: Really?

INTERN: Yes, and do you know what smut level is considered safe?

KARMA: Sorry, I don't.

INTERN: 98 per cent.

CLYDE: Really?

KONG (*using the 3rd Glitz, who is now on all fours, as a throne, and surrounded by fawning Glitzes, now noticing Clyde for the first time*): Hmmmm . . . what heavenly citily-civilized delight have we here?

INTERN: Now if we burn one more maiden in that fireplace without having the chimney stack swept completely clean, the air pollution level in this district will go up to 100 per cent and we'll all croak of cigarette lung cancer.

KARMA: Indeed? How absorbing: statistics always are.

CARRIES: This ain't statistics, it's climatology!

KARMA: Climatology?

INTERN: Yeah, climatology. Y'see, that shows how much you know! And climatology tells us that if it weren't for the stagnant heat pockets which keep the smut pollution about two inches above our nose, because heat rises, we would all have choked and croaked long ago even if the smut level were only 97 per cent.

CLYDE: Ya live and burn.

INTERN: On the wheel of immutable fire. (*Going upstage and placing the jar in the cuspidor.*)

KONG: Hmmmm, who's the handsome young hunter, too prince a Kong at the moment to pay us any mind?

CARRIES: He is an intruder in the dirt, Queen. Permit us to attend to him anon. After such lengthy *explication sur le text*, the matter at present press is the locating of the Chimney Sweep.

BRUTE: Maybe he took da night off.

CARRIE: Impossible—at the salary we pay him?—and at the height of the sacrificial season?

BRUTE: Ya never can tell.

CARRIES: Someone *must* tell! The someone who knows where he is.

CLYDE: How do you know someone knows where he is?

KARMA: How do you know anyone knows where he is?

KONG (*rising to make an ex cathedra pronouncement*): Because someone always knows where someone else is, such is pure Cartesian logic; because anyone always knows where everyone is, as follows in undiluted Carthusian logic based on the well-known specimen theory of the sample that's amply the whole; and because we are all really one and, being one, are some and, being some, are none and so actually one and since one knows none of two, therefore one specimen knows one of one and therefore one of you knows where one another of you is right now, which is authentic cartographic logic so whoever it is had better tell Sister Carries right away and suffer no further delay. (*Heavy exotic accent.*) I haf spoken: let it be written, let it be done!

CARRIES: You heard her!

MAIS OUI: We did, but who writes around here that she can be done?

KONG (*frighteningly*): Sister Carries, We doth ordain you to launch an inquisition toute-suite to scare up the wiley knowledgeable one. I haf spoken: let it be—

CARRIES: Roger! We'll start with you (*indicating Clyde, as Kong makes a throne of 4th Glitz*), you may be the link, O pink one! Brute, get him from his shanks to his shins.

MAIS OUI: And leave the upper Cartesian point to me.

KONG (*to Mais Oui, with the alertness of jealousy*): Mind your behind, low fawning unfavorite . . .

BRUTE (*lifting Clyde to his knees*): Upsa-black-eye-daisy.

KARMA: Got ya out on the carpet now, don't they, snidey Clydey?

CARRIES: Where is the Sweep holed up?—liar, talk quickly!

CLYDE: I wouldn't know, Sister, my job don't usually bring me in contact with sweeps.

CARRIES (*smacking his face: simultaneously, Sweep smacks the face of Venus*): You lie! What is your job?

CLYDE: I'm a sponge.

CARRIES: A sponge? Don't you find it hard to get along being a sponge?

CLYDE: Well, you have to have a lot of openings. As you do.

CARRIES: How dare you? !

CLYDE: I mean, for a chimney sweep right now.

KARMA: Hot damn, what could be duller than night court!

CLYDE: Listen, Sister, I wouldn't tell you where the sweeper was even if I knew, and I do—not.

KONG: Why not, courageous hunter?

CLYDE: Because I don't endorse human sacrifices and I'm thrilled that the sweep is missing so you can't carry out yours. As a matter of chatter, Queeny, I disapprove of your religion in the altogether.

KONG: Show cause.

CLYDE: Cause it's a cult grounded on pain, on banal anal mass masochism and shady sadyism. Isn't it funny, honey, that in two thousand years of worship it shouldn't have occurred to you that pleasure can also be fun?

MAIS OUI (*meandering toward stage right*): Hear! Hear!

KONG (*eyeing Mais Oui evilly*): Fear, fear, he knows no fear, that fruity one!—Ooops, that tickles!

Kong settles back amidst his sniffing pile of Glitzes while Carries smacks Clyde's face and Sweep Venus's face. Mais Oui reaches the site of Sweep and Venus and stares curiously and bemused at Sweep's predicament. Karma is very concerned.

MAIS OUI: Hey, whatsa matter with you?—you ain't been saying much lately.

SWEEP (*gagging*): I don't have too many lines.

MAIS OUI: 'S that a fact? Wonder why not . . . And wondering why not pricketh mine deductive forte to ever higher heights. (*Circling away from stage right.*) Think I'll stick it inta the ol' Sista.

KARMA (*worried*): Wonder what that worm's upta?

MAIS OUI (*goosing Carries who, along with Clyde, is momentarily sidetracked by Glitzes sniffing about them; the much besniffed Kong sighs with stupid satisfaction*): Hey, hot hole, bottoms up!

CARRIES (*annoyed at interruption*): What gives, barren mule?

MAIS OUI (*slowly, importantly, with spy accent*): Inspector,

I imagine that I am capable of invaluable assistance . . .
(*mysteriously*) to you. I beleef I know somethink that
might interest you professionally, very much indeed . . .

CARRIES: What?

MAIS OUI (*meaningfully*): Mind if I sit down, Inspector? . . .

CARRIES: The pleasure's all mine, my mouse; don't be backward, if you can help it.

MAIS OUI (*sitting in the empty chair at the table*): I usually
am backward, in order *to* help it.

CARRIES: Now what is this unvaluable assistance that you—

MAIS OUI (*interrupting, bloated with self-importance, and
gesturing with her head at Karma in the chair beside
her*): Ever dig that dame's chapeau? . . .

CARRIES (*stretching his chin up and peering over and into
Karma's basket headdress*): Hmmmm . . . it's a veritable
horny of plenty . . .

KARMA (*more than anxious*): Clyde, Clyde!—what shall I
do?—the authorities are about to interrogate *me*!

CLYDE: Be as obvious about your activities as possible, Miss
Karma, regardless of what they are. Authority always
looks for something suspicious, not obvious.

CARRIES (*plucking the plantain out of Karma's headdress*):
Hmmm, hello, here's an obvious fruit.

MAIS OUI (*mistaking the reference, incomprehensibly*): Well!
That's Rosey! And after every time I've done—I mean,
everything I've done for him.

CARRIES: It occurs to me that the Mem-sab's objective per-
spective on this play may qualify her as one who might,
with reasonable justification, be expected to be reasonably aware of the whereabouts of the elusive Chimney-
chipper and his broom to zoom.

KARMA (*heavy Portuguese accent from here until specified*):
But, Inspector Carries, you seem to forget zat I was
dancing at zee time zat zee Chimney Sweep disappeared.

CARRIES: Such is factual accuracy. (*Holding up the plantain.*)
Is this your banana?

KARMA: Why, yez, zat's my banana: I must haf dropped it
while I was dancing.

CARRIES (*just too official to be believed*): Quite possible,
Señorita, quite possible. Except for one thing: you see,
Señorita, this is not a banana: it is a plantano.

KARMA: Oh?

CARRIES: And in this district, the only entity possessing a plantano is the Chimney Sweep.

KARMA: Oh—care for a drink, Investigator Carries? Perhaps, some liquor?

MAIS OUI: Lick 'er where?

Carries tosses Mais Oui out of the chair and sits in it himself, the height of affability, debonair beyond words; Karma applies herself to mixing juleps with feverish intensity.

CARRIES: A drink concocted by so porcelain a hand would be hard for a man of my tastes to resist.

KARMA (*straining to concentrate on the juleps*): Do your tastes incline toward zee liquid?

MAIS OUI (*from the floor, up tight*): That depends on how well you lubricate.

KARMA: May I take your headdress, Inspector Carries?

CARRIES: Where ya wanna take it?

KARMA (*straining to affect charm*): Ho-ho; I perceef you are not only wise, but witty, my dear detectif; haf a slug.

CARRIES (*ignoring the glass she offers him, forcing himself closer upon her*): I prefer a hug.

KARMA: But a drink in time safes nine—nine months. (*Quakingly nervous, rattling the table.*) I should be quite offended if you decline my barmaid art.

CLYDE (*warningly, regarding the tête-à-tête with fiancé concern*): Full many a maid by the bar was made.

CARRIES: I'm afraid, Señorita, but I must resist the gratuities. You understand that a man in my precarious position is not infrequently confronted with treachery—in the guise, shall we say . . . of exquisite beauty?

KARMA: Why, Detectif Daring, you could not possibly implicate—

CARRIES (*sudden angry reversal to his old self*): I implicate nothing; I don't swill on the job, that's all!

CLYDE (*wishing to break them up*): How about getting back to the plantain business, Carries?

CARRIES: And so now, concerning the plantano, Señorita—

KARMA: Ah, yez, I find it most divertingly curious zat in this district zee Chimney Sweep alone should be possessed of zee plantano. It makes a most divertingly fascinating conversation piece—especially wit mint juleps, don't you think so, Inquisitor?

CARRIES: It is more than a conversation piece, Chica, it is one of the pointed facts of life!

KARMA: How so?

INTERN: The plantano was a present personally presented to the Chimney Sweep by Her Regal Brutishness, Queen Kong.

KARMA (*subtle sarcasm*): Sounds generous.

KONG (*solemn, profound*): It was. We took it from the tallest tree nest in the majestic bestiary where We cache Our gynecologist-fiitted masturbating material.

MAIS OUI: Wonder how much cash ya could get for it?

KARMA (*shocked*): Gynecologist-fitted *masturbating* material?

INTERN: What is so shocking? Masturbation is America's only innovational contribution to world culture.

KONG (*to Clyde*): Hey, Muskels, wanna make me after court?

CARRIES (*upset*): *Miss* Kong, court has not yet adjourned! Please desist from these spicy interjections and assist me in maintaining the dignity of this seedy proceeding!

KONG: Proceed, Sister.

MAIS OUI (*examining the plantain, which she has picked off the table*): Wonder what the proceeds are on a thing like this? Wonder what kinda seeds it got?

CARRIES: And so, Guwappa, do you still detain your preposterous maintain that you know not the Sweep and did not obtain this plantain from him?

KARMA: Now actually I did spot this zo-call Sweep, but only briefly, and paid him little mind: you see, he was so out of place on this set, what with his weird mime-immodest getup, zat I figured he was just a tourist.

KONG (*working himself up against Karma because of his attraction to Clyde*): How brief could your encounter with him have been, that you had time to con him out of the precious plantain which We personally took from Our parts to bestow on him?

MAIS OUI: Bestowed yer parts on him, did ya?

KARMA (*standing in her fear, reverting to her natural voice*): But this is unspeakably ineffable! It surpasses credence! The Sweep doesn't even know who Kong is! You all, every last loon of you, lack linkage, lack logic.

BRUTE: Naturally, my queer, we're only gibbons. Except for Queeny, she's a grilla.

KARMA: But how does having the Chimney Sweep's plantain mean that I know where he disappeared to?! Somewhere in your reasoning, there's a terrible error!

INTERN: Why do people always think that the thing most difficult for one to effect, is an error?

KARMA (*hysterical, rushing to Clyde*): Oh, help, Clyde, help!

CLYDE (*struggling in his fetters*): Karma! My life's karma! My only karma—huge as it is!

KONG (*with terrifying authority*): We'll take over this obsidianly obliquitous inquisition! Cut that nose-newsing out, will you? Listen, you Brazilian torpedo-hanger, did that Sweeper ever buy you anything?

KARMA (*simpering*): Yes, Mrs. Cross, he did.

KONG: Ah-ha! What!

KARMA: A malted.

Long pause.

INTERN: Chocolate?

KARMA (*simpering*): What does it matter?—you'll find me guilty whatever flavor it was.

KONG (*to Clyde*): Mister Muskels, is this hussy your fiancée?

CLYDE (*meekly*): One might so define her.

KONG: That settles it! Seize her! Seize her! Sacrifice her!

1ST GLITZ (*pushing his way through the crowd toward Karma*): One minx, methinks, is as good as the other mother . . .

INTERN: But Queen K., the air pollution level! The smut rate!

KONG: What care I? I care not! I do not give a good—

CARRIES (*rushing to Kong*): The slut—er, the smut percent Sage—

KONNG (*kicking him with royal fury*): Shut your competitive, repetitive trap! Get the hell out of my hair, fuckface!

CLYDE (*wormwise in his fetters, working his way toward Kong's feet, while several Glitzes lay greedy hands on Karma*): O awesome Ape, reconsider: I at Thy corn-encrusted feet for the lady's life do implore Thee!

KONG (*sudden switch*): Hmm, kinda sexy grovelin', ain't he?

CLYDE: Thou wilt share, er, spare her?

KONG: What balls! Spare her, so *she* can have ya?

CLYDE: For mine unlinked line and pitiable pipe's sake!

INTERN (*pleading*): There are no lines, only a circle, but still, for sake of the smut rate!—on the present date!

GLITZES (*chanting rebelliously*): THE SMUT RATE! WE TOOK OF LATE! FOR KONG-GOD'S SAKE! WE'LL ALL CROAK! IT AIN'T A JOKE!!

Long pause. The chanting echoes out.

KONG: Grrrooooowl! Grrrrrrrrr! Aaaaaagh! Popular opinion seems to run contrary to Our holy Person.

MAIS OUI: And you *do* wanna win next year's popularity poll!

KONG: Such is accuracy. Our august person shall reconsider: Tell ya what.

ALL: WHAT?

KONG: We'll schedule our heathen rite for 10:40. You have a menstruation period of grace from now until then, Prince Kong, in which to bleed out, er, cough up the Sweep. Brute, unfetter him!

BRUTE (*obeying the order*): Jist a minute, Pepe, and ya'll be able to git up and walk away, like a pair o' dirty gym socks, on yer own accord . . .

KONG: If you find the Sweep in the time allotted, this Karma character shall thereby be proved exonerate of guilt and set footloose and fancy-dancing free. And you may marry her.

CLYDE (*freed of his fetters*): And if I fail to locate the Sweep?

KONG: Then the pagan pleasures will come off as scheduled —exactly at 10:40. We shall have a Gemini sacrifice: both Paulet Colbert and Karma Miranda will be spectacularly burnt to death!

CLYDE: But in that event, we'll all suck come to lung cancer!

KONG: Well, We hate to be callous, Maria Callous, but that's how it gotta be. If I can't have you, nobody will. (*Bursting into ditty with sentimental Victorian tune.*)
> If I can not have you,
>   The Rose toward Divine,
> No human shall have you:
>   I ain't asernine!

MAIS OUI AND BRUTE (*singing*):
> Dry Gulch, let me fit you
>   And fill your incline,
> For plantain shall split you

                    At base of the spine.
GLITZES AND INTERN (*singing*):
                    My Spoke, it's to stop you
                    From female supine:
                    A hub soon atop you,
                    A pearl under swine!
CLYDE: It don't make sense. You sing that you want me, but
    the alternatives are—
INTERN: But it does make sense—that's just what's wrong
    with it. Sense, like the mule, manages no young.
MAIS OUI (*near stage right, to Sweep*): You sleeping?
SWEEP: No, dreaming.
MAIS OUI (*picking up a roll of toilet paper next to Sweep's
    unmoving foot*): What? (*Sadly, almost depressed, shak-
    ing her head at Sweep.*) Has it come to this?
CARRIES: It's gonna be a long hot summer, Commissioner!
CLYDE (*confused*): Watts?
KONG: Grrooooowl! Aaaaaaaaagh! Now Our pristine court
    adjerns for supper. Tonight, gourmet treats. (*Suggest-
    ively*) So We'll see a few of you Fubs in Our private
    quarters. Brute, return the Bwana's pistol. He and his
    heart have a confrontation coming up. We reconvene at
    10:30. (*Alter time to exact time of reentrance.*)
CARRIES: Take the broads as hot ages; let's go.

    *Brute gives pistol to Clyde. 1st and 2nd Glitzes revive
    Paulet and then take hold of her and Karma and drag
    them toward downstage left. 3rd and 4th Glitzes refix
    the seats on the bicycle. Intern helps the demoralized
    Carries onto the front seat.*

KARMA: Take yer young paws offa me—I know howda wheel!
2ND GLITZ: Yeah, but we're gonna wheel ya to the last stop!
    And what d'ya mean young? In a few years, I'll be older
    than you.
PAULET: Maybe we'll be rescued by a Buddhist uprising.
KARMA: Buddhist uprising?—what's that—another contra-
    diction in terms?
CARRIES: Thanks, bottle-boy. Hop on, Mae, I'll drive ya home.
MAIS OUI (*complying*): That's what usually happens when I
    hop on.
SWEEP (*shouting across to Mais Oui*): Bring back something
    sixteen and nice, will ya?

CARRIES (*having trouble with the bicycle*): Who *is* he yellin'
to! Gotta get my crotch—crutch relined.

MAIS OUI: The ride I got, but moving I'm not.

KONG (*a bitter dig at Carries*): He'll get that bike started;
he's not a person to rest on his laurels.

MAIS OUI (*kicking-him-when-he's-down*): He's not a person.

CARRIES: There we go; hang on!

MAIS OUI (*hands clasped on Carries' crotch*): Ooo—yer in
reverse!

KONG (*the Glitzes having difficulty in carrying him out*):
Girls, girls, lemme go out on my own gas!

*All head for the exit downstage left: Carries riding the
bicycle out, the Glitzes dragging the women, Kong attempting it on his exhaust like a rocket; they all sing
as they grandly exit.*

GLITZES, ETC. (*singing*):
> If I try to steal you
>   And, Rose, make Divine,
> Ought Smacker conceal you
>   In sexual shrine?

> If I must eschew you,
>   Forever resign
> To be without yoo-hoo,
>   Beware the malign!
>   Beware the malign!
> AND WATCH YOUR BEHIN'!!

CLYDE (*sorrowfully alone and bewildered center stage*):
There is just so much space on this stage, so much and
no more, but I wouldn't know where to begin to look
for that ratty Chimney Sweep. I can't think of a thing
to do. Thank God Kong this is the end of Act One.

*Clyde crosses quite close to Sweep and Venus and squats
on the floor beside them with desolate expression. Eery
mime music plays softly. Clyde rubs his cheek as if in
thought or soothing a smack. Venus intones, but is apparently unheard by Clyde.*

VENUS: Cheeky he to whom is aught
Alien in an'mal thought;
Sim'lar he who beastly instinct

Thinks mere love of licking sin-stink.

KONG (*peering around the corner of the cage, baiting Clyde very coyly*): Yoo-hoo, soldier boy!

CLYDE (*bitchy, as the mime music suddenly stops*): Whatsa matter, forget your purse?

KONG (*coyly*): Oh, please, squeezey please, handsome, don't be curt, Kurt Douglas, with me.

CLYDE: I ain't curt—I'm concerned.

KONG (*emerging from behind the cage*): 'Bout what? Tell mama what's on yer mindy-blindy like a good little boy.

CLYDE: I'm concerned about what's in store for them two peppery numbers.

KONG: Any man worth his salt would be. But there's nothin' to worry about. I seen this play before—

CLYDE: Yeah, I know, and they both die in the end. Well in that case, just stick to the other side of the stage, if ya know what's good for you.

KONG (*genuinely offended*): I really don't know what's wrong with me: people always look at me as if they've seen something I can't bear.

CLYDE: Uglier than a bear. Keep to your corner.

KONG: Oh, please be curt-eous: I readily acknowledge that I was once quite dangerous, but I'm changed now, really.

CLYDE: You're changed now! What were you like *before*?

KONG (*deep alluring feminine advertising voice*): Well, you see, before it was all very like before . . . Compoz . . .

CLYDE: Who *are* you, anyhow?

KONG (*very effeminate*): I'm Brod.

CLYDE: Brod?

KONG (*coyly effeminate*): Brod Crawford. Joan's my sister.

CLYDE (*sarcastic*): Is she? Well, just keep your distance.

KONG: Gawd! you make me feel like Quasimodo!

CLYDE: That's gawd, cause ya look like him.

KONG: How dare you, how double-dare you, how gemini-dare you! I am not Quasimodo, I am Queen Kong!

CLYDE: You may be Queen Kong to them gullible gibbons, but yer just a plain ol' grilla to me. In fact, ya look like a grilla queen to me.

KONG (*feminine indignation*): I am not a gorilla queen—I'm Venus in Furs, I'm a hairy lady, I'm the Lady in the Pelt!—The Lady in the Pelt, do you hear me, care for a little leather and discipline?

CLYDE: No thanks: I'm too young to go out with grillas—
even if they *are* a lady.

KONG: You'll regret this rejection, O cold, short, and unob-
tainable one: remember, only I hold the key to the late
fate of those damsels in distress.

CLYDE: Such is accuracy; I shall reconsider; what do you want
me to do?

KONG: Be a little less chaste; be a little more cha*sing*.

CLYDE: O.K., you call the tune.

KONG (*joyously obsequious*): Oh, sir! Will you be wanting
me for fifteen minutes, sir, or for the whole night?

CLYDE: That depends on the first fifteen minutes.

KONG (*pulling out the nearest chair from the table*): Well,
then, come over here and sit on my face, I mean, my
lap like a good little dog.

CLYDE (*crossing toward Kong seating himself*): I'll screw
anything once. Besides, ya could only screw it up. (*Sitting
on Kong's lap.*) Well, ya gotta eat a pound of dirt before ya die.

KONG (*lifting a doily off the table*): Here, have a derly.

CLYDE: No thanks, I don't go in for that frilly fruit stuff.

KONG: I am certain. (*Trying to employ the rejected doily as
toilet paper, having some difficulty in rising slightly
from the chair since Clyde is securely in his lap and
quite obviously not willing to facilitate matters.*)

CLYDE (*like a psychiatrist*): Now, Madame, since this is your
first visit, please tell me just what is bothering you.

KONG: To begin with, you have too much karma—karma
Miranda.

CLYDE: We'll discuss my philosophical shortcomings at some
future fate, if you don't mind. What else?

KONG: So for another thing, seeing as how us two've finally
gotten ends to meet, so that I be made not to feel altogether too self-consciously hirsute, I'd like to see you
grow a beard; a huge heavy grizzly beard.

CLYDE: What! grow a beard and ruin my eighteen-year-old
image?

KONG (*catty*): Your image is eighteen years old?

CLYDE: A queen is a queen is a queen, isn't he? What else?

KONG: Oh, it's kind of excruciating to put into words.

CLYDE: Well, it should be put into something. Besides, the
Word *was* made flesh; so why not reverse the—

KONG: Yes, that's more or less what I'm trying to get around
to; I do so hate to beat around the bush.

CLYDE: Yes, it's better to go right in. One in the bush is
worth two in the hand.

KONG (*coyly*): You embarrass me, Clydey cutey. I hope you
realize I was innocent until quite recently.

CLYDE: Oh? so you've been making up for lost time?

KONG (*peeved*): Not quite; I've been losing it again:

CLYDE: With a mug like yours, lousy lady, it's small wonder.
You've probably got lice in your face.

KONG (*angry*): Don't get so uppity—just remember, shrimpy
dick, you can always be replaced by a shrinker!

SWEEP: Yeah, don't get so uppity—bail out when you gain
elevation.

KONG: No need!:—he's bailing out right now!

*Kong rises with a swift thrust, catapulting Clyde to the
floor. The table shakes violently in the upset and Kong
bends over it to catch the spilling glasses: in this ma-
neuver Kong's rear end is directly on line with Clyde's
face, sitting as he is on the floor.*

CLYDE (*his nose practically in the huge backside*): Hmmmm
. . . the black hole of Calcutta . . .

KONG: *Quelle insulte noire!* You disapprove of my other side?

CLYDE (*his nose still buried, his hands supporting the huge
buttocks*): Oh, no, I'm glad for *both* of you!

KONG (*turning to face him, furious*): *Both* those girls *will*
perish! I have decreed it and I'll not be deterred from
my decreation!

CLYDE: All right, big boobs, then fend for your front without
my titillations! And that's final!

KONG (*quickly regretful, hovering over Clyde, running fingers
through his hair*): Oh, Clydey-boo, don't be peeved—
your overtaxed nerves are just overwrought, that's all.
I didn't mean to be snappish with you, honest to Betsy—

CLYDE: Get your hairy hand outta my hair.

KONG: But, Diminutive One, I just love your silken locks!

CLYDE: You do?—you oughta try my bagels.

KONG (*purring*): Mmmmmmmmmm, purrrrrrrr, poor bébé,
gimme a kiss?

CLYDE (*calculating*): I'm game . . . turn your back . . .

KONG: But, Princeling, one's ill-advised to turn his back on anything around here.

CLYDE: Now, now, Lady in the Pelt, don't you trust me?

KONG: Of course, but—

CLYDE: Then face the cuspidor and stop giving me a hard time.

KONG: I hope you don't give *me* a hard time.

CLYDE: Few they be, could show hard for you . . . (*He rises slowly from the floor as Kong about faces.*) Yet I can . . . *kick a can!*
(*He rams mightily into Kong's rear with his left boot and, as Kong falls flat on his face, hurriedly picks up the overturned chair and whips out his pistol.*)

KONG (*exotic accent*): You ram treezon! treezon on Her Royal Majesty! Seedy, blood-sucking—

CLYDE (*handling the chair and pistol like a lion trainer as Kong fixes on all fours*): Steady . . . steady, big girl . . . (*Circling slowly about Kong as in a circus ring.*) You have failed to make mental note, haven't you, that famed Clyde Batty is also an accomplished animal trainer?

KONG: How could I? I don't date back to them thirties flicks.

CLYDE: Woulda been worth yer wiles to've sat up and caught a few of 'em on the late show . . . Steady now, big gal . . .

KONG (*twisting torturously within the circle like a baited bear*): Unfledged wingling! Sadistic pipsqueak! I could malleate you with a single blow—they got *that* on the late show too—*Mighty Josephine Young, Daughter Ape*—

CLYDE (*narrowing his circle, nervously, professionally, and altering it as Kong takes several cautious steps toward him*): Quiet, quiet now, enough lip for one act . . . Easy does it, ol' bag, take it easy . . . that's it . . . ah . . . nothin' simpler than animal trainin'—like narrowin' in nervously on the precarious petals of the multifidous rose . . .

KONG: Oh, the humiliation, oh, the disgrace! Royalty debunct! Regality ruined! Majesty in the mud!

CLYDE: Easy, bitch, easy . . . Now—roll over, roll over, baby . . .

KONG (*indignant*): I most certainly will not! (*Making a sud-*

den lunge at Clyde.) I'll stamp you out, you pigmy! you praying manta!

CLYDE (*ramming the chair into Kong's belly*): Back, piglet, back!

KONG (*retreating*): Groooooooooowwwwlllllll!!!! Aaaaaaaagh!!!

Clyde aims his pistol at Kong and is about to shoot; suddenly the Intern drops down from within the chimney stack into the hearth.

INTERN: CLYDE BATTY, DON'T SHOOT!! The Park Department is on strike and there'll be no one to carry off the corpse. The mayor urges you not to litter until further notice.

CLYDE: Glad ya told me. I like to keep an eye on city ordinances. What citizen worth his dicker doesn't?

INTERN: Carry on. Oh, er, Kong, roll over like the man says.

The Intern disappears up the chimney stack. There is a long bewildered pause. Finally, Kong sinks to the floor. Another pause, torturously long, then Kong rolls over, arms and legs thrown in the air. Clyde's glance, scanning the stage, lights on the cage.

CLYDE: Hello, what's this? Ah, yes, the perfect litter basket! (*Edging toward the cage as Kong completes the roll.*) Again, Kong, again, please. (*Backed up against the cage as Kong, all too humanly, repeats his humiliation as best he can, the last vestige of his dignity being his gagged silence.*) Now, Queen, stand on your crown! Facing wing left.

KONG (*pitifully*): But I can't. I'm too fat for that.

CLYDE: Stand on your hard head, I say, or I'll ignore that new ordinance and you'll lie flat on your flabby butt from now till the Forest Forever!

(*Kong, turning his back on Clyde, attempts to obey the command; bulking and clumsy, he cannot, but tries and pitifully tries time and again. As soon as Kong is busied, Clyde puts down the chair and begins hacking away at the foliage that camouflages the huge cage. He topples over one potted plant after another, bulrushes, ivy, and grape vines in particular. Kong is oblivious to all noise.*)

CLYDE: Cumbersome tropical undergrowth! Hack it down
and a day later it's taller than yer tit!

VENUS: Note how, slaughtering, he knaws
Closer to my man-clampt claws!

CLYDE: Lurid vegetation of the torrid zone! Humid, rainy,
salivary climate—that's what shoots it up.

VENUS: But my grappling grasp is full,
Sweep ingesting, cock 'n bull!

CLYDE: Flunky's work this is, chopping the tangle. But if I
savvy that ordinance correctly, I've gotta cut this cage
free—and in a fat-ass hurry. That dumb grilla ain't
gonna be turnin' tricks all day, dig?

VENUS (*trembling*): "Human trap is Zoo of Age
And vice reverses," versed the sage.
Yet Venus Trap by circus cage
Soon shalt be dead foliage!

CLYDE (*reaching Venus and Sweep*): Get a loada that, will
ya! Boy, but they got some strange growths around these
parts. What'll nature thinka next? An Aphrodite in
fly-fur, no doubt!

(*Clyde hacks at Venus with his pistol: her arms, legs
and body fall limp, appear to wither under the assault;
slowly she crumbles to the floor, releasing Sweep who
also seems all but dead.*

VENUS: Moon! at leaf and trap he hacks,
Urine-drinking root attacks!
One! two! three! the fatal cracks!
Dealt as to sane bric-a-bracs
Who, of all the cul-de-sacs,
Chose the right-wing, far from quacks,
Far from the jar of maniacs
Pickled by the zodiacs!

SWEEP (*falling with Venus, but still managing to smack her*):
Female plant! who man ransacks,
Dying, still you merit smacks!

VENUS: Smack thy last, seed-sowing Sweep,
Every night. And now to sleep.

SWEEP (*painfully, before expiring beside the motionless Ve-
nus*):
Love! I lack all lust to rise:
Here must lie till my demise . . .

CLYDE (*pulling on the cage door*): Heavens' Totality! never dreamt a door could be this stuck. Gotta have the pull of a bull to budge it.

The cage door gives begrudgingly with a frightfully loud as well as peculiar [onomatopoeic in keeping with the themes] noise which alerts Kong and curtails his essays at head-standing.

KONG: There's something fishy in the district of Denmark . . . I smell a pussy, I mean, rat! (*Turning around, spotting Clyde busy at the door.*) Ah-ha! guard's down and the table's turned! Aaaaaaaaagh!!

CLYDE (*unaware of Kong's stretching to his full terrifying stature*) The junkel abounds with strange sounds tonight. Many very curious ejaculations.

Kong charges across the stage like an elephant stampede, shrieking and scream-growling at lung's loud top; just as he is about to pounce upon Clyde and shred him, Clyde turns calmly, distractedly, about, daze-eyed at Kong's middle, and says:

CLYDE: Got a dime? I'm short.

KONG (*stopping dead in his tracks, completely stymied*): I'm tall. But hold on a minute. (*Fingering his hairy hips as if searching pockets.*) Gee, I was sure I had one . . .

CLYDE (*circling the preoccupied Kong, so that Kong is between him and the open cage*): Whadda ya doin'?

KONG: Looking for the star in the sapphire.

CLYDE (*landing Kong in the cage with a well-rammed goose*): Back up on a nail and yer flat in rear gear! (*Slamming the cage door shut and bolting it.*) Ho ho! ever consider hibernating, butterfly?

KONG (*turning, grasping the cage bars*): Butterflies come after hibernation. I'm stunned.

CLYDE (*just too satisfied*): Penny for your stunning thoughts.

KONG: From a guy what don't got a dime to his name? Hey, lemme loose!—whatcha take me for, a barmaid?

CLYDE (*smacking his hands together and dusting his finger tip*): Know somethin', Kong baby, I'm gettin' pretty sick and tired of all these double entendres.

KONG: They ain't double, they're triple—triple sec.

CLYDE: Sex?

KONG: Sec, I said. Triple sec. *Ménage à trois.*

CLYDE (*cocking his pistol*): Hummm-gun, a fly trapped Venus with Furs. Ready for a little leather and discipline?

KONG: Hey, wait! whatcha doin' with that plantain, er, pistol?

CLYDE: Ah-ha!—another fraudulent slip!

KONG (*quaking*): Muskels, you ain't bein' very social!

CLYDE: To a grilla? Why should I? Grillas, like chimpanzees and orangutans, ain't social animals.

KONG: But my people, the gibbons, is: they cohabit in herds.

CLYDE (*aiming the pistol*): We ain't discussin' your people now.

KONG (*horrified*): Asocial sore-thumb! Outcast of the cosmos! What gives you jurisdiction over your immanent atrocity?!

CLYDE: I am Clyde Batty, the *great* Clyde Batty, by Hollywood given the jurisdiction to corner, capture, and round up all—to cage, categorize, and define!

KONG (*sinking to his knees, imploring hysterically*): Listen, Mr. Batty, hear me, don't fire! We could still make it, you and I, all things are conceivable, all concei—

CLYDE: Man and manthropoid make it?—don't be sick!

KONG (*arms stretching out of the cage, hands claspt in prayer*): Bide a bit, let me tell you how I've heard of even humans often having sex—one holds the other's hand, lying both in bed, and comes, arrives, achieves orgasm, without further contact!

CLYDE (*unimpressed*): Now dig the hard-on facts, Miss Throwback—Sister Carries, backed by the gibbons, is dead against the burning of the babes because of the deadly air pollution level. That leaves you, and you alone, still motivated to this murder. Which means that if there is no Kong—

INTERN (*voice from within the fireplace*): There'll Always Be a Kong!!!

CLYDE (*unperturbed*):—there is no warming of the hearth. So beat your bubbies and growl your glam-lust last: thy omophagic reign is run!—unles you wanna alter your brainchild right this second?

KONG: I'd sooner alter my string of studs than turn you over to that Karma dame! —Junior, if you slaughter me, you'll be left all alone in the treacherous tropical rain forest:

tell me, just tell me what you'd do if a serpent were to sting your pecker?

CLYDE (*offhand*): Sit down and smoke a cigarette, seein' as how it would probably be my last.

KONG: You do that and you're a better woman than I am.

CLYDE (*stepping downstage, deeply involved and thinking out loud*): Funny, but looking at her locked up in there looking out at me, reminds me of the time I once visited a chicken farm. There was a long, long two-story coop with endless windows on the second floor and on each windowsill a dozen white hens were perched, and all of them hanging out and looking straight down at me, at you. The looniest sight I've ever seen, but all those white chickens were staring me down as if I were the loony one . . . Made ya feel kinda peculiar, it did, ya know what I mean?—sorta crazy . . . (*About facing quickly, firing the pistol directly at Kong*) Fire-arm, speak for me!!!

Percussions echo the pistol shot to deafening pitch. Kong leaps back and stiffens, hands over his bleeding face.

CLYDE: Spit in the cusp!—A perfect shot!—Right in the face!

A moment of pregnant silence. Then drums and percussions of thunderous force; lights blink blindingly like the Lord's wrath come visual; all deaden except for a red spot on Kong who staggers and collapses over a hay heap and banana peels within the cage.

KONG (*expiring, his spot dimming*): Of . . . the sciences . . . anthropology . . . is . . . my favorite . . .

CLYDE (*delivering a funeral oration as the red spot brightens on him*): Ladies and gentlemen of every genus, the Great Kong *was* great: she was a great queen and a great lover. She took over a million gibbons and humans up to her treetop nest during her long and lusty career. But I, myself, just couldn't make it with her: you see, where I come from, animals as well as people are taught to keep their place. For beast is beast and nest is nest and never the sane shall invest in the twain. A line is a line

and division division and woe be to he who holds deri-
sion toward either. And neither shall lessen but both
find a blessin', if brute in the junkel stays and man goeth
separate ways.

*A noisy shuffle within the cage; the spot inky-dinkys
across stage to investigate the disturbance; it picks out
the furry junk pile from which stumblingly emerges
Taharahnugi White Woman, dusting long hairs and
patches of fur off his sarong; a bit shakey.*

TAHARAH: Some costume change, that one—a pain in de
neck. I shed eet like serpent skeen, like steef cacoon. Is
like a woolen dress—beleef you me, eet itches, like a
son of a—

CLYDE (*a second spot on his pale expression, wild, agonized,
as he attempts to escape stage left, but fails, being par-
tially paralyzed; he sings to "A Bicycle Built for Two"*):
      Crazy! crazy! like from a rabies kiss!
      I'm Clyde Batty sighting the savage Miss;
        I have heard of lycanthropy,
        But this can make ya dopey:
            What I had seen
            As grilla queen,
      Was a girl in her chrysalis!

TAHARAH (*unbolting the door, smoothing the bolting bar in
his embrace*):
      Full many a maid by de bar was made,
        But who haf de hole
        Could rigormarole
      A beauty like theez when she laid?

CLYDE: I'm pistil-happy, stigma-stung! A *stone-fuckken-nut!!!*

TAHARAH (*stepping out of the cage*): No, you're not, Bwana.
Theez is de lackadizzical heat-depleting torrid zone: is
not way up Nort where people haf de energy to go mad.

CLYDE: I don't—I won't believe it!

TAHARAH (*lifting up his tight sarong*): What, de torrid zone?
Then, Bwana, allow me to reveal *my* torrid zone.

CLYDE (*as Taharah advances*): From chrysalis to Charybdis!

TAHARAH (*throwing his arms around Clyde, the bolting bar
caught between them*): Junior speak many beeg words.
But Taharahnugi White Woman prefer he carry beeg
steeck.

CLYDE: But, but, Too-hairy-nugi Double Double You, how'd
    you come outta that pen—it was Queen Kong I locked—

TAHARAH: Simple—she married his mama, and out came I.
    You not like the outcame of inbreeding?

CLYDE: No more than Ivan de Carlo likes Mona Liar.

TAHARAH: Taharahnugi no say lie; she not fibber. People who
    lif a fib end their ends on de Bowery.

CLYDE (*tearing himself out of the embrace*): Yet can it be
    that—that after all this, YOU are Kong? Tell me, tell
    me quickly, are *you* Kong? No, no, it can't be, you musta
    been holed up in that cage all along!

TAHARAH: Haf you nefer read *Darwin, dar*-link?

CLYDE: Natural selection is not my specialty, I'm rather in-
    discriminate about whom I choose to ball, but—there's
    such a difference—I mean!—Kong had all that hair, I
    mean where I know for a fact you don't!

TAHARAH: J. R. Marett explains that since iodine deficiency
    causes baldness, humans lost their hair through "the
    need to economize iodine and adapt an anthropoid body
    to a life on the treeless alp of a young mountain system."
    Since salivary tropical rain forest rains in the pluvial
    period engendered an acidity of the soil and an accumu-
    lation of iodine later reduced through the merciless,
    pass-waterless increasing aridity—

CLYDE: Stop telling malicious truths, woman, they're as clear
    as (*shaking the bolting bar at Taharah*) this stick in
    yer muddy hole! Heavens to Betsy's Totality! to think
    that I tried to croak what was actually a human being,
    caged, defenseless—

TAHARAH: Oh, do not keen ofer a dead queen. Instead, be
    oferjoy ofer my emanation from her body like a omniv-
    orous prince from a frugivorous frog.

CLYDE (*jumping on top of the table to avoid Taharah's
    clutch*): I'm losing my bird, that's all: I'm stark raving
    nuts!!

TAHARAH: Talk no more of your nuts, leetle screwel: you haf
    seen nuff movie on de late as well as early show to
    know exactly how theez transformations occur. Nuff's
    too much.

CLYDE: Yeah, but this here's the kinda thing don't matter
    how many times ya see it ya still can't believe it.

TAHARAH (*tugging on Clyde's right boot, pulling it off*):

Muskels, your attenuated nonsuspension of beleef is drag
on de audience: anyone wit haf a brain in theez jernt
figger out my efolution way back in Act One. So quit
labor—

CLYDE (*concluding, imitating*): Wit de pernt? Hey, whatcha
doin'?—Hopin' against hope for a prehensile foot?

TAHARAH (*pulling off his sock*): Generally, I'd stoop to con-
quer more confentionally, (*pointing his chin up toward
Clyde's thighs*) but you too-too high up and too-too
far ofer for that!

CLYDE: Then jist which innovation have you in heart, Miss
Mange?

TAHARAH: I thought I'd get a leak, er, look at de nur between
yer toes—

CLYDE (*yanking his naked foot away from Taharah's grasp
and bending it up into the cupping protection of his
own hands; shocked*): The nur between my toes?????

TAHARAH (*his feelings hurt*): Ees only natural. Ain't us all
de go-between angel and earth, expression and suspension?

CLYDE (*cringing as before a leper*): Now wait a minute—
what other talents in this category do you decline toward?

TAHARAH (*intimidated, very tentatively*): . . . I could eat de
cottage cheese out of a dead gibbon's jockstrap . . .

CLYDE (*letting go of his foot in catatonic disbelief*): The
only thing wasp about *you* is yer waist!

TAHARAH (*seizing the foot*): What's theez? You've a webbed
toe!!

CLYDE: A web between two toes: not much room for nur, is
there?

TAHARAH: How long haf you had theez?

CLYDE: Since I was born. What of it?

TAHARAH (*to audience*): Girl, deed I get roped in! Not so
high up on de tree of efolution himself, is he, theez Mr.
Muskelar Halfback!

CLYDE: Never claimed to be more than halfway back; but
that's still a branch above you, a grilla girl!

TAHARAH: Or beneat me: depend which met-trick system you
exploit.

CLYDE: Here, man, help me down.

TAHARAH: How can I?—I'm not your inferior.

CLYDE: But you are, because I've asked you to be my butler.

TAHARAH: That's not your subtlest, but it ees at your best.

*Suddenly the "Tales from the Vienna Woods" waltz is
heard, "sung" to by the Hartz Mountain Master Ca-
naries [whose sound may be approximated by toy bird
whistles]. Clyde and Taharah listen to the first chorus
in bewilderment, acknowledgment, and finally ecstasy;
they join to sing the chorus as it is repeated.*

CLYDE AND TAHARAH (*singing*):
    The Forest, Forest Forever,
    The Forest, Forest Forever,
    As brought to you by Hartz Mountain,
    Is sung by Master Canaries,
    Hartz Mountain Master Canaries.
    Hartz Mountain Master Canaries
    Sing the Song of Kong clad in white sarong
    And the empty cuspidor
    That contains the World and more:
    Urine specimen, urine specimen,
    Ample sample of the hole;
    Trinity of sex and soul:
    Plantain, the jar, and the rose—Amen!
TAHARAH (*singing to "Yes, We Have No Bananas Today,"
    and dance-stepping toward right wing as at the end of
    a vaudeville soft-shoe routine*):
    Yez, we haf no buwanas today,
        (—I better beat it!)
    We lost both our gambit and lay!
CLYDE (*jumping down from the table*): Hey, where you
    going?
TAHARAH: Just going, not waiting.
CLYDE (*grabbing onto Taharah's long wig*): Wait a minute.
TAHARAH: What for?
CLYDE: I need you.
TAHARAH: I mean, what are you waiting for?
CLYDE: I'm waiting for the Chimney Sweep to show; or for
    those Glitz Ionas to get here ahead of him. —Gulp!
TAHARAH: Hear me, Bwana, hear me good: ain't no such
    think as waiting *for* any-sink: waiting *ees.*
CLYDE: How d'ja mean?
TAHARAH: Some pataphysician! I taught you went to Barn-
    yard? Ain'tcha heard?: waiting is our position longer;
    there's nothink to wait for, all thinks are as ees now.

CLYDE (*clamping onto Tahara's neck*): Get it, Charmer, I got plans 'n sizzling ol' sarong-clad you figgers in 'em!

TAHARAH (*hitting and kicking fiercely to escape*): Lemme go, weel you—I gotta beat it! Blueballs usually do.

CLYDE: A privates break, eh? I—

TAHARAH (*sudden switch*): Oh, when you're back in New York, weel you sent me a pair of dungarees?

CLYDE (*taken aback*): What for?—ya can buy 'em here.

TAHARAH (*feeling his biceps*): Yez, but you can understan' de sentimental py-chology behin' my request . . .

CLYDE (*appreciative*): Gosh, Sweets, I suppose I do.

Sister Carries, looking even more neurotic than before, sweaty, blear-eyed, appears downstage left. He is wearing a circus ringmaster's top hat in place of the nun's headdress, and a whistle dangles from a string of shrunken heads around his neck.

CARRIES (*smearing war paint on*): So do I. She has no money.

CLYDE (*sardonic*): Now, if it ain't sanguinolent Sister Soft Heart, the latest in anthropological mysticism!

CARRIES: Oh, go crap in a quonset hut! Is this here your plantano plantation?

CLYDE: Not exactly. It's actually just a place ya can check into without a toothbrush. —Why?

CARRIES: Nobody's checkin' in; we jist wanna use the fireplace concession.

CLYDE: Precisely what business I wanna haggle over—

CARRIES (*raising Eddie Cantor eyebrows*): When it comes to the business, I'm a sharp shooter. Find the Sweep yet?

CLYDE: Looky, Sis, ya can case the jernt yerself, but Queen Kong ain't nowhere in the theatre: so why go ahead with the barnfire? It'll only raise the carbon monoxide—

TAHARAH (*released and sizzling*): To speak nothink of de temperature, and it's sizzling nuff round theez parts (*indicating which*) wouldn't you say?? . . .

CARRIES: Nothin' doin'! During the coffee break, I went out and danced me a no-holes-bare war dance and got me plenty enthused and sweated up about this finale bit. Then I boosted me falt'rin' courage with a couple o' peppies, er, pepsi's and am right rear to go! (*Demonlike, looking suspiciously about.*) Who cares if Queen Kong's here or not to oversee the succulent sights?—I'm as good

as her any night!!! (*Expanding his narrow chest and
pounding on it.*) In fact, my unsuspecting ninnies . . .
I AM KONG! ! ! !

CLYDE: Apecock!

TAHARAH: Peacock, perhaps; or a typographical error.

CARRIES (*breaking uncontrollably into a distinctly American
Indian war dance, chanting*):
Big barbaric barbecue
Make good eatin', b'lieve me you!
Me work up heap appetite,
Me big Injin dynamite:
    Pow-wow! Pow-wow!
Smokin' signals, smokin' hash,
Gonna bust me heap big bash!
Plenty footwork, plenty keen,
Me damn good like ballet queen:
    Pow-wow! Pow-wow!
    Pow..
(*Stops, suddenly embarrassed by his manic display.*)
Bring in the babes!!

*The Glitzes converge on the set from all the various
entrances, grunting, squealing, smearing war paint over
their hair masks and patched fur costumes; some are
still in the process of putting on their costumes; Karma
and Paulet, arm in arm, enter unescorted downstage left,
chatting like two neighbors on a shopping tour; Karma
with her bonnet full of flowers, Paulet in her bikini.*

KARMA: And so finally, I must reiterate how very much I en-
joyed taking in the cinema when we weren't called for
on stage.

PAULET (*not too adept at sophisticated chit-chat*): Quite,
quite so, my fair. Gee whiz, it's noisy around here.

KARMA: I do believe the cinema is superior to the theatre,
because whereas in theatre, which may be defined as the
quickest way to lose the greatest sum of money, every
thing is replaced, in cinema the curving cinemascope
screen is actually the circumference of the earth, or to
speak more accurately—

PAULET: The curvature of space, itself.

KARMA (*shouting above the Glitzes' racket*): Quite. I just
love a girl friend with whom I can hear mouth to ear.

PAULET: I just love a girl friend.

CLYDE: Hi there, Karma; now how ya diggin' the play?

KARMA (*preposterously affected*): Oh, Clyde, dahling! This piece is simply so frothy, so trifling, so airy—I believe I might liken it to a dandelion—

TAHARAH (*jealous*): She mean you got a dandy's loin—

KARMA (*as Carries lays hands on her*): And truly have the feeling that if I were to breathe heavily upon it . . . were to *blow* on it . . . (*Carries winks deliciously at her*) it would all blow away . . . light as air—

CLYDE (*angry*): Pollution! So ya blew on it, did ya, was he (*indicating Carries*) any good?!

KARMA (*thick Chinese accent*): Ah so, yes, he cum quarts (*correcting*) quats.

CARRIES: Enough of this interlay, er, delay: let the rain dance, er, the ritual begin! (*Looking at his wristwatch, stating the exact time.*) It's precisely———. Mister Beauty and Master Beast, (*indicating Mais Oui and Brute*) please to take in hand the soon-to-be-late lovelies, Miss Karma Miranda and Mrs. Paulet Colbert.

PAULET: *Miss* Paulet Colbert!

CARRIES. *Miss* Paulet Colbert.

MAIS OUI: One L— Scott, one flower pot, coming up!

Mais Oui and Brute hasten toward the women; Clyde leaps quick into the medley and fends them off, stands with arms akimbo before the threatened two, a cartoon superhero to the rescue; confusion.

CLYDE: Hold your hair pieces, you Sugar Commies!! Your whole hirsute outfit is postulated on a preposterous falsie! a Piltdown hoax!

TAHARAH (*edging offstage right*): A putdown! a showdown! Oh—

MAIS OUI (*laying it on thick*): We don't believe it!

CLYDE: Ya betcher boobs ya will, 'cause I can prove it!

BRUTE: None o' dat soft salami, you!; lemme spread 'im out!

CARRIES: Show cause!

CLYDE: I will! (*he yanks out of the crowd and darts after Taharah.*) Heads down, I got a date who don't rate!

TAHARAH: Why ees eferbody looking at me? I ain't de star— oh!

CLYDE (*seeing Venus' arm shoot out and grab Taharah's*

ankle): A confederation of its composites is junkel jus-
tice! That's ironical!

VENUS: And botanical.

TAHARAH: Protect the proprieties! release me as I haf done
no wrong! Beastly plant!

CARRIES: We know that snatch. What's the big deal?

CLYDE (*gripping Taharah around the waist, yanking him
free*): There's no big deal, that's just the lack of point.

TAHARAH (*fighting*): Unband my waist! In deference to—

CLYDE (*pulling Taharah's sarong down to the waist; since the
falsies are built into the sarong, bare-chested, Taharah is
a man*): There ya go—contemporaneously Topless!!

GLITZES (*severally, chaotically*): WHAT HATH GOD
WROUGHT!!! WELL, I'LL BE A MONKEY'S
AUNT!!! UNDERSEXED!!! UNDERFED!!! OVER-
MILKED!!! NEEDS PASTURING!!! etc., etc.

The cries of dismay peter out into a long shocked silence.

TAHARAH (*sniffling*): What's wrong wit all you guys?! Ain't
cha never seen a naked white woman before??!!

CARRIES (*crossing to examine Taharah*): Lucky thing my li-
cense is for mind reading and not body-reading powers.

TAHARAH (*bitch-back*): Oh, I read *you*, Maude!

CARRIES: I thought you were of size and then some trouble
(*his hands palm-flat on Taharah's flat chest*) but I suppose even a witch doctress can be wrong. How come you
chose *this* kind of life, Taharahnugi?

TAHARAH: Well, er, er, you know how straight people are—
one of them leads to another.

CARRIES: Certainly. O.K., everybody, that was an edifying
diversion, and now let's get on with the finale.

CLYDE (*pushing Taharah aside*): Whadda you mean?! I just
exposed what a fake this entire development is!

CARRIES: All you exposed is an underdevelopment.

TAHARAH (*licking his wounds upstage*): A figger ain't eferthink. A man who's really a man can appreciate a
woman for her mental development, her culture, her
talents, etc. . . .

CLYDE: But don't you see? Taharahnugi White Woman is
Kong!

GLITZES (*stunned chorus*): SHOW CAUSE! SHOW
CAUSE!

CLYDE: Cause she's, I mean, he's a queen.

CARRIES (*incrdeulous*): And just how does his being a queen make Taharahnugi White Woman Kong?

CLYDE: Because Kong is a queen.

CARRIES: Of course, she is! What nonsense—there are millions of queens, but there is only *one* Kong. Logic, at this point of the tale, may be a vestigial structure, but what's above *your* buttocks, Mr. Batty, I have no idea! We shall suffer no further delay: to postpone the proposed another two minutes will be to dispose ourselves to pejorations on the part of neighboring packs. Seize that birdbrain and cast him into the canary cage!

TAHARAH: Thought you haf it all figgered out, dincha, stool pigin!

CLYDE (*bewildered*): Gee, I thought I had it all figured out . . .

KARMA (*to Taharah as several Glitzes toss the catatonic Clyde into the cage*): He had your figure figured out.

PAULET (*disappointed*): Yeah, damn.

MAIS OUI (*to Taharah*): He probably *had* your figure.

TAHARAH: Shut up! You've got *hair* on *your* flat chest.

CARRIES (*disarming Clyde and bolting the cage*): So ends your screaming weak end: you won't be needing this pistol now: you see, Pepe, I told you you'd never adjust.

BRUTE (*peering with amazement into the cage*): It's like an inverted zoo, ain't it? Us bein' the—

CLYDE: Inverts.

MAIS OUI (*brandishing the plantain which she has constantly carried about*): Have a plantain; here, boy, here, have—

Carries blows his whistle and the Glitzes scurry to starting positions. They sing and dance in three groups; Brute is part of the first third, Mais Oui is part of the second third, and Carries is part of the third third. The three groups begin by singing and dancing together "The Frickadellin," whose music and choreography is an illogical extension of whatever is the latest in the long line of social dances inaugurated by the Twist; its particular flavor, however, its gestures and footwork, imitates the nature and movements of the gibbon. The lyrics suggest many of the steps and appropriate action should accompany any line indicating it.

Karma and Paulet, now two British tourists, squat near stage right watching the festivities. Taharah looks on from the left. Clyde rattles the cage bars. This spectacle should be amended and continuously augmented until it has the effect of a three-ring circus:

GLITZES *(sing, dance)*:
  Do The Frickadellin!
  Do The Frickadellin!
  Lotsa stompin', lotsa yellin'!
  Gibbon-steps you'll find compellin'
  Witchy footwork for dispellin'
  All the hang-ups that ya fell in!
      Bash your sole upon the groun'—
      Scratch an armpit up 'n' down—
      Let your roommate search your hair:
      See if any salt is there!
  Sui generis rebellin',
  Let's go do The Frickadellin!
      Let's go Frickadellin! —Dellin!
      Let's go Frickadellin!   Dellin!
KARMA *(as the Glitzes dance the frenzied "Frickadellin" without singing)*: You can't conceive how rewarded I feel about our decision against skipping these native ceremonies in our touring sheduel, pressed though we are for the exact time.
PAULET: Oh, I shouldn't have missed this for a month of catlick cathedrals.
KARMA: This will certainly be something to yack about back in Es-sex.
PAULET: How but they do make you homesick, don't they?
GLITZES *(sing, dance)*:
  Do The Frickadellin!
  Do The Frickadellin!
  Lotsa stompin', lotsa yellin'!
  Sounda chestnuts that yer shellin'
  Adds to muzac parallelin'
  Snappin' toes the dance is swellin'!
      Gambol on the void of veldt;
      Pinch the Princess in the Pelt;
      Swing from twig to twig in trees,
      Give a free ride to your fleas!

Pyromaniacs rebellin',
Let's go do The Frickadellin!
   Let's go Frickadellin!—Dellin!
   Let's go Frickadellin!—Dellin!

PAULET:Their costumes are so natural, so unusual, what?

KARMA: Their choreography worthy of Cunninghamlingus.

*The first third of the Glitzes leaps up on the shelves
between the fireplace and the table, and proceeds to
unhook vine ropes that are attached to the ceiling and
chaotically scalloped over the shelves; then they com-
mence swinging back and forth across the stage. The
second and third thirds begin to sing and dance "The
Cockamanie," a thirties ballroom extravagance with pre-
tensions to ballet; the dancers attempt to emulate the
poses and lowbrow "gracefulness" of bathroom and
kitchen-can decals.*

2ND AND 3RD THIRDS OF GLITZES (*sing, dance*):

Plant, perform The Cockamanie!
It is ballet; classic! zanie!
Loved by audiences brainy
Or by dolts, the weather rainy,
Worried glad rags might get stainy,
Ent'ring opry house complainy.

*While the second and third thirds of the Glitzes dance
a romantic underline of "The Cockamanie," Taharah
notices Brute swinging blissfully, idiotically on a vine
rope above, and tugs on his leg.*

TAHARAH: Hey, you, dopey, I understan' you're interested in
fruits, from time to specific time, that ees . . .

BRUTE: Yeah, but I don' find you too excitin'.

TAHARAH: If you was a beet more mature, you'd realize that
money ees more importan' than excitement.

BRUTE: But you ain't got no money.

TAHARAH: No one person can haf eferthink.

2ND AND 3RD THIRDS OF GLITZES (*singing, dancing, half like
ballet swans, the other half like river reeds caressing
them*):
The ghostly swans in triple claque
   Do The Cockamaniac,
While faithful bull-rush 'umbly slack

Also Cockamaniacs
Caressing pizzle-frizzled backs.

Carries blows his whistle to begin the third song-dance theme, "Pyromania." Several Glitzes roll a six-foot in diameter, nonspoke but hollow-hub, wooden wheel into center stage from out of the right wing. This wheel is both an Indian mandala and a Chinese Yin-Yang circle: i.e., the full flat wood with hollow-hub suffices as a mandala, while the curved black and white semispheres of Yin-Yang are painted over it:

Karma is seized and bound against the black half of the wheel, her full shepherdess' skirt filling out the wider bottom, her arms tied above and to the side of her head in the narrow portion. Paulet is bound with her hands behind her back into the white half, from head to waist slightly bent, filling the wider portion of the white; and her tapering, curving legs filling the narrow portion at the bottom of the wheel.

"Pyromania" is a musique concrete choral, stepped to with erratic modern-dance technique. The Glitzes sing and dance while they bind the women; then, rolling it upstage so that the women go topsy-turvy, they plant the wheel securely within the fireplace.

PAULET: Heavens, what's that?
MAIS OUI: It's a mandala, smarty.
KARMA: And just *what* is a mandala?
CARRIES: Oh, it's a mystic symbol that tells you where It's at. (*With absolute flatness, an afterthought.*) So what.
KARMA (*being bound*): Oh, tourist participation! How quaint.
PAULET (*being bound*): It ain't.

First third of Glitzes sings, and second and third sing and dance.

GLITZES: Pyromania applied
In the drought-hit eventide
Will ignite the shadowed camp
Better than a Tiff'ny lamp!

Rub two dicks till you've a spark
Shot off through the virgin dark;
Then some tissue paper use
So wet print may not abuse
Your intentions with a damper
Like the lust for month-old hamper.

Teach these cherry tarts a trick
Who with chilly arsenic
Frost our vision till it's sick.
Boy, this beats a grade-B flick!

Karma and Paulet are now fixed in the fireplace; the first third of the Glitzes continue swinging on their vines; the second third dance insanely "The Frickadellin"; the third third gracefully dance "The Cockamanie." During the ensuing scene, Taharah manages to coax Brute down from his swing and the two of them get intimate on the shelf between the fireplace and table. Carries blows his whistle. Against this counterpointed complexity, Queen Kong stirs within the cage: his huge bulk laboriously rises to all fours.

KONG: Grrrrrrrrrrrr . . . Aaaaaaaaaaaaagh . . .
CLYDE (*freezing with incredulous terror*): YOU! No! No! I thought you were dead, I mean, transformed!!
KONG (*awesomely*): I *am* dead. I am the Corpse of Kong!
CLYDE: But, but, his corpse is out there, in the guise of Taharahnugi White Woman, currently making time with—
KONG: Grooowwwl!!! Shut up, Piss-a-bed, I am The Corpse of Kong and I have arisen in Her core-ish behalf to ravish you and rape you gutless!!!
CLYDE (*backed up against the cage door, to Carries*): Help, lemme out, Maria Tall Chief—save me!
CARRIES: This is quite a blast; those attending are stunned.

KONG (*full height*): I am The Corpse of Kong, bigger than life!

CLYDE: I'll take yer word for it.

KONG (*flinging himself at Clyde, grabbing his crotch*): Aaagh! Queen Kong surpasses Queen Anne—now!—try this Chippendale cabriole on for size, O he who would be hung too high for Her Majesty!!! Aaaaaaaaaagh!!!

CLYDE (*thrown to the cage floor on his back; Kong leaps on top of him*): Eeeeek! What does one in a fix *comme ça*?

MAIS OUI: Come too. Or close your eyes, and think of Brooklyn.

CLYDE (*giving up under the superior weight*): Ah, me! Which do you prefer: screwing men or screwing women?

KONG (*pumping like a nanny goat*): Such is a question improperly put; ask rather: "Which do you prefer, at the present moment?" Hmmmmmm.

CLYDE: Remedial zoology! Oh, the interspecial ignominy!! Beasts of the Kingdom Come, bring K. Y. e're I die!

KONG (*in the heat of passion*): Intercourse! interrun-fun! interrush! intermix! intermingle! interseed! interzone! interbone! inter ONE BY TWO!!! . . .

The second third of the Glitzes breaks off dancing and bounds up on the shelves between the fireplace and the cage: there they unhook vine ropes attached like the previous ones, and quickly join the first third in swinging back and forth, but from the opposite direction. The counterswingers occasionally ram into each other, pinch those crossing them, pluck a hair or two, smack a passing face, etc. The third third remains downstage to continue dancing and singing "The Cockamanie."

3RD THIRD OF GLITZES (*sing, dance*):
Apeman, mark The Cockamanie!
Lift your limb and learn the pain we
Find in pelvic hern-ya strain—see?
Squat upon your squeamish sitter,
Leap up then to toe-point—titter!—
O, Act Two's perversely bitter!

The swinging Glitzes throw gigantic black and white balloons down to the third third, each of whom retrieves one and dances with it as if he were a bubble dancer; on the last line of the next stanza, each bursts another's balloon with a pin.

TAHARAH (*fondling Brute*): If you care to join me in de cuspidor, Brutey, you'll fin' a surprise waits for itchy-bitzy you!

BRUTE: What?

TAHARAH: Napalm.

3RD THIRD OF GLITZES (*sing, dance*):
Them bubble babes who lap all lack,
    Split in The Cockamaniac:
At least their bubbles show a crack
    During The Cockamaniac
When Truth procures a prick and—WHACK!!!

The first third of the Glitzes jumps down from their ropes; the third third rushes to the shelves, grabs the ropes and swings in their place along with the second third; Mais Oui also descends in this exchange, running over to the prostrate Sweep, nudging him.

MAIS OUI: Quick, quick—who was the intern?

SWEEP (*lifting his head slightly, annoyed*): Was? A brute.

Mais Oui runs back to her swing as the first third of the Glitzes lustily resumes the frenetic singing and dancing of "The Frickadellin"; their first stanza is a bridge, in which they go about listening at each other's stomachs for the innocent offender.

1ST THIRD OF GLITZES (*sing, dance*):
Herr Carter's little liver dumplin's
Consumed, cause gastric stomach rumplin's:
Yet playing it by ear oft stumbles
In puzzling out whose belly grumbles:
Alas, we fear we'll never figger
Exactly whose emits which snigger!

Do The Frickadellin!
Do The Frickadellin!
Lotsa stompin', lotsa yellin'!
Soon you'll cease yer mildew smellin',
Axial division dwellin':
Ego solo arts farewellin'!

Anchor up! ascend! embark!
Roommates in the Noah's ark:
Both your places, vacant, paired,
Safely separate, simply shared.
Salvagees ain't infidelin'
When they do The Frickadellin!
    Let's go Frickadellin! —Dellin!
    Let's go Frickadellin! —Dellin!

*The first third of the Glitzes dances "The Frickadellin";
the second and third thirds continue swinging; Carnes
blows his whistle.*

KONG (*rocking motion as in a rocking chair, sighing as an old
    grandmother*): Push away, Vinyl Vuman, push away
    . . . push away . . . push away all the pain . . .
TAHARAH AND MAIS OUI (*singing*):
    Rock-a-bye bottle fulla pee sop,
    You plant a plantain, I'll reap the crop . . .
KONG (*to Clyde*): How do you like my can-opener?
SWEEP (*aroused by the commotion within the cage*): Seems
    to fit in the rim like a rose the nose.
KONG: Mind your own mate.
SWEEP: How can I, with you kids making all that noise?
MAIS OUI: Whatsa matter Sweep, can'tcha sleep?
SWEEP (*rubbing his eyes in disbelief*): Heaven's Contradiction!
    A big ball in full swing and me hung low! (*Looking at
    his wristwatch.*) Wow, am I late in coming so to speak!
VENUS (*turning over but not rising*): Quit kickin', will ya,
    can't stomach a restless sleeper.
SWEEP (*standing*): Don't recall being hot to trot with you
    —must've been plenty soused. Sorry, but I gotta pull
    out.
CLYDE: Pull out! Pull out!
SWEEP (*yawning*): Honey, I'm late for work.
VENUS: Deposit a token of yer esteem on the dresser, will ya?
SWEEP (*exiting right*): Later, mater.
BRUTE (*to Taharah*): I gotta hand it to you guys, ya really
    know howda work it up.
TAHARAH: Yez, work eet up an' hand eet to me.
KARMA (*to Paulet*): Am I cracked, Bric-a-brac, or is a horn
    of the Billygoat-legs-Lieutenant-and-Major-General-War-
    Commander-Sergeant falling down?

PAULET (*peering up the chimney stack*): Either that, Shepherdess, or it's drizzlin' soot!

KARMA (*peering up the stack*): Something's coming down; headsup.

PAULET: If drawers are coming down, heads *are* up.

A narrow ladder drops from the chimney stack and is grounded in the grate next to the wheel; then a foot, two feet of the Sweep appear on its rungs; then a broom sweeping hither and dither.

SWEEP (*singing*):
Cremated ashes Indians plunder,
Lessen ya sweep 'em a carpet under.

KARMA: Why, if it ain't the rock dropping May-son and smacking thief!

SWEEP (*reaching awkwardly down from mid-ladder and smacking Karma's face twice*): Take two, a sign yer true.

PAULET: What d'ja say he was?

MAIS OUI: A chimney sweep to you.

PAULET: A chimney sweep! —It's THE Chimney Sweep! Hey, there, Karma, you're saved! Oh, Honey, I'm so glad for you!

TAHARAH (*greatly disappointed*): Conratulations.

KARMA: Never mind!! Whadda ya doin' *here*, Skinny? I thought we had a date for 10:30 under the Venus Fly Trap!!

SWEEP (*busy sweeping*): Did we? Gee, must be living a double life. The pollution's probably affecting my brain. Junkel rot setting in.

(*Singing.*)

When dick splits the May-son halves asunder,
Sweep the cracked twosome a carpet under.

KARMA: You rot rat!! You unicorn!! You forgot our date! And I! I risked all, dear life itself, to keep it quiet!!

SWEEP: Then please keep quiet now, will ya, China-doll? I got a gig to do, and I'm late enough starting as is.

KARMA: And yer late showin' here to boot! Why *are* you so late?

SWEEP: I believe, Mother-Source, that I was victimized by the tse-tse fly; whereupon a rather heavy nap by a normally light sleeper ensued.

PAULET: Are you the "heavy" in this play?

SWEEP: Mr. White, I weight 98 pounds. Have a smack.

PAULET: Watch it, buddy, I can handle you!

SWEEP (*poking the top end of the broom handle toward her*):
    In your present Promethean state of being, it is I, on the
    contrary end, who can handle you.

*The second third of the Glitzes descends from its vine
ropes and joins the first third in singing and dancing
"The Cockamanie."*

1ST AND 2ND THIRDS OF GLITZES (*sing, dance*):
    Man, mix in The Cockamanie,
    On one peg let love profane be!
    Karma lax your lap resistance,
    Lessen twixt us mating distance:
    "Animals for Co-existence"
    Advocate we, sex persistents!

*The swinging third third of the Glitzes tosses huge white
fans to the dancers below, each of whom, catching a fan,
tips off a très fey Sally Rand fan dance. The goings-on
in the cage are now blocked from view by a build-up of
the furry junk piles. Mais Oui comes dancing down to
the very edge of the audience.*

MAIS OUI (*very thick exotic accent*): Theez play weel nefer
    cloz!

1ST AND 2ND THIRDS OF GLITZES (*sing, dance*):
    Fandangle dancers, tits so stack,
        Started The Cockamaniac;
    Bow wow now how to bivouac
        After The Cockamaniac
    In a single dingle dangle's sack?

*The first and second thirds of the Glitzes leap onto the
shelves and join the third third in swinging chaotically
above the stage; all hum and sing at once snatches of the
three different songs; happy chaos.*

KARMA (*shouting*): You there, Sister Cynosure, mind land-
    ing for a minute? Earth errand.

CARRIES (*jumping from his rope, annoyed at the interrup-
    tion*): It's protocol to permit virgin condemnees a last
    utterance, but don't overenter my good ear.

KARMA: Hate to steal yer time during the juballie, know just how Carries away you are, but if it please yer Doctress-ship, the Chimney Sweep Lost has been rediscovered, and I'd appreciate being unbound. —Cut me loose!

CARRIES: Life's lack of ironies! The Sweep is here?

SWEEP: How do there, Ph.D.?

KARMA: Hurry, please: I gotta beat it home and start supper.

PAULET: Yeah, remember big Queen Kong's ex cathedra bull!

CARRIES (*untying Karma*): A technical knockout, a whim of the wheel of fortune. Well, one tittie toasted is still a branch above none.

PAULET: Congratulations, Karmy, good luck to you.

KARMA (*rubbing her wrists and body cramped from the bonds*): So long, Paulet, bikini-clad, keep a stiff clit, try harder in yer next reincarnation.

CARRIES (*remounting his swing*): When the day's come that even a witch doctress gets bogged down in all the red tape involved in a simple propitiation—

GLITZES (*all swinging, all singing a thunderous chorus of "Pyromania"*):
Teach the Tomish heretic
How to lay a cosmic brick:
She'll lay off her candlestick
Once within our fire's flick!

Pyromania! Torch Song!
Gibbons to a herd belong
Chimpanzees've heard headstrong.
Torch song! night long! right-wrong! torch song!

Carries and Mais Oui descend from their ropes and ignite a torch; they step menacingly, then coyly teasing, toward Paulet.

PAULET: At last! I can see the light.

MAIS OUI: Ya could practically feel it, it's so real.

GLITZES (*singing, swinging*):
Pyromania! Torch Song!
Light the cold the dark night long
Taking out of right all wrong.
Torch song! night long! right-wrong! torch song!

SWEEP (*to Karma*): Betcher glad to be in the bleachers.

TAHARAH (*to Brute*): Betcher glad to be in my breeches.

A clattering and rattling of the cage bars accompanied by ear-splitting drums; everyone turns toward the cage. Clyde-as-Kong, i.e., Clyde dressed in Kong's gorilla costume, is roaring to be released. He is radically shorter than Kong and has a rivet held against his back from his waist up to the top of his head by straps about his hips and neck, which prevents him from being able to bend: he stands up absolutely straight. All assume he is Queen Kong.

CLYDE-AS-K (*roaring*): Stop the stupid muzak! Get me outta this marriage broker's Bronx Zoo!

CARRIES (*aside*): O Queen, thou comest when I had thee least in mind and matters most in hand; my power-grab's gummed-up! (*To the Glitzes.*) Why, it's kitsch Queen Kong! Stop the repetitive muzak!

CLYDE-AS-K (*as the music and swinging halt; all attention focused on him*): What are all you guys starin' at? Ain'tcha never seen a queen before? Mais Oui, undo this bolt!

MAIS OUI (*hastening to obey the order as the Glitzes all descend from their ropes*):
From rope she rode to all-four floor,
   And thence unlatched the door,
Let out a Queen that in a Queen
   Hadn't gone before.

CLYDE-AS-K (*released*): Douche, er, douse that torch, Master Carries. And now, everybody, it's final curtain marriage time!

Carries, suspicious of Clyde-as-Kong's identity, quietly disobeys, hands the torch to Mais Oui. Suddenly the Intern appears from behind the wheel carrying another quart jar, this one empty.

INTERN: Void a specimen, Your Majesty?

CLYDE-AS-K (*taking the jar and turning around, making gestures as if he were urinating into it*): Anytime. And, er, please don't forget a blood sample also. We, Kong, Queen of all the cage can convey, are mightily pleased that you, O Miss Karma, have come safely through this savage spectacle in one piece (*indicating Paulet*), or

half a piece; and, as was decreed Our right if the Sweep
were found, We do desire to marry with you. (*Handing
the jar to Intern who takes it upstage to the cuspidor;
he extracts the first jar and begins performing medical
tests on both.*)

KARMA: We do?

CLYDE-AS-K: Yes. Americans have always evinced absorption
in the pressing question: "Are the great apes women-
stealers?" This play goes a long way toward begging
that question and, to be sure, other adjacencies.

KARMA (*winking maliciously at his rear*): Speaking of adjacencies, how does your other feel?

CLYDE-AS-K: By this point, I'm closed for alterations. But
how's about yer big self? Has this harrowing experience
in any way changed your life?

KARMA: Actually, yes; I've had my menopause.

TAHARAH: And now men pause before rerequesting your hand.

CLYDE-AS-K (*emphatically*): They do not! May I rerequest
your hand, Mem-sab?

KARMA: Really, Queen Kong, how could you possibly expect me, a mere woman, to requite your request? What
would our children be—grillets?

CLYDE-AS-K: But lovely light 'n you're Karma, don't you recognize me? I'm your fia—

KARMA: Fiasco! A woman wants a man who's a man, not a
man who's a queen. (*Putting on her shepherdess bonnet.*) No, Kong, I prefer to marry the Chimney Sweep,
an able stable stud and a he-hero, he who is responsible
for snatching me from the tongues of fire. For his time-
liness, I reward him with my hand. (*Putting her hand
to a rewarding spot on Sweep.*)

SWEEP: I receive, er, accept. As a man, you have, er, I have
made mine cherce.

CARRIES (*to Clyde-as-Kong, with squint-eye suspicion*): Any
objections to his directions?

CLYDE-AS-K (*unable to nod his disapproval because of the
rivet*): Let me not stoop to go between lovers hard
and fast. Two lovers fastened hard. Now, let's look . . .
(*Looking with difficulty about, spotting Paulet.*) Douse
that torch; spare the Tom; I ain't picky, I'll marry *her*
instead.

MAIS OUI (*putting out the torch, holding the burnt stick up to Paulet*): Pyrotechnical flamboyancies aside, hon, this could still be of use to you.

PAULET (*being untied by several Glitzes*): Fresh freak! wise guyess, you'll get yours with gauze!

CLYDE-AS-K: Well, m' nervy Paulet, queen of Our heart, can you picture us both on a bicycle built for two?

PAULET: Sorry, Queen, I ain't a queen: I can't marry you: I'm a lezzy: wanna marry a lezzy?

CLYDE-AS-K: A man had as well marry a celibate and beget imaginings. But let me look around the set: we do have to find someone for you before curtain call. (*Peering about, everyone peering brow-knit about.*) Don't see any comers . . .

INTERN (*busy with the tests*): How about the Venus Fly Trap?

MAIS OUI: Yeah, how about her? Like Marilyn Monroe, she's forgotten, but not gone.

Clyde-as-Kong, Carries, Paulet, and Mais Oui rush en masse downstage right to the motionless, recumbent Venus.

PAULET: She done gone out!

MAIS OUI: Who does her hair—the elements?

INTERN (*his back still turned*): She needs an aphrodisiac.

CLYDE-AS-K: Quick, Glitz Ionas, bring flies to revive her!

The Glitzes converge, form a tight circle around Venus; sounds as of a commode flush feedback are heard; then the circle of Glitzes breaks, and Venus, rejuvenated, is helped to her feet.

CLYDE-AS-K: Venus, revived when administered to by fount-filled cods and swordtail steaks, won't you consider this salmon-slender spoke of your—

VENUS (*appraises Paulet with immodest velocity, then*):
I of flies have had my fill,
Wishing bones and pickles dill;
This Paulet is scented dish:
She renews my nose for fish.

As Venus and Paulet come together, Clyde-as-Kong moves away toward center stage, his back presented to

Carries who suddenly is alerted by the obvious rivet:
Carries cocks the pistol.

CARRIES: Wait, hold everything! Queen Kong is kinda spineless.

CLYDE-AS-K: So?

CARRIES: Yers looks like it could give ya a cerebral hemorrhage!

MAIS OUI (*examining the rivet, brandishing the plantain*): Funny place to hang yer umbrella. What a man!

CARRIES: Man, no doubt! Kong!—are you a *poseur*?!

CLYDE-AS-K: Just for *Phyzeek Magazine.* Why?

CARRIES: Let me stare at you . . . scrupulously . . . like someone who's just discovered that monkeys have faces . . .

CLYDE-AS-K (*heavily scrutinized by all*): Why do people always look at me as if they've seen something I'm afraid of?

CARRIES: All right, Chinaman on the make, who ARE you?

CLYDE-AS-K: I am the product of the rape of Clyde by the Corpse of Kong, as well as all that remains of those two.

CARRIES (*lifting his face mask, seeing Clyde*): Eeek! *You are* . . .

CLYDE-AS-K: I am Clyde-as-Kong.

ALL: CLYDE-AS-KONG???!!!

CLYDE-AS-K (*meekly*): What's so strange? It has alliteration.

CARRIES (*suddenly resigned*): Such is accuracy. And I suppose that makes him legitimate.

KARMA: Really, Doctress?

CARRIES: Yes, my child, there is nothing I can do. The product of a rape by Kong-as-Corpse is always the Rapee-as-Kong; and "as" as the go-between two alliteratives in the product's name is always the birthmark of legitimacy. Such is our gibbon law. I haf spoken.

INTERN (*coming downstage with the two quart jars*): And Clyde-as-Kong's specimen is medically identical with the specimen of Queen Kong which I mystically had the foreskin, er, foresight to procure back in Act One.

BRUTE: Which means wha'?

INTERN: Which means that the specimens, as ample sample of the whole, bear out Clyde and Kong as identical, as wholly one. I haf spoken.

TAHARAH (*tossing Brute aside*): Oh, Holy One, ees it really

you, Muskels? I haf been waiting so patiently for you to
evolve. Leetel unprecocious me!

MAIS OUI (*tipping Taharah's flat chest with the plantain*):
My, but yer unprecocity leaves something to be desired!

TAHARAH (*haughtily triumphant*): Second fiddle, piddle!
piddle!

CLYDE-AS-K: And now that my lawful stock has been improved, I mean, approved, who'll wed me? I'm a find in
any behind.

TAHARAH: I weel! I weel wed you, Queen Clyde-as-Kong!

CLYDE-AS-K: But—but—how can you, my love? You are the
Living Kong, his transformation!

PAULET: Is such, den, veracity?

TAHARAH: Yez, woman, it ees. Clyde shot Kong, and I resulted. Kong-Shot raped Clyde, and he resulted. I am
Kong-as-Kong-Shot; he is Kong-as-Kong-Shot's-Load-Shot.
You haf heard of cell-cleavage?—well, try to keel a
Queen (*squeezing his flat chest together*) and she
cleaves. No rose that fades, but pressed, it haf two
shades.

KARMA: But, Taharahnugi White Woman, wasn't it you who
was smoldering around the verandah before Kong got
shot?

SWEEP: Ever hear of astroprojection?

KARMA: I thought a medium was needed to conjure it.

SWEEP: Your anticipational jealousy was the medium.

KARMA (*still jealous*): But if you marry *him*, don't you marry
back into your previous half?

INTERN: She does. But why shouldn't she? If he marries her,
he too marries back into his previous half. Two halves
so identically destinied are well healed, er, wholed, are
they not? and augured well for future compatibility?
(*Mumbling to himself as he wanders back upstage.*)
Or does he marry back into his previous half's half?

CARRIES (*ex cathedra*):
Kong clove into Taharah and Clyde,
But Taharah weds Clyde is Kong simplified.

VENUS: And reincubied, and considerably fructified.

CARRIES (*holding out the pistol as at a shotgun wedding*):
And now, with the power invested in me by the Union
of Witch Doctresses, I pronounce you man and wife,
or man and man, or ape and man, or queen and woman,

or queen and man, or queen and queen, or ape and ape
up and up. And now, if it please the cast, could we all
canary the finale. There's a great flick on the Late Show
and I don't wanna miss it. —Maestro!

The new pairs hold hands and all sing. Several Glitzes
begin removing their costumes and makeup while others
of them bring the bicycle back on stage. Clyde-as-Kong
and Taharah mount the bicycle and ride off through
the audience with the entire cast singing and following
them.

ALL (*singing*):
Can this corny triplethink,
Better nab a nipple pink:
Art about your life is plot,
But your life 'bout art is not!

Soooooooooooooo:
If it's got a mind, stump it.
If it stands too high, slump it.
If it willn't budge, bump it.
If ya don't like it, lump it.
But if it's got a hole, hump it!

Clear the aisle, we're ridin' through,
Locomotive, make adieu!
If your mores still you'd trover,
Please, tight patrons, bend right over!

If it's militant, jump it.
If it's got a pipe, pump it.
If it smells too much, dump it.
If it hymen has, rump it.
But if it's got a hole, hump it!

Reservations we eschew,
Ne'er accept, "The heck with you!"
Narrow-minded: rend fright over;
Spotless—(THE spot!)—bend right over!

Brute disengages himself from the singing, exiting parade,
and hops back up on the stage. He scampers over to the
cuspidor and extracts the purple rose.

BRUTE: Ladies and Gentlemen of every genus: Forget dem

dirty-minded fakes: art ain't never 'bout life, but life *is* only 'bout art. Dis rose?—oh, it ain't no symbol like ya mighta thought, an' dat's cause it ain't got nothin' to do wit life either. Dis here rose is all 'bout art. Here, take it—

(*He throws the rose into the audience.*)

ABOUT THE PLAYWRIGHTS

SAM SHEPARD was born in Fort Madison, Illinois, on November 2, 1943, and raised near Los Angeles. He acted his way to New York with the Bishop's Company Repertory Players and spent five years writing plays for Off Off-Broadway, among them *Chicago, Red Cross*, and *Icarus's Mother*. *Melodrama Play* was produced by La Mama Repertory in Europe, *Fourteen Hundred Thousand* was seen on the National Educational Television network, and *La Turista* was presented at the American Place Theatre. Mr. Shepard is the recipient of numerous "Obie" awards and various grants and is currently in Hollywood writing movies and playing drums.

ROBERT HEIDE (Sun in Taurus; Moon in Virgo) studied theatre at Northwestern University with Alvina Krause. He worked with Stella Adler, Uta Hagen, and The Living Theatre. Acting experience included The American Shakespeare Festival in Stratford, Connecticut. He has written a number of plays, including *West of the Moon, Hector, The Bed, Why Tuesday Never Has a Blue Monday, Statue*, and *Moon* which have been produced at New Playwrights, Caffe Cino, Café La Mama, The Cherry Lane, Sullivan Street Theatre, and at the Washington, D.C., National Arts Festival. His scenarios, *The Bed* and *The Death of Lupe Velez*, were made into films by Andy Warhol. His new play *Duck's Blood, or Within the Context of Cities* will be a La Mama production.

MARÍA IRENE FORNÉS was born in Havana, Cuba, in April, 1930. She came to the United States in 1945 and started painting in 1949. She lived in Paris from 1954 to 1957 and began writing plays in 1960. Her plays include *The Widow, Tango Palace, The Office, Promenade, The Successful Life of 3*, and *A Vietnamese Wedding*. She has worked closely with the Judson Poets' Theatre as costumer and director as well as playwright.

MICHAEL SMITH was born in Kansas City, Missouri, on October 5, 1935. He wrote theatre criticism for *The Village Voice* from 1959 until 1968, and was associate editor of *The Voice* from 1962 to 1965. With Nick Orzel he edited the anthology *Eight Plays from Off Off-Broadway*, and a collection of his criticism has been published by the University of Missouri

255

Press. He has directed Off Off-Broadway productions of plays by Gertrude Stein, Sam Shepard, Soren Agenoux, and H. M. Koutoukas.

SOREN AGENOUX was born in Hollywood, California, on March 5, 1936. His plays include *Geoffrey and Leona, Silver Miner, Silver Thief, Even So Is Even So, Quarters for the Head, Quarters for His Marble Bag, A Glutton Eats a Good-Looking Peach, A Fool Rejects Philosophy, Donovan's Johnson, Donovan's Braine,* and *Love's Fear of Hunger.* He published *The Sinking Bear* in New York and helped the Free Speech Movement sit-in at Sproul Hall in Berkeley in 1964.

DONALD KVARES was born in the Bronx on January 28, 1938. He attended the High School of Music and Art and served in the United States Army in 1959–60. He studied playwriting with Jacob Weiser and Barbara Miller. Beginning with *Modern Statuary* in 1963, fifteen of his plays have received Off Off-Broadway productions. They include *Bust of a Lunatic, What Did You Say to Me in the Last Scene?, Smarty Party, The Chronicles of Hermos,* and *Couchmates.*

RONALD TAVEL is a Taurus and the founding dramatist of the Theatre of the Ridiculous, which produced his plays, *Shower, The Life of Juanita Castro, The Life of Lady Godiva, Screen Test, Indira Gandhi's Daring Device,* and *Kitchenette.* He has written screenplays for fourteen of Andy Warhol's movies, including *The Chelsea Girls* and *Vinyl.* His most recent play, *Arenas of Lutetia,* was produced by the Judson Poets' Theatre in the fall of 1968, and his novel, *Street of Stairs,* is being published in New York by Olympia Press.